AVID

READER

PRESS

Convent *Wisdom*

How *Sixteenth*-Century Nuns Could Save
Your *Twenty-First*-Century Life

Ana Garriga *and* Carmen Urbita

Avid Reader Press

New York   Amsterdam/Antwerp   London
Toronto   Sydney/Melbourne   New Delhi

AVID READER PRESS
An Imprint of Simon & Schuster, LLC
1230 Avenue of the Americas
New York, NY 10020

For more than 100 years, Simon & Schuster has championed authors and the stories they create. By respecting the copyright of an author's intellectual property, you enable Simon & Schuster and the author to continue publishing exceptional books for years to come. We thank you for supporting the author's copyright by purchasing an authorized edition of this book.

No amount of this book may be reproduced or stored in any format, nor may it be uploaded to any website, database, language-learning model, or other repository, retrieval, or artificial intelligence system without express permission. All rights reserved. Inquiries may be directed to Simon & Schuster, 1230 Avenue of the Americas, New York, NY 10020 or permissions@simonandschuster.com.

Copyright © 2025 by Ana Garriga and Carmen Urbita

All rights reserved, including the right to reproduce this book or portions thereof in any form whatsoever. For information, address Avid Reader Press Subsidiary Rights Department, 1230 Avenue of the Americas, New York, NY 10020.

First Avid Reader Press hardcover edition November 2025

AVID READER PRESS and colophon are trademarks of Simon & Schuster, LLC

Simon & Schuster strongly believes in freedom of expression and stands against censorship in all its forms. For more information, visit BooksBelong.com.

For information about special discounts for bulk purchases, please contact Simon & Schuster Special Sales at 1-866-506-1949 or business@simonandschuster.com.

The Simon & Schuster Speakers Bureau can bring authors to your live event. For more information or to book an event contact the Simon & Schuster Speakers Bureau at 1-866-248-3049 or visit our website at www.simonspeakers.com.

Interior design by Ruth Lee-Mui
All interior art by Clay Smith

Manufactured in the United States of America

1 3 5 7 9 10 8 6 4 2

Library of Congress Control Number: 2025933763

ISBN 978-1-6680-6551-8
ISBN 978-1-6680-6553-2 (ebook)

To Laura Bass, our mother superior.

For always being a mentor, a haven, and a friend.

Because we could've never thrived without her trusting care.

Contents

Introduction: Nuns Knew Best   1

Girlfriends   7

Work   46

Body   78

Love   103

Money   125

Soul   149

Fame   175

Epilogue: A Portable Convent   203

Acknowledgments   209
Character Guide   213
Notes   221
Selected Bibliography   235

Convent *Wisdom*

Introduction: Nuns Knew Best

You wake up in your overpriced apartment slightly hungover, bleary-eyed, and once again regretting saying yes to last night's date instead of staying in with your friends. You promised yourself you'd start the day with some stretching on an empty stomach followed by hot water with lemon and ginger, but you find yourself rotting in bed, mindlessly scrolling through the most analgesic corners of the internet. Your algorithm, too aware of your disillusionment with a crumbling world, shows you an unexpected recurring theme: nuns.

The memes of a group of joyful nuns overlaid with the words "I have one more situationship left in me before I join the convent" spark a smile of recognition. Another nun, this one with a sassier habit, stares you down beneath the caption: "Me, if I get ghosted for 8+ hours then get a random 'hey' text." You sigh in acceptance. A nun holding her rosary: "Me, if I hear 'it will happen when you least expect it' one more time." You nod in your empty room. Nearly an hour has passed, and you're still in bed, still scrolling. You realize your feed has been possessed by a nun fixation that is no longer just the airy, ironic remarks of a generation under the spell of conventual fantasies: the Endless Scroll has shepherded you to the addictive realm of content created in actual enclosure. Nuns choreographing Karol G and Nicki Minaj covers. Nuns rescuing axolotls in Mexico. Nuns teaching you how to make sushi. Nuns with impossibly radiant skin. Nuns sharing the wisdom of centuries-old sisters—nuns radiating a calm that feels more aspirational than ever. You scroll back to the meme of an ecstatic nun blissfully levitating over the rubric "When you and your friends claim the nun lifestyle." You read the endless thread of comments left below—"Don't give me ideas," "I've already applied LOL," "Girl I'm thinking about it," "Never been closer"—and you're tempted to write your own: "This is not even a joke anymore."

Nuns are everywhere—from Chappell Roan and her band flaunting their nun habits on the stage of a massive music festival to the Bad Bunny "Convent Meeting" SNL sketch. But behind every meme advising us to get ye to a nunnery and every mocking interpretation of convent life, there lies a nun fever that transcends mere satire. It's not simply a wistful glance at a utopian past or a fascination with a restrained nuncore aesthetic. Rather, this revival of convent culture feels revolutionary and joyful: a checkmate to the isolation and alienation of our twenty-first-century lives. You've never seriously considered taking a vow of chastity. But how often have you fantasized about finding refuge from the chaos of the world in the tranquility and warmth of a sustainable close-knit community with your friends? Soaring rents, tech bros pulling the strings of international geopolitics, relentless work schedules, the labyrinthine hierarchy of global corporations, the rabbit hole of online dating . . . As you keep scrolling, the simplicity of convent life feels oddly tempting.

Full disclosure: this is not two nuns talking. We never took religious vows. We did, however, feel some kind of calling when (not knowing each other yet) we both decided, against the better judgment of our agnostic parents, to get baptized at age nine. It must have been the unquestionable allure of Catholic imagery assailing us from our grandmothers' Virgin-crowded walls, the magnetism that the religious ethical toolkit had for two girls obsessed with doing the right thing, or simply the first hints of our latent lesbianism kicking in at the mesmerizing sight of Saint Joan of Arc's butchy armored splendor. Whatever reason had driven us to make that unexpected public confession of our faith wasn't strong enough to usher us to the convent. And yet, it didn't go away entirely, and we did end up committing to a different cloistered kind of life. At some point in our mid-twenties we both decided (still strangers, at this point) to join the ranks of academia. The vow of poverty we took when we resolved to be PhD candidates was virtually no different from the one assumed by the austere Discalced Carmelites. The academic submissiveness to professors and thesis supervisors wasn't any less unyielding than the negation of one's will inherent to a nun's vow of obedience. We didn't, in case you're wondering, take the chastity vow, but you'd be surprised at how easily six years of graduate life in Providence (Rhode Island) can get you quasi-celibate status.

We didn't choose to consecrate our lives to the obscure deities of higher education after being seduced by internet bits about joyous academics (there's a meme genre that'll never exist). And who knows if, had the nuncore frenzy stormed our phones ten years earlier, we'd now be writing these words in between prayers and behind latticed windows. But what actually brought us to the self-flagellating retreat of academia was our first encounters (still not knowing each other) with sixteenth- and seventeenth-century nuns. As remote as they first seemed, we were immediately struck by how relatable their voices were. It wasn't just that their autobiographies, letters, and spiritual treatises made it unexpectedly easy to put ourselves in the place of women who lived four centuries ago. It was, above all, the uncanny realization that convent wisdom had an assuaging answer for every contemporary malaise. It soon dawned on us that a clique of sixteenth-century Spanish Discalced Carmelites could analyze the intricacies of the current dating scene with a finesse that no *Sex and the City* episode could ever achieve, that a Capuchin Poor Clare fasting in seventeenth-century Italy may help you more than any body-positive guru, and that Oprah Winfrey's career advice could never live up to a Mexican Hieronymite nun's lessons on boss-handling. When we finally met at Brown University, we thought our studies would be exclusively academic, but in fact, during our years in Providence, we would mostly learn how to survive. Our readings there taught us that, from the twelfth to the seventeenth century, nuns built together a transhistorical book club of readers and counselors— one we suddenly felt part of. Sometimes, bored in the Rockefeller Library, we liked to picture ourselves stacking up all those letters, autobiographies, spiritual treatises, and government manuals just to try to gauge how huge the pile would get. It was a ridiculous mental game, given our lack of spatial vision, yet there was something comforting in knowing that all those pages were there, like a soft cushion, ready to catch us when life threw something unpredictable our way, from the mundane to the existential. An assertive email? An infidelity? A body that just wouldn't cooperate? A divorce? A nun always knew best.

Whether Poor Clares, Discalced Carmelites, Hieronymites, or Dominicans, our nuns had amassed a collective wisdom that seemed tailor-made for us. Much like those who sneak into the exclusive (and cringeworthy) dating app The League by faking their college degrees, we had inherited a self-help guide crafted centuries ago without having taken the vows of poverty, obedience, and chastity. But we didn't feel like intrusive voyeurs; we were true believers. Over time, we learned to see ourselves like the rightful heirs in this long line of role models. And, as is usually the case, a nun had already said it better. Mistreated and silenced by the male hierarchies of her order, the Discalced Carmelite María de San José, a favorite of ours, was determined to turn her writings into an enduring legacy—one that we felt like a gentle tap on our shoulders, an affectionate whisper in our ear: "I write this, as I said before, to tell the virtues of our Sisters so that their memory and example may endure for the nuns yet to come." Maybe we weren't the "nuns yet to come" that María had imagined, but her words felt like they were meant just for us: "I have wished, my Sisters, that all persons might know of this angelic Life."

Life, you must be thinking, is everything but angelic, and any of our nuns would agree. That's why, we realized, we all need this not-so-saintly handbook for handling our daily predicaments. Because this is a book about cloisters, candlelight, mortifications, and hushed prayers, but it is also a book about friendship, money, FOMO, love, lesbianism, procrastination, impostor syndrome, work, fame, and pop culture. It is a book about the two of us and our nun-flanked surviving years, but it is most of all a book about you—because we're certain that anything you may be going through right now already happened to a nun living in the sixteenth and seventeenth centuries. "I confess," wrote María de San José, "that whatever I do know, I learned from these nuns." It is our hope—and we're two very hopeful creatures—that by the end of *Convent Wisdom* you'll be able to make her words yours.

Girlfriends

If only you will love me as much as I love you, I forgive you all you have done and will do.

Saint Teresa to María de San José

How a Friend Crush Might Change Your Life Forever

The nun is in her cell. She knows she should be praying for her sisters, considering Christ's suffering at the cross, or writing a repentance letter for her confessor, but all she can think about is Teresa. No one forgets the sudden onset of a friend crush—not even a sixteenth-century nun dealing with a massive retaliation executed by the ecclesiastical hierarchy. This is not the first Resurrection Sunday that María de San José has spent locked up in the prison of the Portuguese convent she founded herself six years ago. The thought of yet another Holy Week estranged from her sisters and deprived of all exterior communication is a miserable one, but luckily she still has a scrap of paper and some drying ink. She needs a morale boost: "He [God] is overjoyed, / and so I find contentment, / even if I'm cornered / in this sad confinement." It's a rather poor sonnet, she knows, but for now, it's enough to keep her entertained and prevent the bitterness of her unjust imprisonment (imposed by certain friars of her own religious order) from consuming her. On her desk lies the letter she wrote two days ago, filled with rage: *Letter Written by a Poor and Imprisoned Discalced Nun to Console Herself and Her Sisters and Daughters Who Are Afflicted by Seeing Her Thus.* She takes pride in the title—dramatic, self-congratulatory, and promising. Though she cannot share it with her companions just yet, she hopes that one day it will be published and serve as a lesson for generations of Carmelite nuns to come.

As she rereads the letter, each word transports her back to the beginning of it all. During her two years of isolation, María has spent many sleepless nights reliving the memory of that first moment when she witnessed Teresa in the midst of a mystical rapture. For a girl born in 1548, the enchanted choreography of an ecstatic body can't have been any less mesmerizing than the well-rehearsed moves of Dua Lipa today. The languid gesture, the faraway gaze, the parted lips, the hands contracting to the rhythm of the spiritual rapture: a repertoire of masterful expressions that every aspiring mystic knew how to replicate and that María analyzed with the devout attention of a newly converted fan. What she didn't know was that she would one day become best friends with the great star of mysticism. When they first encountered each other, Saint Teresa had not yet become a saint, and María de San José was going by another name.

In 1562, María was simply María de Salazar, a fourteen-year-old student enjoying a pampered adolescence at the opulent palace of a distant, wealthy relative named Luisa de la Cerda. Vainer than most, María preferred hobbies like maintaining the starched rustle of her dresses and the impeccable whiteness of their lace. That night, however, she didn't mind putting all that puffed-up pomp aside and dragging her skirt along the ground, hurting her knees just to peer through the keyhole of Teresa's room. Much like someone elbowing their way to the barricade of a crowded festival, she fought to position herself well among the throng of curious courtiers, all kneeling and struggling to catch a fleeting, sparkling glimpse of the palace's most popular and intriguing inhabitant: Teresa de Jesús.

Teresa was a forty-seven-year-old Carmelite nun. After two decades of living in anonymity, her mystical charisma, stubbornness, and revolutionary ideas began to set her apart from the countless other religious women scattered around sixteenth-century Castile. Teresa is that friend you look at with bemusement when she decides to leave everything behind and invest all her energy in a self-managed collective housing project—but in the end, against all odds, she succeeds. Teresa had made the decision to found a new religious order, the Discalced Carmelites, enemy to conspicuous religiosity and ostentatious displays of wealth. For forty years, mental prayer, austerity, and intimacy—as opposed to the two hundred nuns who lived in the convent where Teresa had professed when she was twenty, the Discalced Carmelite houses would never have more than thirteen nuns—would be the cornerstones of Teresa's ambitious dream. Rumors were beginning to circulate that she was more than just a nun—she was a saint in the making.

Many centuries would pass before Teresa became a global icon, with statues of her adorning churches across the world, but her reputation for holiness already preceded her enough for the noblewoman Luisa—hoping to alleviate the sticky tedium of her recent widowhood—to become enamored with the idea of having this spiritual celebrity stay at the palace for a few months. While Teresa shared whispered consolations with the widow, a swarm of dazzled teenagers followed her around every corner. They peered through curtains and tapestries to spy on Teresa's gripping conversations, her prayer exercises, and the gruesome spectacle of violent self-flagellations performed by someone who was, at her earthly core, a frail lady pushing fifty. It was impossible not to look. The entire palace was in an uproar, but María had a hunch that although these unusual displays were captivating everybody, they were meant more for her benefit than for anyone else's. María was never Teresa's least toxic friend, but she would end up being the most loyal.

From the confines of the convent prison where she now found herself, and with that yearning for the carefree and exhilarating days of youth that haunts you as soon as you hit your thirties, María could not stop thinking about those spying escapades of her girlhood that had forever altered the course of her life. Years earlier, in her 1585 *Book of Recreations*, she had already tried putting the sudden rapture of her friend crush into words: "I was then thirteen or fourteen years old, she was in the house, on that occasion, about six months or so. Now, Sister, I wish another tongue than my own to tell of the transformation wrought in us all by her holy conversation and her practice of prayer and mortification." Before it was too late, she wanted to leave a testimony of the first time she saw Teresa that would capture the bewitching, relentless character that everyone had recognized in the future saint. Although she feigned humility behind a vague "us all," what María truly wanted was to feel like an exception by revealing the unique whirlwind of emotion that had, for more than twenty years, formed the backbone of her relationship with the most esteemed woman in sixteenth-century Spain. Had María been able to foresee all the future torments into which her loyalty to Teresa would drag her—including slander, the ordeal of founding new convents, and her current seclusion—she wouldn't have changed a thing. And neither would we.

Our first meeting also took place among ornate draperies and molded ceilings. Lacking the corridors and chambers of a Renaissance palace, we settled for the lobby of a once grand 1920s hotel, long since fallen into decline. To reach the Biltmore Hotel in Providence, Rhode Island, one must cross a bleak square, cursed by a poor government decision in the 1980s to live out its days as an open-air bus station. Now, the bravest students from Brown and RISD (Rhode Island School of Design), the two wealthiest universities in Rhode Island, wait for their buses, making great effort not to touch anything, all the while thinking about how insightfully they will discuss the opioid crisis once they are safely on the other side of the city. One March night in 2016, overcome by an unnerving sense of newness, we both crossed that square with a light step, determined to impress each other. Every budding friendship is in part a courtship.

In *Instruction of Novices*, her manual for novice nuns, María de San José provides very precise guidelines about the protocol two religious women should follow when meeting for the first time: "Between equals, they will make a slight bow to each other, giving way to one another." Luckily, we had a cocktail menu to help ward off the initial threat of Carmelite stiffness. The chandelier, dusty carpet, and plastic flowers in the Biltmore's lobby lent a sense of unease that the $16 dry martinis could not quite shake off. Rumor had it that Emma Watson had lived in one of the Biltmore suites during her years as a student at Brown and, for some strange reason, imagining the actor of our childhood riding the elevator that unsuccessfully tried to evoke the city's bygone splendor gave us a much-needed sense of coziness. Officially, it was our first-time meeting; in reality, without any way to spy on each other through the crack in a door, we had both succumbed weeks earlier to the embarrassing ritual of stalking each other through Instagram. Instead of mystical theatrics or mortifications, we found the illusion of intimacy that kept us equally captivated as we tried to decipher in each other's gestures the key to our own incomprehensible life decisions. At just twenty-six years old, we had already spent too much time in academic seclusion, dedicated to meticulously dissecting the intricacies of the Catholic Counter-Reformation, the politics of sanctity, and the sensory fervor of Renaissance demonological treatises. This trove of knowledge might eventually help us win some prizes on quiz shows or even score some points on a Tinder date with someone with a fetish for scholarly minds, but it proved largely incompatible with a happy twenties. Without any intention of steering our lives toward more rewarding paths, that night at the Biltmore bar we made a toast to our unusual, shared decision to cloister ourselves for the next five years (eventually seven) in the solitary silence of a doctoral program four thousand miles from home:

—Carmen, let's have a toast.
—To the PhD?
—To Saint Teresa.
—You're right, always to Saint Teresa.

And then we exchanged some religious cards we each kept in our wallets.

The truth is that we had spent more time picturing the aridity of a sixteenth-century nun's cloistered life than our own desolate journey through academia. The claustrophobia of the narrow cell; the stomach growling in despair after weeks of zealous fasting; the best hours of the day lost to prayers and penance; the bloodshot eyes squinting helplessly at a half-embroidered altar cloth—we thought we knew everything about the rigors of convent life. But we chose to ignore the daily martyrdom that awaited us in the following years: fourteen harrowing hours a day sitting in a chair, our eyes forever locked on a ruthless, uncompromising screen, our gaze getting lost too often on a scratch in the damp wallpaper; the guilt of disobeying the sacrosanct mandate to escort an exquisitely toned body through the marvels of a vitamin-infused prime of life; hearts perpetually torn between the isolation of academia and the tantalizing lure of cultivating a personal brand on social media. On that first night together, we were unaware that within a year we would begin to see our own peculiar paths mirroring the sacrifices of our sixteenth-century idols.

The names of many nuns came up during that first conversation. Once we got past the uncanny feeling that sitting opposite a doppelgänger of convent research induced, all sense of wariness faded and we began sharing names of religious figures with the same irrepressible fervor as stamp collectors in their sixties, and with the same personal and incomprehensible zeal of teenagers swapping Magic: The Gathering cards during recess. In the increasingly deserted lobby, we spoke about Saint Teresa and María de San José. We expressed our joint admiration for the Mexican Sor Juana Inés de la Cruz and reminisced about the juiciest excerpts—her steamy dreams about the town's confessor, the unruly behavior of her 666 demons—from the autobiography of Jeanne des Anges, the possessed Ursuline nun. We did not, at the time, discuss any of the nuns hailing from the Venetian convents of the late sixteenth century, as figures like the Benedictine Arcangela Tarabotti would become part of the extensive catalog of discoveries we would unearth together in years to come.

Later, we learned that out of the 135,000 people living in Venice, Italy, in 1581, 2,508 were cloistered nuns. At that time, the city was a bustling commercial center, thriving on the textile industry and the production of sought-after luxury goods, including the famous Murano glass. The city was also becoming an elaborate urban recruitment office for convents. With the cost of dowries going through the roof and wealthy families fearing the fragmentation of their dwindling wealth, many found little incentive to continue feeding the city's marital circuit. As a result, thousands of Venetian teenagers, with or without a calling, ended up behind the walls of convents. Much like how retailers, families, and brides conspire in the TV show *Say Yes to the Dress* to turn the quest for the perfect wedding dress into the tearful prelude to the marriage contract, sixteenth-century Venice, with a few shrewd branding decisions, managed to seduce an entire generation of women with a vastly different kind of contractual celebration. To avoid the hassle of domestic disputes and quell adolescent rebelliousness, the city's upper class devised an enticing package meant to convince their daughters that only by entering the novitiate could they have the wedding of their dreams: an exceedingly lavish ceremony for taking the habit. The sight of each new batch of novices parading in white silk dresses to the convent doors, ready to become brides of Christ, gradually infused the Catholic liturgy with a dramatic allure unrivaled by even the Met Gala. These rituals became known for decadent banquets, exquisite gifts, and trousseaus overflowing with satin undergarments, embroidered veils, and the occasional piece of gold jewelry. Faced with a reality that offered few generous options, many Venetian women learned to eagerly anticipate the day of their entry into the convent. It was a wedding done right, without the added inconvenience of a husband. Had we also waited with anticipation for our own initiation ceremony? We would have never admitted it, but at the very least we were intrigued by Brown's Opening Convocation and its procession of incoming students through the legendary Van Wickle Gates—only open three times a year with rigorous solemnity. So, casting our graduate students' insouciance aside, we gave in and passed through those symbolic gates. Though the rite itself certainly felt less glamorous than a Venetian nun's profession of vows, we were, just like them, unwittingly saying yes to a life of strife only assuaged by the affection and devotion of new friendships.

Not all teenage girls in Venice were persuaded by the promise of a day teeming with feasts and haute couture. Throughout the city the young swapped eloquent verses capturing the disillusionment of a generation in a manner not dissimilar to trap lyrics: "Mother, please, don't make me take the habit, / I don't want to talk about it. / Don't make me a tunic that I don't want to wear. / All day long at vespers and all day long at mass / With the abbess yelling, it just won't pass." It was clear that beneath all the nuptial frenzy, there was an awareness that, as soon as one took the habit, the romantic mirage vanished, replaced by the austere discipline of the novitiate. Perhaps, if we had known that little verse while slowly sipping the most expensive dry martinis of our twenties, we wouldn't have been so receptive to the snobby charms of a private university. Before that first trip to Providence, we had both devoured *The Marriage Plot*, the Jeffrey Eugenides novel in which he imbues Brown University with an aura that made us see the research contract as something akin to a most stimulating marital agreement. Besides—although no one had ever presented us with anything resembling a Venetian trousseau—we soon discovered that we both shared a spirit easily swayed by the offer of indulgences, however insignificant they might be. We confess that on the two university-funded nights we spent at the Biltmore, we were not immune to the pull of a four-poster bed and room service platters of Manchego cheese and quince jelly. If that was Brown's strategy to seduce prospective grad students into choosing its programs, it certainly did the trick for us. Had we already encountered Arcangela Tarabotti's *Convent Life as Inferno*, the autobiographical manuscript in which the Venetian Benedictine nun condemned the tyrannies of monastic seclusion, we might have more cautiously considered the hell we were committing ourselves to: years of tiny apartments plagued by millennia-old filth, ascetic sleeping habits, cruel crises of intellectual faith, library halogens wrecking our once-smooth skin, a perpetual FOMO we could not shake, and aesthetic ravages (pitiful dark circles around the eyes, a sickly pallor, premature gray hairs) that we now carry around with us with the dignity of survivors. Still, we regret nothing.

╬

María de San José never regretted the path she chose after that first night she caught a glimpse of Teresa. She had plenty of opportunity—a year of isolated confinement in a microscopic cell, without the escapist refuge of scrolling at her fingertips. With her gaze lost in the blue tiles of the Portuguese Convent of São Alberto in Lisbon, María must have mixed up the bells that rang for lauds, the Eucharist, vespers, and for all those services she could no longer attend, while she wondered where she might have been at that moment had she not said yes to the Carmelite habit at the age of twenty-two. After securing a favorable marriage for María, Luisa de la Cerda might have funded her dowry. In this alternate reality, María could be staring down a future of perpetual pregnancy and long, cloying afternoons receiving courtesy visits from distant relatives in the upholstered sitting room of a more or less stately home. But what about her friends now? In that cell, she was isolated, but not alone. She knew she had an entire group of Carmelite nuns outside, encouraging her to write. She was motivated, as she would say, by the duty "that love and tenderness towards them incline me to care for the comfort and well-being of the Sisters, as if they were daughters of my heart." The path of her cloistered life had dragged her into a hellish captivity, that much was true. But just as Arcangela Tarabotti described her own monastic hell in *Convent Life as Inferno* and its luminous opposite in *Convent Life as Paradiso*, María never lost sight of the fact that her friendship with Teresa had also given her decades of dizzying thrills. Embedded in the shared biorhythms, collective strategies, and spiritual ambitions of the convent, María found the love and tenderness that we all seek.

Generally, one reaches one's fourth decade on all fours, bewildered by a tumultuous twenties and relieved to have avoided greater disaster. With varying degrees of self-forgiveness, we all must ultimately accept that, within the absurd and oppressive landscape that we're forced to negotiate, there is no choice but to reconcile with the arbitrariness of a path that has plopped us in a sufficiently good place in the present. For the nuns of the sixteenth century, options might have been more limited, but that did not lessen the vertiginous bedevilment of decision-making. Some took vows out of obligation, others out of vocation, many to avoid marriage, and more than a few because they fancied the idea of wearing one of those Benedictine habits described by a seventeenth-century traveler touring Venice as "an outfit more suited to nymphs than to nuns dedicated to a life of penance and prayer." Some sought fame through sainthood, and many, perhaps the majority, simply took vows because their aunts, friends, and cousins had done so before them. All roads through life are capricious, but those who are guided by a desire to be with their girlfriends face uncertainty with a different kind of calm. María de San José could have taken the Dominican or Benedictine path, but from the moment she felt that deep infatuation for Teresa, there was no option but the Carmelite way.

In that spring of 2016, we could have chosen Harvard, Yale, or Columbia, but in the end we decided, almost at the same time, to stay in Rhode Island. Blame it on the Biltmore, Jeffrey Eugenides, and even Emma Watson, but most of all, blame it on that night when we let the intuition of a budding friendship dictate the next years of our lives. No matter what century you're reading this in, never let the promise of a lucrative salary or the varnish of a prestigious career overshadow the prospect of a life built in community when making important life decisions. The nuns brought us together forever that first night in Providence. They soon ceased to be an object of research and became our most valuable survival tool, imparting a wealth of therapeutic teachings on how to endure isolation by navigating the stormy waters of friendship. As we often say: "Anything you are going through right now has probably already happened to a nun living several hundred years ago." The euphoria, the sleeplessness, the turbulence, the caring, the rigor, and the devotion of friendship too.

How to Survive Your Friend's Tantrums Without Banishing Them from Your Life

Every friendship has its triangulation. We all know that moment when the phone trembles in your hand and your lips burn with the need to unload all the gripes of wounded loyalty onto the friendly vertex of a neutral, understanding third party. Because you can only really speak ill of a friend to a mutual friend, just as you can only really speak ill of a mother to a sibling. For Lindsay Lohan and Paris Hilton, Britney Spears was the third vertex that completed their iconic Holy Trinity. Between Teresa and María de San José, the third piece of their triangulation was always Jerónimo Gracián.

Jerónimo was the provincial of the Carmelite order and Teresa's main ally in all her endeavors. Their mutual devotion was so deep that when the nun's tomb was opened nine months after her death, revealing her body to be completely incorrupt—who needs Botox when you have sainthood?—the friar, as her closest friend, rolled up his sleeves without the slightest hesitation and cut off the corpse's left hand so that he could take it to the Carmelites in Lisbon. But the acolytes in Portugal did not receive a full hand: Jerónimo kept the pinkie for himself. Nearly ten years later, still carrying the little finger with him, he embarked on a journey from Naples to Rome that was dramatically intercepted by Barbary pirates. Jerónimo had the sole of his foot branded with a red-hot iron and was held captive for two years under threats of being burned alive, but nothing pained him as much as the moment the pinkie was confiscated. When he was finally released in 1595, the thought of leaving Turkey without Teresa's digit never even crossed his mind. Later on, he wrote in a marginal note on the first printed biography of Teresa: "I recovered it [the pinkie] for about twenty *reales* and some gold rings I had made with some small rubies that adorned the finger." Jerónimo knew that, regardless of its size or macabre nature, the relic of a close friend, and the memories it contained, was worth the peril of a life-or-death haggle.

The friar had many reasons to cling to Teresa's anatomical

amulet for support. That ill-fated journey was part of a pilgrimage to the Vatican meant to persuade Pope Clement VIII that Jerónimo was being subjected to a ruthless and baseless persecution by his own order. In February 1592, after a humiliating and very public judicial process, Jerónimo had been expelled from the Carmelites. Behind this campaign of harassment was a complex amalgamation of personal grievances and radically opposed views on how external or autonomous the governance of the convents and the spiritual direction of the nuns should be. There was also long-standing concern about the friendship between the friar and María de San José. As early as 1578, when María was the very young prioress of the Seville convent, two of her nuns, Beatriz de la Madre de Dios and Isabel de San Jerónimo, began having visions and prophecies (just another day in sixteenth-century Spain). In the investigations that followed, Jerónimo himself became embroiled in the scandal, accused by his enemies of being a Carmelite Sean "Diddy" Combs, dancing naked in front of the nuns and spending less-than-devout nights with María de San José. Those allegations came to nothing and were dismissed as mere tabloid rumors. In 1585, however, the whispers resurfaced. The leadership of the order grew wary of the time Jerónimo spent with María at her convent in Lisbon. It was rumored that the friar let the nuns there wash his shirts and cook his favorite dishes because—as has always been true—male feminist allies always have a secret self-serving agenda. Shortly before his kidnapping, Jerónimo received a papal brief that officially approved his cancellation. María, who had already made significant enemies by defending Teresa's legacy, also caused quite an uproar with her letters defending her friend Jerónimo. On September 25, 1587, she wrote a letter—nothing short of sassy by sixteenth-century nuns' standards—to Provincial Vicar Antonio de Jesús threatening him and all the high-rank friars who were willing to ruin her reputation: "It has come to our attention that they say the whole province is scandalized by the familiarity and conversations that Fray Jerónimo Gracián had with us during the time when he was Vicar General here. For that reason, our conscience compels us, for the sake of the Father's honor as well as for our own, to seek a means for the truth to be acknowledged and the scandal to disappear." That's how she ended up imprisoned and isolated in her Lisbon cell.

Teresa knew that Jerónimo loved María as much as he loved her. That is why, when her closest disciple tests her patience and she finds herself gripping a pen until her knuckles hurt, he is the only person to whom she can imagine venting. On October 4, 1579, Teresa wrote to Jerónimo the kind of message that makes you wish iMessage shall never get hacked and your treasons revealed:

> It is with great sorrow that I am troubled by the folly of that prioress [María de San José]. She has lost much credit with me. I fear that the devil has begun to work in that house, which I cannot endure, and this prioress is more cunning than her position demands. Thus, I fear she deceives us, as I once told her, for she never dealt plainly with me. She possesses much of the Andalusian nature. I tell you, I endured much there with her. As she has written to me many times with great repentance, I thought she had reformed, for she seemed aware of her faults. I have written her terrible letters, but it is no more effective than striking steel.

The letter is brimming with ire. Teresa has received news that María, driven by an itch for acquiring real estate, is considering moving the Seville convent to another building. Teresa tries to remain calm, but she is already overwhelmed by too many impertinences from a friend who, she sometimes thinks, no vow of poverty can ever free from the indulgences of a pampered childhood. Only four years have passed since they secured the building where the Carmelite nuns of Seville now live. Under the cover of night, Teresa, María, and two other nuns had squatted in the vacant building that a group of Franciscan friars were reluctant to sell. Teresa believed that none of them would ever forget the "great fear" they endured during those first nights when "all the shadows they saw appeared to them friars," nor the nightmare of the following month, when they were forced to live together in a cramped basement while workers renovated the building's main structure. What surprises her most is how quickly María seems

to have forgotten their shared enthusiasm for completing the property in Seville, with its orange blossom water fountain and panoramic views that Teresa misses so dearly. Teresa doesn't know where María is planning to move next, but she knows, and tells Jerónimo, that in any new house, "they will not have the views they enjoy from this one, which is a great delight for the nuns and the best feature of the place. Over here, they are quite envious of it." Teresa's anger is like the frustration any of us would feel watching a friend abandon a rent-controlled apartment in the heart of a city ravaged by speculation. Yet her outburst conceals something deeper: the pain of realizing that María is discarding, without any shred of remorse or longing, the emotional territory of a shared project.

Today, Teresa would be the friend insisting that everyone enable location tracking in shared apps for safety reasons, the one who knows everyone's work schedules, vacations, and the dates of their gynecological appointments by heart. Sometimes, Teresa managed to conceal her need for group surveillance under the guise of affectionate words. At other times, she couldn't maintain the pretense and ended up unleashing her more controlling nature: "I tell you," she confessed to Jerónimo, who was already more than accustomed to his friend's authoritative nature, "that I am terribly upset that I do not have the freedom to do myself what I am telling others to do." To be fair, María didn't make it easy for her. Her often sly and secretive ways were a constant burden on the relationship. When Isabel and Beatriz, those nuns who in 1578 had landed with their visionary howls the entire Seville convent in an extremely uncomfortable situation, Teresa had only three pieces of advice for María: Isabel should eat meat for a few days, Beatriz should tone down the intensity of her fasts, and María should do everything she could to smooth things over with the nuns' confessor to avoid tensions that could further raise the suspicions of the Inquisition. María read Teresa's letters, responded affectionately and obediently, and then capsized the plan by rudely dismissing the confessor. Teresa never understood why she did this behind her back. Why look for another building in secret and why not tell her about the tumultuous dismissal? Also, why hide the fact that she was negotiating for money with Fray Nicolao de Jesús María? (Perhaps María would have been more cautious had she known that, in a few years, that same scheming and manipulative friar would end up sabotaging the Carmelite reform.) "What has displeased me," Teresa reproaches her in a letter, is "that you both in the end acted against my wishes." Deep down, Teresa knows why. Because María is a spoiled and malicious girl, a "cunning fox," as she tells María herself, almost splintering her quill against the paper with the same rage that must have driven Paris Hilton to maliciously laugh at her friend Brandon Davis's calling Lindsay Lohan a "firecrotch." Teresa's vocal cords contract in a spasm as she holds back the urge to cry. María was a cunning and slippery creature who they should never have trusted.

This sudden estrangement between the two Carmelites was as melodramatic as the fallout between Lindsay and Paris, but unlike the warring nuns, the twists and turns of the celebrities' friendship strayed far beyond the privacy of letters. Sensationalist magazine coverage no doubt intensified their conflicts, but for generations lacking a collective image of female friendship, two decades of media immortalization publicly demonstrated the subtle complexities that have always been a part of the story of female friends. Reading that the famous pair reconnected after Lindsay's engagement in 2021—"We're not in high school anymore," Paris stated—any twenty-first-century girl can aspire to see her friendship breakups mended. But where was Teresa supposed to look for role models?

Teresa often thought about the final embrace of two particular friends, Saint Felicitas and Saint Perpetua, Carthaginian martyrs who died together in a third-century amphitheater after refusing to worship pagan gods. (If you live in the times of classical antiquity and your best friend refuses to worship pagan gods, then you refuse too.) She also frequently reflected on Saint Justa and Saint Rufina, two sisters from Seville who, also in the third century, chose to endure the torture of the rack and iron hooks rather than renounce Christ by venerating a figurine of a Babylonian goddess. The end of a friendship was supposed to be marked by the defiant and fanatical courage of a Counter-Reformation Thelma and Louise, not marred by murkiness and secrets. Truth be told, Teresa had wished to replicate the guiding relationship that Saint Anne had with her daughter, the Virgin Mary, in her friendship with María. She longed to see in her friend the same dazzled disciple she had first inspired years ago in the palace of Luisa de la Cerda. But María was no longer a child; she was a prioress with her own agenda. The model of Saint Anne no longer applied. In fact, it only served to exacerbate old insecurities.

Teresa never had access to formal education. As a child, she had to learn on the fly from her mother's readings and prayers. She never mastered the intellectual refinement of Latin and could never quite rid herself of the envy she felt watching María flaunt her education. For her friend, the palace of Luisa de la Cerda had served as an elite boarding school where she learned to conquer Castilian grammar, ace French and Latin, dabble in the metrical forms of the Italian sonnet, and interpret the Bible as she pleased. A bit like us. We've often found comfort in imagining how the eccentricity of our academic sacrifice might have served us well in captivating María. But this wasn't always the case. The ghosts of impostor syndrome hovered over many of our days that first year at Brown; the possibility of blanking during the Q&A session at a conference was enough to give us cold sweats. Faced with such self-doubt, one of us elected to give up a summer of friends, beer, and vitamin D to seek her own palatial erudition at an intensive three-month Latin course hosted by a prestigious New York university that advertised the opportunity to acquire a level of skill that would usually take a decade. We were both equally seduced by the promise of intellectual validation that comes from mastering a dead language. Who knows, together, we might have been able to make it through the language boot camp. But that was not to pass:

—Carmen, will you still love me when you come back in September a Latin native?
—Ana, I can't take it anymore. This tyrannical military discipline required to learn Latin is absurd. A misstep in a declension means unbearable public humiliation. If at 4 a.m. you're not sweaty on the phone with the professor, discussing various versions of a Catullus translation, it's like you're doing something wrong. I don't want to spend my summer crying because of these Latinists with sociopathic tendencies, but I don't know how to quit.

Fortunately, friendship can save you from almost anything, including this. Between sobs, we assured each other that no one deserved to risk their sanity for a few crumbs of scholarship. Better not to know Latin at all than to go through such an ordeal. Besides, would our friendship have survived an imbalance in Latin proficiency? Teresa and María's almost didn't.

Generally, Teresa viewed María's intellect with pride and affection, referring to her as "my little scholar" on many occasions. There were, however, times when she wanted to slap her for being a "know-it-all," such as in 1576, when María wrote a letter to Father Ambrosio Mariano de San Benito, a Discalced Carmelite renowned for his engineering and mathematical knowledge, and tried to flaunt her learning by peppering the lines with Latin quotes. Teresa's reprimand was swift: "God spare all my daughters from showing off their Latin," she wrote at once. "I much prefer they take pride in seeming simple, which is very saintly, rather than rhetorical." This outburst carries a whiff of anti-intellectualism that doesn't represent the true spirit of Teresa's foundations ("I prefer having her [a smart nun with no dowry] to taking in foolish nuns," she had also said.). She also didn't want them to be conceited or arrogant, nor did she want them to boast about having more education than she did. Above all, she could not stand the idea of the prioress being able to comprehend codes that eluded her. How did the future saint know that her friend had stuffed that letter with Latin phrases? Because María, her intentions known only to herself, had deliberately sent it unsealed.

—✢—

And then there's a painful truth: It's never been possible to keep the thorny issue of money out of friendship. Not even the endless wealth of Beverly Hills prevented Lindsay and Paris from stumbling over the tricky topic of finances in 2006 when a squad of paparazzi captured Paris laughing gleefully, her veneers sparkling, at Lindsay's alleged financial problems (the "problems" being that the actress's assets, tragically, did not exceed $7 million). The equalizing, communal setting of the convent should not lead us to believe that the Carmelites could keep their relationships free from financial concerns. With María de San José, as Teresa well knew, it was impossible.

One hot day in 1576, the convent of Malagón, Spain, receives an unexpected package containing half-squashed quince jelly, some tiny fish, and a little tuna from María. Teresa smiles appreciatively at the gesture, but her smile fades as she begins to count the costs of delivering this relatively modest care package—María's gift doesn't seem so cute anymore. While the novices buzz around her, tearing into the package and smearing their cheeks with stray jelly in their haste, the founder realizes it would be pointless to reprimand María, just as she didn't expect much from the letter she had scribbled angrily only two days before. She had reluctantly thanked her for the surprise shipment of orange blossom water for the nuns and the veil for the Carmelite friar Juan de la Cruz. But she could not do the same for the money. Money meant something else entirely. When she opened that package, the sight of coins stung her eyes like an open sore: "How can you presume to send money already! This struck me as funny"—she wrote, disguising her exasperation as sarcasm—"since I am so worried about what you are going to live on." Remember, the founding of the Seville convent had been a nightmare. The squatting of the property had been a success, but the faith the nuns had placed in the charitable spirit of the city's wealthy families for their sustenance had proven to be a tremendous miscalculation. No one had offered them financial support. For months, all they had were fragile wicker structures strewn across the floor and a couple of mattresses eaten away by grime and bedbugs. Even now, in Malagón, Teresa spends many early mornings burning the convent's candles as she scrawls away on crumpled papers, trying to balance the accounts to support her sisters in Seville. It drives her to despair that, during all this, María indulges in the arrogance of exorbitant gift-giving.

"You must dream of being some kind of queen," she will scold María a year later. "Don't presume to do such things again. When I need something, I'll let you know." The unspoken rules of the gift economy have always put friendship at risk. Teresa knew that behind every act of generosity lurks the possibility of incurring an eternal debt, that in any friendship, extravagant gifts are often a red flag or a red herring.

In December 1577, still unsure how to handle María's impudence, Teresa learns that her friend has been house hunting. She's managed to quell her anger up to this point, attributing it to María's openhanded nature. But when she starts tallying up the ducats that the foolish María will have to spend to cover the move, her irritation thickens into a bile reserved only for financial betrayals involving friends and family. "I do not understand," she writes to María on December 10, 1577, "with what money [you] plan to buy another house." Finally, abandoning any restraint, Teresa gets petty: "If you have so much money, don't forget what you owe my brother." We'd give up the privilege of a lifelong gift card to the home section of our favorite department store (and we are both ardent fans of all things domestic) just to see María's face when she read that letter. The prioress knew perfectly well that the building in Seville was theirs thanks to the fortuitous investment of Lorenzo de Cepeda, Teresa's brother. When the convent's financial situation improved, María continued to procrastinate on repaying the loan. More painful still, in 1579, Teresa asked several times for the funds needed to build a small chapel in memory of her recently deceased brother. María never sent the money.

-+|-

In the last letter Teresa sends to María, the paragraphs of the saint's exhausted handwriting, ravaged by the uterine cancer that will take her life a few months later, are interspersed with the light script of a scribe. Despite Teresa's "tired head" and mounting tensions between them, María's well-being is top of mind, especially in light of the horrifying news out of Seville: The plague is decimating the city's population. The thought of María, thirty-three years younger, wasted away from unending headaches and vomiting, her body covered in purulent buboes, plunges Teresa into indescribable anguish. When she finally receives a couple of hopeful letters from María, assuring her that she and all her sisters are safe—enforced seclusion was a very effective way to ward off the plagues—Teresa finds the peace she seeks to surrender to her body's frailties: "Your letter was a great consolation in that you tell me the nuns are not sick—not even a headache. It doesn't surprise me that they are well considering the prayers that are offered for them in every house; they even ought to be saints after so many supplications. I at least am ever concerned about all of you and will never forget you."

Caring for others so that they are never forgotten was always a feature present among the Carmelites, as embodied by Teresa, María, and many others, who fought tirelessly to secure the survival of their little patch of the world. This didn't mean that betrayals didn't hurt or that slights were forgotten. The pact of enclosure and the shared devotion to their project created a small, intimate circle of mutual vulnerability and dependence. In this setting, occasional moments of toxicity were not enough for its members to abandon attachments that were meant to last forever. Perhaps that is why, when Teresa received a letter from María in July 1576 saturated in remorse for not having spent more time with her during the months they spent together at the Seville convent, Teresa hastened to reassure her with a love bomb that neither would ever forget:

I assure you that I am touched at the loneliness you say you feel at my absence. The enclosed letter was already written when yours arrived. I was so delighted to get it that I felt softened and ready to grant you pardon. *If only you will love me as much as I love you, I forgive you all you have done and will do*, for my chief complaint against you now is that you cared so little to be with me.

Neither of us would have handled the years of our PhD program without the survival manuals of our nuns, nor without the professional help of our therapists (who, incidentally, are also friends with each other). It is precisely because of this that we remain wary of certain therapeutic approaches that encourage severing relationships that we deem too toxic, too unproductive, or unworthy of energy. In a community of thirteen Carmelite women, none could have followed such ideas without turning the convent into an unbearable war zone or fatally disrupting the collective spiritual project. Reclaiming the convent for the twenty-first century might be less about attending choir together or withdrawing from secular life (though that too retains its allure), and more to do with maneuvering the terrain of friendship with the interdependence of the Carmelites: maintaining the bonds of friendship with the care one gives to a delicate miniature, even when the temptation arises to cut someone loose.

How Teresa of Jesus Created the Commune of Female Friends You've Been Dreaming Of

Romanticizing independence is difficult in a 269-square-foot apartment where economy is not a choice, but a matter of survival. Nor is it easy to idealize communal living when you share a bathroom with a complete stranger whose shaving habits have become etched in your mind because every third day your sink becomes a graveyard of facial hair. Living under the same roof can be a blessing or the greatest of agonies. We would ban forced cohabitation projects that attempt to cover up the plunder of gentrification, but we celebrate utopian attempts to live with our girlfriends. All of a sudden, returning to the convent doesn't seem like a bad idea. Remote work has intensified the sense of demoralization and absurdity we feel during our nine-to-fives while increasing the appeal of collaborating with others to achieve something tangible and meaningful. Those mired in the hell of heterosexual dating have always needed a Carrie Bradshaw–like guiding light to navigate its nine fiery circles, but apparently—according to a *Financial Times* report on a widening ideological gap within Gen Z that separates the genders—more women have simply given up trying. (Everybody has a friend who unknowingly echoes the complete disinterest in men expressed by a seventeenth-century Mexican nun: "I never kept company with a single male, because I have always felt an unspeakable horror and dread of them, which has always made me flee as soon as I could at times when I had to speak with some man.") This stubborn pushback against certain societal norms is perhaps, in part, why the nun-core aesthetic seems to have enjoyed such a revival. We see it on the runway at fashion shows for major brands like The Row, the Olsen twins' company; in the photographs of Rihanna portrayed as a sultry nun shot by Nadia Lee Cohen for *Interview Magazine*; and in the memes that your girlfriends send you, threatening to leave it all behind and relocate the group chat to a convent. As Maria Stanchieri put it in her 2022 article for *NSS Magazine*, "We may have officially entered the nun-core season." The joke is becoming more and more common—and much more serious. We all have reasons, beyond religious vocation or the expense of a dowry, to fantasize about living in a convent. Saint Teresa had them too.

✢

Ten successive pregnancies had driven Beatriz de Ahumada, the mother of Teresa, to her death when Teresa was only twelve years old. Teresa's thoughts were forever haunted by her mother's screams during childbirth, and the memory of her frail body suffering alone in a house overflowing with children. If you were a woman, Teresa learned, the exhaustion of managing a household could consume you and take your life before you were even forty. So we can imagine how, years later when Teresa rang the bell to inaugurate her first convent in 1562, it felt like a collective victory: thirteen women living together, free from the tyranny of reproduction. Eight years later, inspired by this communal passion and enchanted by Teresa's self-aggrandizing performance, María would adopt the Carmelite habit. By then, Teresa was adept at plotting her way through the intricate corridors of palaces and convents, artfully handling disputes with men of the ecclesiastical hierarchy and engaging with the controversies surrounding mental prayer. (It's true, as Teresa believed, that praying in silence without a repetitive formula might be a more authentic and meditative approach to prayer. However, who could guarantee that the nuns, perpetually silent, were truly engaged in prayer rather than trying to remember how many eggs were left in the convent kitchen or daydreaming about the upcoming Christmas party?) Teresa managed mortgages and loans with the cunning of an experienced moneylender, wrote compulsively, and was resigned to the physical toll that constant travel between the numerous convents she had founded levied on her body. At fifty-five, retirement was far from her mind. Her life before becoming a nun had faded into a jumble of distant memories: the floral scent of cosmetics, reading knights' tales with her mother, occasional frivolity, debilitating illnesses, and the emotional pain of seeing her brothers flee to the Americas.

At just twenty years old, with the fervor and eagerness only a recent teenager can muster, Teresa committed herself to life in La Encarnación, a monastery crowded with two hundred wealthy girls who never tired of receiving visitors or candies. Why would they? In *The Life* Teresa confessed that, in the almost three decades that she spent in that convent, even she could not help but "indulge in one pastime after another, in one vanity after another and in one occasion of sin after another." Life in La Encarnación was never as sinful as that party where Nicole Richie played Paris Hilton's sex tape, nor as wild as the Jay-Z listening party where someone bit Beyoncé's cheek, and it is highly unlikely that, even in their worst and most dissipated days, Teresa and her nuns would have stirred up the convent's parlor with a challenge even half as bawdy as Katy Perry's when she offered her guests the chance to pose with a photo of a paparazzied, paddleboarding, naked Orlando Bloom. But still, the discipline in Teresa's first convent was loose enough to lead its women astray. "Youth, sensuality and the devil," she reflected, "invite and incline them to do things which are completely worldly; and they see that these things are considered, as one might say, 'al right.'" Teresa must have felt like someone who knows she's chosen the wrong sorority in college. But who could have blamed her? A sixteenth-century religious woman had the same chances as your high-school self of ending up with the mean girls. Young nuns, wrote Teresa, "wish to escape from the world, and, thinking that they are going to serve the Lord and flee from the world and its perils, they find themselves in ten worlds at once, and have no idea where to turn or how to get out of their difficulties." Internally, Teresa always felt "unliked" in La

Encarnación because she was the type of person to prefer a living arrangement with not even a hint of debauchery, no lavishness, and, above all, a much more intimate, less crowded atmosphere where true confidence and affection could blossom. Although she "knew neither how nor when," she was "very certain" that what she wanted to do was to "found a convent more strictly enclosed." Founding a religious order based on poverty and contemplation in sixteenth-century Spain as a woman with mystical tendencies and Jewish ancestors was an unsurprisingly difficult undertaking. Teresa nurtured her idea for two decades, knowing that since "I was quite alone [. . .] there was so very little that I could do." So she started talking. She spoke and negotiated tirelessly with bishops, confessors, sisters, friends, and colleagues. During the course of this process, she came to learn, as many do, that you cannot achieve much on your own. Grand plans need great friends. By the time she died in 1582, Teresa had successfully founded seventeen convents. If she'd lived several centuries later, we are certain she could have maintained a lucrative side hustle giving TED talks about her Carmelite achievements.

†††

The itch of coarse fabrics and the chafe of hemp sandals would periodically remind Teresa, María, and countless other sore nuns of the vanities they had left behind. Yet the companionship, comfort, and conversations offered by their sisters more than compensated for the trials of life behind the lattice windows. And there were many trials. The stifled yawns after the early morning call to lauds, the hands chapped from tedious domestic work, and a palate bored with the same food day in and day out—not to mention the condescending attitude of certain confessors, the economic backflips necessary to keep the convents afloat, and the arrogance of the many capricious widows who sought refuge in the calm of a cell but were unwilling to bow to the demands of community life. But bland spoonfuls of lentils in a freezing refectory or harsh scoldings from prelates could never diminish the pleasure that Teresa's nuns discovered in the convents when they shared moments of fun, cared for one another, read together, or sang the catchy four-line stanza "The founding Mother / comes to recreation. / Let's dance, let's sing, / let's rise our intonation." These innocent pastimes surely sound less provocative than the mischievousness of La Encarnación's party girls, and certainly less costly than María's teenage palace distractions. And yet the writings of both Teresa and María speak of the incomparable joy of connection formed at an intimate sleepover while everyone else is slaying at the club. Their conviction helped us see our joint academic confinement as an unexpected blessing—and it wasn't easy.

Many months had passed since our first meeting at the Biltmore Hotel. Memories of plush canopy beds and plasma TVs often breached our minds as we struggled to find remotely comfortable positions on our IKEA mattresses from which to squint at blurry photocopies of obscure theological documents. We didn't have to deal with the itchiness of rough habits or blisters from hemp sandals, but our dreams of grandeur had been largely buried under grueling schedules that would challenge even the most dedicated Carmelite. We were truly miserable. Maintaining the image of an impeccable student meant sleeping five hours a day, analyzing sonnets by Sor Juana Inés de la Cruz over breakfast, losing patience with convoluted poststructuralist texts, and socializing with patronizing professors at events that drained our will to live. Like María de San José, we missed the life we had left behind at the doors of this deceptively idyllic confinement. Yet, just as María had found, no amount of haggard eye bags, unremitting financial insecurity, or tomes of laborious writing could overshadow our elation at having found, amid the groans and yawns, the camaraderie of a true ally. Would we have given up everything, a few Friday nights, just to spend a couple of hours being two Encarnación sort of girls? Probably. But at heart we knew we would always hold dear to this friendship of ours, born and nurtured in the hardest of cloisters, and that we wouldn't change the way things were for all the decadence in the world.

☩

"For charity's sake, I beg you to write me through every means you can so that I may always know how you all are." It is June 15, 1576, and Teresa has found a moment of peace to sit and write these words as she adjusts to life at the convent of Malagón in Toledo. She is over sixty years old, and the aftermath of the arduous 220-mile journey from Seville has kept her from her correspondence for several days. The scene that greeted her on arriving in Malagón is distressing: The convent is so dilapidated that the nuns can barely live within its walls. The prioress, Brianda de San José, is bedridden with a severe and mysterious illness. Meanwhile, Luisa de la Cerda, Teresa's widowed friend and now sponsor of the convent, is reluctant to fulfill her promise to pay for the necessary repairs. For a few days, all this commotion distracts Teresa from her nostalgia for Seville. After all, she reminds herself, the city was not for her: the "lack of honesty," "injustices" and "hypocrisy" of its people, and the "abomination of sins you find there" never alleviated her feeling of being a stranger. But now that she knows she will never return, she cannot stop thinking about the Andalusian convent she left behind. She hasn't had time to shake off the cloying sensation of sweat under her habit, nor the fond memory of the nuns in Seville whispering together as they admired the spectacle of galleys arriving at the Guadalquivir River from across the Atlantic. She tries not to dwell on it too much—she was the first to detest "melancholic" and "gloomy" nuns—but bidding farewell to María de San José, whom she left in charge of the convent in Seville, reverberates relentlessly in her mind. She wants María to write to her constantly, *out of charity*, to try to reconstruct the oasis of her friendship.

They will never see each other again.

We have often fantasized about this farewell: Was it controlled and sterile, or emotional and tearful? It's unlikely to have been a private occasion, because everyone would have wanted to accompany the founding mother to the gate. María, let us not forget, was trained in aristocratic restraint and concealment, and given she needed to project enough authority as prioress that no one would doubt her leadership, she had more reason than ever to hide her emotions behind an inscrutable expression. Sometimes it's just impossible to serve sensitivity and authority at the same time. Teresa, for her part, was already deeply invested in the persona she had created for herself, bound by a tyranny of well-being that she hoped would inspire the people around her. She likely downplayed the farewell, perhaps even encouraging the nuns to smile or improvising a quick *copla* to lighten the mood. Maybe they reminisced about that eventful trip they took to Seville the year before, a journey that had strengthened their friendship as nothing else could have.

Seven nuns, two friars, and a layperson composed the expedition that traveled to Seville in unbearable heat. Teresa's fevers, which left her "as if delirious," kept everyone on edge, unable to rest at the intermittent Castilian inns, which were less inviting than even the worst roadside motel. All of them barely made it out alive. While crossing the Guadalquivir River, one of the carriages was swept away by the current, leaving the nuns unable to do anything but scream and pray for a miracle, which duly came: "the boat happened to turn on sandy ground, where was little water, and thus a remedy was provided," Teresa would recall with relief. What could have been a disaster ended up only a shocking fright. The less traumatic scenes were ones of ordinary warmth: the morning rush to gather firewood, egged on by María's friend who directed the routine with the agility and contagious zeal of a Pilates instructor; the songs Teresa composed according to each new episode of their adventure—a sort of musical that was part epic, part convent story, and part autobiography that drove away the fear and melancholy of the younger nuns; and then there was the silent but meaningful glance they all exchanged by the Guadalquivir River when Teresa broke the group's stunned silence with a joke about the accident, instantly raising everyone's spirits. As we all know, a look exchanged between two friends facing the tragedy of lost luggage, a missed life-or-death connection, a nightmare vacation rental, or a bout of food poisoning miles from reliable plumbing is the blood pact that guarantees a lifelong friendship.

In 2017, a year after we met, we boarded a plane to Puerto Rico, determined to break the monotony of our studies by adding some lush Caribbean landscapes to our lives. The people we traveled with were poorly chosen, we overestimated our tolerance for alcohol after a year of monastic sobriety, and we shared a windowless room that provided not only shelter for us but also for 90 percent of the island's mosquitoes. To make matters worse, Hurricane María hit. Amid the clatter of trash cans and streetlights snapping, we remembered the journey of Teresa and María de San José. If they had overcome such hardships to reach Seville, and if we knew of nuns who had managed to evade pirates and survive maritime storms to travel from Toledo to Manila, then we could certainly endure the calamities of having planned the worst vacation ever. At least we realized that we were no longer just PhD companions. Like María and Teresa, we were finally true friends.

Since a shared obsession with nuns first brought us together, we have never been apart for more than a couple of months. Our worst nightmare is a separation that cannot be bridged by instant messaging, video calls, and the occasional meme shared during sleepless bouts of procrastination. It was the same for Teresa. From the last of those farewell hugs at the gates of the Seville convent, she spent her days tormented by separation anxiety. Religious life had given her a sense of belonging through the comfort and protection of friendship, but her thirst for spiritual fulfillment brought with it an ache of longing. Desperate after weeks of waiting for mail, she would imagine what her María might be saying in the letters that frequently got lost along the way, or in the ones in which her friend's poor handwriting made it impossible to decipher a name or adjective. "They [the letters]," writes Teresa in a letter of her own dated July 2, 1576, "arrived in good condition, but whenever you try to improve your handwriting, it gets worse." She demanded more and more letters all the while painstakingly attempting to commit to paper a scrap, no matter how small, of her yearning for María's presence. A letter sent by Teresa on January 3, 1577, is both an exquisite display of first-class guilt-tripping manipulation and an alluring lullaby of friendly seduction: "I was very glad to see your letter, but should be far more glad to see you. It would give me special pleasure just now, for I think we should be close friends. There are few with whom I like to talk on many matters as I do with you, for you really suit me exactly, so that it delights me when I realize from your letters that you have realized it too." It was the letter every girl dreams she'll get from her friend crush.

※

It is September 1576, and Teresa and María have suffered a summer full of worries: The Seville convent is overwhelmed by debts, María is suffering from an illness that only Ozempic-like purges can relieve, and the Inquisition is closely watching the Discalced Carmelites of Seville. Upon hearing the mail approaching, Teresa rushes to the turnstile and smiles when she discovers that a package from María has finally arrived. The quince jam, small fish, and tuna that María sends add color to the dismal food landscape in Castile, but as we know, Teresa can't help but resent her friend's brazen squandering. However, she almost forgets everything as soon as she finds that María has enclosed two letters folded together for the price of one: "I can truthfully say that your letters are such a consolation. When I read the one and thought there were no more, I myself was surprised by the happiness I felt when I discovered another one; it was as though I hadn't received the first. You should then realize that your letters are a kind of recreation for me." She confesses: "You should know that at times I have such a desire to see you that it would seem I have nothing else to think about; this is true."

In the years that followed our dry martinis in the Biltmore lobby, we devoured Teresa's letters to María de San José with the same dedication we once possessed as ten-year-olds grappling with the nuances of friendship by watching coming-of-age TV movies. We discovered that piloting the complex desires of friendships in our thirties was made unexpectedly easier by reading how sixteenth-century cloistered nuns expressed their affection in intricate equations of love and how they were always ready to painstakingly build convincing mirages of proximity. Each time she begins a letter to her friend, Teresa is eager to acknowledge the truth that she deeply misses María. She sheds any semblance of moderation, rejecting the pretense of coldness and indulging in confessions of exclusivity that are toxic but unavoidable because, as she will soon admit: "It would be a great consolation for me to see you, for I find few nuns so pleasing to me, and I love you greatly."

Teresa of Jesús died on October 4, 1582, when María was just thirty-four years old. Her profound grief at the loss of not only a woman she esteemed and enraged in equal measure but also the trove of memories they had shared since she was a fussy twenty-something soon alchemized into a powerful yearning for emulation. Teresa had been her friend, confidante, and teacher. How many others could say the same? It maddened her to think that for decades, Teresa had been the object of a parasocial relationship nurtured by hundreds of nuns who only wanted a bit of her fame to rub off on them. And behind the myth of Teresa lurked a group of recalcitrant theologians and envious friars who had been lying in wait for years. They eagerly anticipated the death of this "restless, wandering, disobedient and obstinate woman" for an opportunity to dismantle her convent.

In October 1582, Teresa's advice echoed in María's mind like mantras: "Better to indulge oneself than to be unwell"; "Women understand one another's language best." María found solace in knowing she was not alone in her spiritual orphanhood. She sensed that at that very moment, there was a squadron of scattered Carmelites who, while watering their vegetable gardens or scrubbing the tiles of their cells, muttered Teresa's mandates of joy with pursed lips, hoping to soothe their sadness. She liked feeling accompanied in her mourning—to a certain extent. Just like that friend of yours who "doesn't get" polyamory, María didn't believe in hierarchy-free relationships. She took a perverse pleasure in knowing she would never have to blend into the background behind a vast army of anonymous nuns. None of them could claim as many letters from a woman who, everyone agreed, was on the brink of achieving the most exclusive status of the sixteenth century: sainthood. To no one else had Teresa written, with the trembling handwriting of someone nearing death, that "you say everything so well that if my opinion were followed, they would elect you foundress, after my death. And even if I were living, I would be eagerly in favor, for you know much more than I do, and are better; that is the truth." María valued this letter so much that, in 1588, she called a notary to make an official transcription, the closest thing at that time to a backup copy, in case she lost the original.

Had they been able to leaf through them, Teresa and María would have read with disdain the thousands of lists that flood today's women's magazines with advice on how to cultivate friendships in lives overwhelmed by the demands of productivity. They both knew that no tie is more invincible than one born from sharing an ambitious and delirious strategy for geo-religious expansion. Lacking any grief management manuals in 1582, María sensed the sorrow she felt would only be alleviated if she got down to work on some of the many tasks that Teresa had left unfinished. "What joy it would bring me if Portugal were to happen!" Teresa had written to her, almost in a whisper, a couple of years earlier. It was decided: If María devoted herself wholeheartedly to leading a small group of Carmelite nuns to Lisbon, she might feel closer to her friend.

Three years later, in January 1585, María de San José inaugurated the convent of São Alberto in Lisbon. Shortly after its founding, the convent received a gift from the provincial of the order—the inauguration present every Carmelite nun dreams of: the incorrupt hand of Teresa, a piece of flesh so worshipped that it would later end up preserved in an ornate shrine (gilded silver, precious stones) strikingly identical to Thanos's gauntlet. Everything was progressing perfectly, but the happiness would not last long.

—⫶—

Years later, locked away in the cold prison of Lisbon, María would feel fear as a splinter in her throat—and yet, she would convince herself that she was not alone. Setting aside her obsession with an exclusive friendship with Teresa and with the tricky "best friend" narrative that every girl has to face at some point in her life, María found courage through the distant yet impassioned company of all her companions. These lines from her sixteenth-century *Letter Written by a Poor and Imprisoned Discalced Nun* should be our collective twenty-first century reminder to always surround ourselves with a squadron of—maybe not so virginal—friends:

> I do not know, my dearest sisters and daughters, whether to give in to the passion and tenderness of a woman and join you in your tears, or to follow the light of my heart and lament your sorrow, for it is not fitting, according to the *law of the close friendship we share*, that you should cry over what makes me laugh . . . I will always take pride, if I may, in being *surrounded by a squadron of virgins* who, though few, are great in valor. In their strength, I feel the power of your valiant arms against our common enemy, who, seeing my defenders, has not dared to approach the prison door as he would like.

In her *Spiritual Conferences*, many years after Teresa's death, Ana de San Bartolomé, another of the saint's dearest disciples and friends, faced the challenging task of instructing the novices at a newly founded convent in Antwerp. Although Teresa had already been canonized and was widely praised for her mystical prowess, Ana chose to teach her novices the lesson she thought would help them the most when they encountered spells of sorrow and needed to ease their estrangement: "And you will see for yourselves that sometimes you will go reluctantly to recreation feeling sad and melancholic, but you will find that the joy and good spirit of the sisters will distract you from your sorrow and turn it into happiness." No matter what century you're reading this in: The most reliable cure for ailments of the spirit is always a good time with your girlfriends.

Work

> *It seems impossible, given my circumstances, that I can write as much as needs to be written.*
>
> María de San José

"The Greatest Repugnance" for Work: How to Turn Your Problems into Prayers

Sixteen square feet had never felt so suffocating. Juana Palacios Berruecos (1656–1719)—renamed María de San José upon entering the convent, conventual naming conventions having very little fear of repetition—paces back and forth, barely managing three steps in one direction and three back, certain that her despair echoes like thunder throughout the immensity of the Santa Mónica convent in Puebla, Mexico. A true Taurus, she is not one to be easily swayed by sudden flashes of anger but, when sufficiently provoked, her displeasure can be irreversible. After that day's particularly frustrating showdown, the nun has good reason to believe that her superiors have done everything in their power to drive her mad. If María were a corporate woman trapped in some twenty-first-century multinational company, rather than a poor, seventeenth-century Augustinian Recollect, her righteous fury would drive her straight to HR, resignation letter in hand.

The nuns of the seventeenth century knew just as well as you or us that nobody can survive forty hours a week—whether it's manning Excel spreadsheets or baking hundreds of Communion wafers—without resorting to complaining into the ether. They also knew that working in vain for a bunch of clueless, incompetent bosses is wont to ignite the dangerous engines of indignation. As two small creatures in a tiny academic bubble, our relationship with our superiors—thesis advisors, professors, editors—has always felt much more like the intimate vassalage of feudalism than the cold dynamic of corporate logic, a way of thinking that remains largely alien to us. It might seem strange, but the truth is that nothing has helped us decipher the noisy confusion of corporate jargon (bonuses, KPIs, COOs) quite like the life and work of this particular Augustinian Recollect. Much to María's misfortune, while religious institutions lacked a human resources department, the rigid hierarchies that managed the convents did resemble the organizational structures of most modern multimillion-dollar corporations. Between the confessor who extended a hand under the guise of friendship to ensure your spiritual writing did not stray too far from the order's party line and the bishop with the final say on whether your excessive vocation was mere theatrics or a genuine divine calling, there stretched a Russian doll of often talentless men. Cardinals, CEOs, order visitors, account managers, archbishops, CFOs: different titles for the same tyranny.

⸘

Back in her cell, María struggles to dismantle the Russian doll in her mind. With their robes and ridiculous hats, they all seem the same: Fray Plácido de Olmedo, Juan de Cárdenas, Bishop

Fernández de Santa Cruz, Father Piñero.... As the names pile up in her head, she finds it difficult to fix her righteous anger on any one face. All she knows is that somehow they have lost or ruined the notebooks they themselves commanded her to write. (If you lived in a convent in the seventeenth century and had literary ambitions, you were almost always forced to submit to the only genre available: the autobiography commissioned by suspicious confessors. It did not matter whether you were a Capuchin, Hieronymite, Augustinian, or Carmelite—if you wanted to be creative, you had to conform to the constraints of this format, which could either lead you to the fame of sainthood or the punishment of the Inquisition.) María, who had only grudgingly complied with this mandate in the first place, couldn't believe that just as she was finally getting the hang of her writing, her overbearing superiors seemed to be conspiring to spoil the job.

Her path to writing hadn't been easy, but neither had her path to the convent cell. As the youngest of seven siblings in an impoverished family of farmers, the two thousand to four thousand pesos needed to enter the convent were an impossible expense for María. Like many others, she depended on fickle scraps of benevolence from bishops and prelates. (No matter what century you're reading this in, achieving your dreams is always easier with a healthy bank balance.) Thus, María was a late bloomer: She didn't manage to take her coveted Augustinian Recollect habit until she was thirty-one. Before she could embark on her spiritual journey, she spent more than a decade knocking on the doors of prelates, pleading for mercy, and begging for favors with the same naive enthusiasm that drives us all to agonize over cover letters, accept thankless unpaid internships, and send groveling LinkedIn messages to thousands of unresponsive employers. This hunger to begin a life of workplace exploitation is astonishingly timeless, and María, like everyone else, soon discovered that the path to the delights of vocation is paved with humiliating exercises in subordination. When she was finally in a position to say yes to the habit in 1687, Bishop Manuel Fernández de Santa Cruz, the very same man who had previously obstructed her entry into the convent, was the first one to waste no time in commanding her to write an account of her life and visions. María would never forget his sadistic, bullying methods:

> I went back a third time not to his home but to the cathedral. I found him [Fernández de Santa Cruz] seated at one side of the great altar, and seeing that some women approached as if to confess . . . I too made my way to his feet. And as I was entirely wrapped in my shawl, he did not know me at first until I began to speak to him. As soon as he recognized me, he asked, "Why have you come here?" I told him why I had come, to ask him for a place . . . I had no sooner spoken these words than he pushed me away from his feet, saying "Leave here at once, and do not bother me! Have I not told you there is no place for you?"—in a very loud voice, as though he had grown angry at my impertinence . . . My fright and astonishment were so great upon hearing him that I could not raise myself from his feet and did not know where to flee, because the fright robbed me of all my strength. I got up as best I could, so stunned that I neither knew nor saw where I was setting my feet, and as I was going down the steps of the altar, I missed a step or level. I fell headlong and slid down I don't know how many steps . . . There I lay a short while until I had recovered somewhat. I cried a great many tears, and though I suffered this mortification, I had courage and valor to undergo still greater trials to attain what I so desired, which was to become a nun.

If you think there's nothing more excruciating than that awful interview that didn't land you the job, just remember it could always get worse: You could fall down the stairs.

The convent walls failed to protect her from the "great many tears" and "greater trials." Now in her forties, María has spent what feels like an eternity striving to fit her life and visions into a legible handwriting and a (more or less) coherent syntax. The absence of those thirty notebooks echoes in the overwhelming hollowness of her small cell.

†

It was a disaster of project management. The poor Augustinian nun obsessively tracked the chronology of the failure with the incredulous calculations of a stock manager enumerating too many inventory discrepancies and the desperation of an artist watching her best work pass from one incompetent person to another. Eventually, she learned the truth. After her confessor's death, all María's notebooks ended up in the hands of the infamous Bishop Manuel Fernández de Santa Cruz. He ignored the nun's attempts to discover the whereabouts of her papers and ordered her to leave the convent in Puebla. She was sent to establish a new convent of Augustinian Recollects in Oaxaca and left without knowing if she would ever see the fruits of nearly seven years of work again. Six years and two confessors later, Fray Ángel Maldonado and Fray Plácido de Olmedo entered her life. These two religious men took pity on her plight and agreed to break locks and lift cassocks across the spiritual map of Mexico until the notebooks were found.

The story of the investigation doesn't end there. More religious figures were involved in the misplacement of María's papers than there are names cc'd on a work email. After contacting the dean of Puebla, a sort of vice president of the cathedral, Fray Ángel

Maldonado and Fray Plácido de Olmedo chased down Chaplain Juan de Cárdenas, the confessor of the convent where María lived. He had the notebooks. In fact, he'd had them all those years but had chosen to say nothing, despite being fully aware of the nun's tireless search, as María notes in her journal:

> This priest, Fray Plácido de Olmedo . . . has assisted me with great charity, for which I am greatly beholden to him. I informed him of the state of my conscience and especially how when I set out to come to found this convent [Oaxaca], I left behind the notebooks I had written in the possession of Bishop Santa Cruz; that it had been almost three years since God had taken him; that I had heard not a single word of what had become of those papers . . . for only if our most Illustrious Father the Bishop, don Ángel Maldonado, took the matter in hand could they be tracked down. Thus it was that he soon wrote to . . . Cárdenas . . . who was the one who had them in his possession. He had denied them to me, refusing to send them to me in spite of all the efforts I made.

The deep sense of dispossession and alienation imposed by the capitalist mode of production were already well understood by nuns of the seventeenth century.

During those six years in which her notebooks were lost, María did not write another word. She had been ordered not to. In a way, the mandate granted her something approaching a paid vacation, a leave of absence, a well-deserved sabbatical. Those years were "spent with rest and relief at being spared the great travail I always have when I am writing," Maria wrote in her journal. But then, one day, Cárdenas finally hands over the notebooks—only for María to realize that ten have been irretrievably lost: "This Father Cárdenas had been my confessor for a short time, and he bore down very hard on me; and though he no longer is, he still does so whenever he can. As soon as he saw the handwriting of our . . . Bishop, he handed over the notebooks, although not all of them came, because of the thirty there were, he sent only twenty." And if her anger over their loss was not already enough to justify a hunger strike, María is pushed to her limit when she learns that, due to her superiors' negligence, her years of rest and relaxation are to be brought to a most abrupt end.

> Seeing how much is missing, and that no hope remains that they will ever reappear, my confessor has ordered me to write over again everything that was written in those ten notebooks. I feel the greatest repugnance at doing this work again, for many reasons and causes that I will not include here so as not to get too long: the main one is that my health is so poor that it seems impossible, given the condition I am in, that I can write all that must be written.

It was 2017 when we first read María's lament, and her words took root within us like a consoling prophecy of our own future: It truly was impossible to write as much as needed to be written. We knew little about corporate culture, but, much to our own dismay, we knew all too well the muscle strains of a perpetually hunched back, the terrifying specter of deadlines, and the torture of writing for the judgment of superiors. From that day on, we began to whisper María's "greatest repugnance" like a prayer, whenever we sensed the approach of another long, soul-crushing day in New England. We had found the perfect litany for our peculiar call to matins. It could be, in fact, a very handy prayer, a source of solace and relief for anyone who faces the grinding monotony of salaried work each day. *The greatest repugnance* when the alarm destroys your spirit every morning. *The greatest repugnance* when your new boss cancels working from home. *The greatest repugnance* when you return home in a subway car crammed with more souls than a saints' day calendar. Oh, such great, *great repugnance* every day we are required to work as much as we need to.

―⧾―

Around the time we were reading María's spiritual autobiography, our procrastinatory TikTok scrolling introduced us to entrepreneurship 2.0 and its terrifying cast of productivity gurus. The secret, they claimed, was to submit to a truly monastic routine: "Waking up at 5 a.m. will radically improve your performance"; "A cold shower every morning increases your chances of becoming a millionaire"; "Meditate for ten minutes before going into the office and watch your productivity soar." In this deranged vision of success, complaining is an unforgivable sin and a shortcut to the worst kind of failure. Fortunately for us, within the framework of spiritual autobiographies and the letters of nuns, complaints are not pathetic. They are shared incantations that harbor within them the first stirrings of rebellion. Little by little, we learned to legitimize our grievances thanks to our nuns. As we approached the dreaded age of thirty, we found comfort in reading Saint Teresa endlessly tell her companions: "I am old and tired." We were energized to read her critique of the necessity of holding down several jobs—like us, Teresa was "exhausted at times by so many tasks together." When we discovered that the Chilean Poor Clare nun Úrsula Suárez (1666–1749) woke up day after day "as tired and sore as if I had worked beyond my strength," unable to avoid "complaining about the weariness I felt in my body," we realized that the Fordist production chain of the PhD process deserved the constant reinforcement of our bitching.

Not one day passed in which we did not soothe ourselves with the balm of those two words: *greatest repugnance*. When the inertia of work became too unbearable, that shared mantra made us feel less guilty for setting aside our writing and surrendering to the numbing pleasure of vegging out. Three years into our PhDs, we had mastered the university's administrative maze and the art of achieving two fully funded goals in one. Proud of our ability to craft research proposals compelling enough to secure a competitive Summer Research Award, we arrived in Seville in July 2019. Each time we declared, "We're going to the Archive of the Indies for a week to conduct research," we felt motivated by an exotic allure that somehow compensated for the challenges of life in Providence. However, we soon realized that while such a pronouncement might sound impressive to those outside our hellish bubble, the prospect of spending even only seven of our summer days restricted to a dim archive without internet access was far less appealing. After three years of enduring "the greatest repugnance" of academic productivity, that hotel with a rooftop pool and AC became far more attractive than our efforts to decipher the calligraphy of a seventeenth-century inquisitorial lawsuit:

—Carmen, how about we go to the archive later? It's still pretty early.
—Yes, please! Besides, it's superhot outside, and we said we'd watch *Ru Paul* together this summer.
—I can grab some breakfast first. Let's watch one episode, and then we'll head out.

We never set foot in the archive. Day after day, we indulged in Takis, ice cream, and sparkling water while watching Violet Chachki showcase her vintage glamour and nail every lip-sync challenge. In her journals, María described her own version of vegging out as allowing herself small concessions that felt less alarming than our reckless use of research funds: "I felt very weary and fatigued, both in spirit and body, because one must toil and work hard, very hard, in all ways, and so the poor old donkey drags its feet . . . the thought came to me that it would be better to write these things in brief and succinctly . . . For it causes me great travail, and it is not necessary to write as much as I am writing." She's right. In the end, it is not necessary, because nothing is so essential. The world will not collapse because a page of spiritual autobiography is handed in late, or because that email you forgot to send was left in the drafts folder. María understood this three hundred years ago, we felt it in our moments where we abandoned our work ethic and binged Ru Paul, and the idea has since been celebrated by countless online champions of "girlrotting"—women who have turned their backs on the hectic and theoretically empowering culture of "girlbossing" to simply embrace the softness of their sheets, watching the hours slip by, the only work in evidence being performed by the body as it moves toward its own inevitable decomposition.

We don't know if it was thanks to the therapeutic power of complaining, the secret pleasure of criticizing her bosses in the very pages she sent to them, or a perverse drive toward productivity, but over the course of thirty years, María ultimately managed to write and keep more than two thousand handwritten pages. No one knows how that immense amount of paper ended up in one of the libraries at Brown, but there they were, just as we were there, somehow. María's manuscript was before our tired and myopic eyes: twelve bound volumes filled with lamentations about the merciless work of writing. In that dark winter, we endured thousands of pages of weekly readings, a seminar on pedagogical methodologies so unbearable it would have made Maria Montessori herself give up her didactic passion, and rambling office hours of self-important professors bent on recounting endless anecdotes about every writer from the Latin American Boom. Our abject lives were a mirror image of that reclusive Augustinian woman we had just come to know.

As we turned manuscript pages under the watchful eye of the archivist, engrossed in María's delicate handwriting, we came across a stain that slightly obscured the text. The archivist looked over the rim of her bifocals with a mischievous gleam in her eye, inviting us to go back to the first page, where María devotes a whole paragraph to the mark.

> [As] the Guardian Priest was reading this notebook, which is the first part, a boy came to give him a cup of chocolate and, handing it to him, spilled it on the notebook. It was heavily stained, though it could still be understood clearly. This Guardian Priest did not want to return it like that, stained as it is, but set about transcribing it with his own hand just as it is written. And when my Confessor, Fray Plácido, saw these two notebooks, one stained and one transcribed, he told me in the confessional that he had received the new one, but that none would serve but this one because it is written in my own hand. And this is why I have included this here, that it may be clear and all may know how this happened.

María had learned to write at thirty-two. The pride she felt when her confessor chose the chocolate-stained manuscript—simply because it was written in her own hand—must have been akin to the exhilaration of receiving an A+ on a paper that has driven you to the brink of madness for weeks. But seeing that blotch spoiling her oeuvre must have also infuriated her. One can easily imagine María (whiny as she was) grumbling about the clumsiness of that chocolate-addicted priest. It's highly likely that, as a secret protest and vowing to honor her "greatest repugnance for work," María decided to extinguish her lamp and refused to write a single word that night. We like to think that instead she spent the night rotting in bed.

When we left the library, it was already dark. We walked gracelessly through the snow, still learning how to handle the boots and puffers we had bought a few months ago. Then, we began to complain because perhaps our complaints, like María's, could also become acts of subversion. We complained about the snow, the pedagogy seminar, our students, our professors, about how it truly *seemed impossible, given our circumstances, that we could write as much as needed to be written.* But we did it, embracing María's valuable lessons: Complain for fulfillment, lament with pride, grumble without remorse. The greatest repugnance for work; rapturous praise for vegging out.

How to Say No to Your Boss with the Intricate Yet Unyielding Rhetoric of a Nun Putting Her Confessor in His Place

In the Museum of Religious Art, housed in the former Convent of Santa Mónica in Puebla, Mexico, there hangs an oil portrait of a sorrowful María. Her hands gently carry a bouquet of flowers, but they also seem to be scratching each other, as if in reaction to a nervous rash, and her eyebrows, though perfectly shaped, draw together, wrinkling her expression and casting a shadow over her gaze. It's a look of subtle misery, the expression of someone who knows they have an unbearable workday ahead, more painful even than the torment of a cilice belt. María's drawn little face is as unknown as the vast majority of nuns' features from her century. They constituted the faceless labor force of Catholic spirituality. There is, however, one face from a seventeenth-century convent that endured to haunt many corners of contemporary culture.

Sor Juana Inés de la Cruz (1648–1695), who features on the Mexican 200 peso bills and often appears in soap-opera-y fictions such as the 2016 series *Juana Inés*, is arguably the most iconic figure in Latinx pop culture. If the Hieronymite nun has managed to escape anonymity and oblivion with enough force to warrant a Netflix production, it is because she spent her lifetime doing everything in her power to ensure her posthumous fame. Sor Juana was a nun, but she did not limit herself to writing devotional literature. She took a vow of enclosure, committing to stay in the convent forever, yet found a way to ensure that more VIPs passed through her convent's parlor than backstage at Coachella. She took a vow of poverty, too, but her cell in the Convent of San Jerónimo was a duplex staffed by servants. She also, obviously, took a vow of obedience, but she ignored her confessor's directives in order to engage in theological debates. Almost everything she did in life seemed part of a meticulously calculated operation to claim the entire market share of exceptionalism.

We can confidently admit that Sor Juana's impenetrable texts were the source of the biggest headaches of our PhD. From the Aristotelian shadows in her verses to the deeply obscure metaphors inherited from the Jesuit and polymath Athanasius Kircher, it was that same inscrutability that ultimately established the nun as the most hypnotic and enigmatic author of the seventeenth century. The moments when we believed we had cracked Sor Juana's code (which were few and far between) made us feel as invincible as when we finished a particularly grueling spin class. But the most valuable instruction we learned from Sor Juana, the one that has endured the longest, the one that has saved our lives countless times, has nothing to do with lofty philosophy or the theological mystery of the Eucharist. If we keep a special place for Sor Juana in our conventual altar, it is because she showed us how to master the task that overwhelms us all in the twenty-first century: writing emails.

The first thing we discovered about each other was our shared love for nuns. The second was that we both trembled at the thought of communicating a message with even the slightest assertive edge. One day, after surviving the defense of our thesis proposals, we decided to treat ourselves to a minor cosmetic procedure. In the long minutes that stretched from the moment the girl asked us to lie face down on the treatment bed while she adjusted a bright white lamp to inspect our backs (which were, by the way, spotless) to the moment she explained how she was going to proceed to exterminate the almost nonexistent blackheads on that forgotten part of the body, we were incapable of clarifying that what we actually wanted was a facial. We walked out of that expensive Providence spa with our backs gleaming and our faces just as decrepit as they were before we had paid $140. It was dismal proof that we were undeniably members of the people-pleasers club—two pathetic, accommodating little worms. If something as inconsequential as a beauty treatment mix-up could lead us to such extreme self-flagellating, writing a difficult message to a member of our thesis committee or supervisor was enough to rob us of an entire night's sleep. That was our soft underbelly: the inability to execute those emails that seem to imbue a computer keyboard with all the tension of a bomb defusal. To collectively manage the stress, we soon developed a system, still in use, that consists of creating shared documents that we edit side by side. Like two nuns taking turns with the embroidery cloth to ensure that no stitch is out of place, we suggest words, reorder clauses, and garnish each other's sentences with adjectives, until we arrive at a text that causes us the least anxiety to send. This eased our paralysis, but we never quite managed to send a completely anxiety-free email. That is, until we read Sor Juana.

In March of 1691, the Hieronymite nun faced what would have been, by today's standards, the most difficult email of her life: the *Answer to Sor Filotea de la Cruz*. A few months earlier, the always-meddling bishop of Puebla, Manuel Fernández de Santa Cruz, had published a text filled with convoluted theological casuistry written by Sor Juana without the nun's consent. The text was Sor Juana's rather heated refutation of a sermon by a Portuguese Jesuit, which had come to her attention through gossip circulating in one of the many chaotic gatherings in her parlor. Like one might get carried away after a few drinks at a party among friends, the nun delivered an impromptu speech at that same gathering, mercilessly criticizing the Jesuit's stance on what was Christ's greatest quality. (Nuns and bishops could spend hours arguing on whether it was his death for the sake of humanity or the gift of the Eucharist that counted as Christ's greatest quality, just as you can now spend hours debating whether you'd rather run into a man or a bear in a deserted forest; you just don't write a treatise about it—though you probably should.) It was only after much urging that Sor Juana agreed to put her thoughts into writing, in a manuscript that was passed around until Manuel Fernández de Santa Cruz—the same bishop, mind you, who had made María's life so difficult—unilaterally decided to share it with the entire world. For Sor Juana, who had a Kardashian-like vise grip on the control of her public image, this was a misstep of biblical proportions.

Her unscripted argument provoked a number of incendiary pamphlets damning the author, but that wasn't the worst part. The most humiliating aspect of the affair was the fact that, under the pseudonym Sor Filotea de la Cruz, the bishop decided to preface the text with a letter admonishing Sor Juana. He praised her for the elegance of her reasoning and the breadth of her erudition, but he also loudly chastised her for dedicating her time to the writing of secular verses instead of devoting herself, as she had in the text he was prefacing, to strictly sacred matters. (It had been two years since Sor Juana published *The Castalida Flood*, a volume of more than three hundred folios that included, among other literary feats, her greatest poetic hits—some with verses too ardent to comply with the modesty that, in the eyes of Fernández de Santa Cruz and many others, a nun of the Counter-Reformation was expected to embody.) Here's a line from the bishop's preface dripping in seventeenth-century levels of passive aggression that could serve as evidence in a workplace harassment lawsuit: "It is a pity that such a great intellect should stoop to the petty concerns of the Earth, without aspiring to penetrate the mysteries of Heaven; and that, if it humbles itself towards the ground, it should not sink lower, to contemplate what transpires in Hell." If your boss threatens you with ending your days in hell, you know it is time to roll up the sleeves of your habit and unleash your full rhetorical arsenal to defend yourself.

And so Sor Juana decided to write her 1691 *Answer to Sor Filotea de la Cruz*. The letter, which took her a full three months to write, is that exquisite rhetorical juggling act you perform when you need to put your boss in their place without jeopardizing your livelihood or the viability of your project. More than three hundred years later, we once again turned to Sor Juana's trusty *Answer* the day we had to write the most difficult email of our lives. It was the summer of 2024. We had just submitted the first chapter of this book to our editors, and the feedback was harsh. The sentences were too long, they said, we overloaded each page with too much information, and, most importantly, we were being overshadowed by the nuns. A rewrite was needed. We were tempted to cave, to default to our familiar people-pleasing tendencies. But the thought of ending up with a book that didn't feel like our own was too much to bear. And, honestly, the prospect of rewriting tormented us as much as it did María: *It was impossible, given our circumstances, that we could write as much as needed to be written.* As students of the Hieronymite's guidance we opened our shared document.

Step One: Win over your audience with a touch of self-criticism and self-pity. "It has not been my will, but my scant health and rightful fear that have delayed my reply for so many days. Is it to be wondered that, at the very first step, I should meet with two obstacles that sent my dull pen stumbling? The first (and to me the most insuperable) is the question of how to respond to your immensely learned, prudent, devout, and loving letter," Sor Juana wrote. Nuns' *captatio benevolentiae*—their strategy for winning their confessors' goodwill—should always be a staple of any conventual guide for delicate email-writing success. Apologize (even if there's no reason to), overexplain (no matter what), and mislead your reader with a mesmerizing string of flattery.

Step Two: Reaffirm your vow of obedience. "Yet I protest that I do so [writing my *Answer*] only to obey you; and with such misgiving that you owe me more for taking up my pen with all this fear than you would owe me were I to present you with the more perfect works." Is it your editor? Your chief marketing officer? Your spiritual director? It doesn't matter—they are all at their most vulnerable after a convincing pledge of vassalage.

Step Three: The defense. For Sor Juana, this meant systematically listing evidence in favor of her desire to continue writing nonreligious works from the convent. Hers was a straightforward argument—no woman wants to endure the fierce reprimands that could result from a theological misstep. "And thus I confess that often this very fear has snatched the pen from my hand and has made the subject matter retreat back toward the intellect from which it wished to flow; an impediment I did not stumble across with profane subjects, for a heresy against it is not punished by the Holy Office but rather by wits by their laughters and critics with their censure." Sometimes you just don't prioritize the tasks you are assigned in a given week, resulting in unmet KPIs and an unsatisfied confessor. Don't fret. You can always defend yourself by role-playing their airheaded fantasy.

Step Four (the most-feared step): The unexpected counterstrike. Sor Juana knew better than anyone how to confuse her audience with a veil of submission, humility, and feigned ignorance, only to suddenly tear through it with a whiplash of audacity. She directly challenged Fernández de Santa Cruz: "If it [my work] is heretical, as the critic says, then why does he not denounce it [to the Inquisition]?" This may sound civil enough, but when you're a seventeenth-century nun, you don't go around teasing your superiors into denouncing you to the most lethal corporation on Earth unless you really mean business. Steps one to three are just a mitigating strategy to now finally say what would otherwise get you in immediate trouble: Now it's your moment to point to those failures in their marketing strategies, threaten with a resignation letter, or defend in a firm voice your vision for your book about sixteenth- and seventeenth-century nuns.

Step Five: Time to gaslight your reader. Return to your softest, most adorable self and apologize for any possible missteps, as if Step Four had all been but a bad dream. "If the style of this letter," Sor Juana writes, "has been less than your due, I beg your pardon for its household familiarity or the lack of seemly respect . . . And hold me in your own good grace, so as to entreat divine grace on my behalf; of the same, may the Lord grant you great increase, and may He keep you," which must be the equivalent to adding a smiley emoji to your refusal to assume any more responsibilities.

Adrift in our inertia, we devoured Sor Juana's emboldened and insolent letter with the nervous enthusiasm of someone daring to emulate their alter ego. Yet she wasn't always so strategically savvy. In an attempt to test her learning, a teenage Sor Juana had been subjected to a public examination orchestrated by the most esteemed intellectuals and clergy of New Spain. At that time, in her more arrogant and careless youth, she had relished silencing all those men with her self-taught knowledge. But now she was in her thirties, burdened by two decades of persecutions, slights, challenges, and affronts, and she had reached her limit. In 1682, Sor Juana allowed herself an outburst, a compelling fantasy for any people-pleasing coward: "I can't do this anymore . . . And so I beg you . . . if you no longer wish to favor me (which is voluntary), then please forget about me." We all know there are moments when the camouflage of a well-wielded vocabulary and hyperbolic sleights of hand are insufficient, and you simply have to shout at your boss, your confessor, the bishop, or your thesis advisor. Among all the men in cassocks who baited such shouting, none made her life

more unbearable than her Jesuit confessor, Antonio Núñez de Miranda. A militant misogynist and a prime example of envy, Núñez de Miranda had shadowed Sor Juana's every step and dissected her writings with increasing disapproval since she entered into the convent. When the jet-setters of Mexico City began flocking to the nun, speaking in hushed tones of her wisdom and blushing at her verses, Núñez de Miranda decided to launch a campaign to discredit the woman who had once been his protégée.

We were in a seminar led by a brilliant and exuberant professor, a woman who had found her own way through the minefield of 1970s American academia to become one of the first women to earn a PhD in her Ivy League department. It was the late afternoon of a particularly dull Friday, and she was doing everything she could to ignite the class's enthusiasm. For some, the convoluted labyrinth of Jesuit disputes in which Sor Juana was embroiled was more than enough to engross us. For others, not so much: It was a little difficult to reconcile all that with the apocalyptic fall of 2016; it felt too distant from our growing desire to start planning where to have our self-prescribed one beer of the week a few hours later.

Toward the end of the session, we finally arrived at what is possibly the harshest passage Sor Juana ever wrote—so audacious that we all found ourselves crumpling the page out of sheer shock as we read a paragraph that resounds like a howl directed at Núñez de Miranda:

> What is the cause, then, of this anger? What is the reason for discrediting me? For portraying me as scandalous to everyone? Have I burdened your reverence with anything? Have I asked you for anything to aid my needs? Or have I troubled you with any other spiritual or temporal matter? Is my correction

your responsibility due to some obligation of duty, kinship, upbringing, authority or something similar? If it is pure charity, let it appear as pure charity and proceed as such, gently. *Exasperating me is not a good way to correct me for I do not possess a servile nature that would make me yield to threats rather than to reason.*

There was applause. There were even a few shouts. We were just a few months away from the explosion of the #MeToo movement, and encumbered by the ubiquitous weight of academic machismo, Sor Juana's baroque rebuke made us feel like the descendants of a genealogy of female anger, still thunderously relevant.

Sor Juana taught us to cloak our emails in rhetorical finesse and to at least flirt with abandoning the conciliatory route when the situation calls more for a shout than for a scheme. But the linguistically masterful nun also showed us that sometimes silence can speak the loudest. At the end of 2021, we were so exhausted that we just stopped meeting our theses' deadlines. We saw the days go by in our calendars, the chapters stuck in the very same page while our Sor Juana posters watched us with a sympathetic eye. Those last months of the year also saw more than four million Americans leave their jobs in a wave that the business world—so fond of labels—dubbed the Big Quit or the Great Resignation. Stagnant wages, rising living costs, the greatest repugnance for doing insubstantial tasks day after day, and the panic-inducing prospect of returning to the office during the COVID pandemic are some of the triggers that labor market analysts offer when discussing this trend. Simply put, people, like Sor Juana, *just couldn't take it anymore.*

Instead of shouting it, however, millions of workers quietly drifted away from their positions, like phantoms, changing jobs, becoming freelancers, or finding caves to hunker down in. Libraries and archives were temporarily closed, so it was easy for us to just keep silent, never admitting to our supervisor that our theses had come to a halt—that we had, at least for now, quit the job.

On February 8, 1694, Sor Juana, who had a sense of spectacle we sadly lack, reaffirmed her vows as a Hieronymite nun in a telenovela-worthy act: adding to her signature a dramatic "I, the worst in the world." On March 5, 1694, she took it a step further—Sor Juana signed a declaration of faith with her own blood, in which she also pledged to abandon her studies and writing to devote herself solely to God. This last gesture has always seemed highly suspect to us, and we are skeptical of interpretations that see the letter as a true act of surrender. In fact, in 1995, an old inventory of the convent was discovered, proving that Sor Juana continued to read and write the kind of verses she enjoyed, even after this bloody pledge. She simply stopped publishing; she continued on her path, but in silence. We will always choose to believe that Sor Juana's Big Quit was not a reactionary conversion, nor anything resembling a defeat. It remains, however, proof that when language is insufficient and shouting is not an option, there is still a quiet, subtle way to reach freedom.

How to Lead Your Union with the Dignity of a Sixteenth-Century Discalced Carmelite

Every uprising needs an enemy. Distinguishing one Carmelite friar from another based on their surviving portraits is almost as impossible as telling apart the besuited gentlemen who pose each year in group photos at the Davos economic forum; the identical tonsures merge their features, and the plain habits and capes smudge them into a single indistinguishable mass of white and brown. No matter how much you stare at them, they always end up looking like interchangeable silhouettes. Except, that is, for one man: Nicolás Doria. An aquiline nose, mischievous smile, eerily symmetrical cheek dimples, and eyebrows pressed too close together over very dark, tiny eyes, all conspire to render him unmistakable. When, just a few months after the founding of the Carmelite convent in Lisbon, the general chapter of the order appointed this Genoese friar as head of all the convents in the province, María de San José (Teresa's best friend) knew for certain that it would not end well.

We all have a Doria in our life. Doria is that man from a bourgeois merchant family who, at thirty-one, experiences a crisis of conscience, abandons his lucrative career as a banker, and retreats from the world to become a Discalced friar under the pious name of Fray Nicolao de Jesús María. Once inside the order, however, he knows only how to operate by the mechanisms of the world that has shaped him. He may have been born in the sixteenth century, but Doria had the spirit of a twenty-first-century consulting bro who viewed the Carmelite order as a hierarchical multinational in which he could rise up through the ranks. It is no surprise then that he loathed Teresa, who had been implementing methods of organization based on gentleness and the freedom for women to choose their prioresses and confessors. So, when he was appointed provincial superior, the first item on his agenda was to destroy the legacy of Teresa that all her Carmelite friends treasured. Doria's policy was simple: rigor, fasting, and discipline.

How was it possible that this banker-turned-friar, with neither spiritual sensitivity nor affection for the sisters, had the power to destroy in a second what Teresa and María had spent two decades building? Unmoored by the nightmare that was unfolding before her, María de San José took a deep breath and recalled the most valuable lesson she had learned from Teresa: "It is a great evil for a soul beset by so many dangers to be alone." María knew that many of the sisters wanted to continue living in communities where, despite the hardships and persecutions, "everything passed in laughter, composing ballads and *coplas* about all the events that befell us." "Strive to be loved in order to be obeyed," advised the *Constitutions*, a sort of internal corporate rulebook for the Carmelites that Teresa had managed to print in 1581, and which Doria now wanted to completely overhaul. "After meals, the prioress may allow all to converse together about whatever pleases them," it also said. The Carmelites knew that if they could keep their rulebook intact, Doria's misogynistic impulses would be reduced to mere childish tantrums.

╬

In 2016, Brown's graduate student union had just formalized its organizational structure and was actively recruiting new members. Although we felt slightly uncomfortable waving the flag of indignation while cradled in the privilege of an elite university, we did believe it was fair to equalize the conditions between students in the sciences and the humanities, increase wages for staff, and establish some control over teaching hours, so on certain afternoons, we set aside our writing to attend the meetings. The sessions were disheartening—overwhelmingly male, with an antiseptic and dispassionate tone. When we were assigned to create an Excel sheet ranking each student in our department on a scale from 1 to 7 based on the level of union involvement we sensed in them, we drew back from this particular activism. We admit that this came close to snuffing out our union enthusiasm. It doesn't matter what century you read this in: If they demand you work in Excel, it is not your revolution.

Workers with more patience than us did manage to bring the effort to a successful conclusion and secured improvements from which we later benefited. But even now, we are certain that the movement would have attracted more supporters (including us) had it been led by someone who was sufficiently charismatic. *Charismatic*, in common language, refers to someone who has the gift of captivating those around them. *Charismatic*, in Carmelite terms, means spending little moments of prayer together and, by extension, emphasizing the strength of the community. Every labor movement needs the charisma of someone like Fran Drescher, the creator, producer, writer, and star of the 1990s television series *The Nanny* who, after assuming the presidency of the Screen Actors Guild in 2021, sparked a highly publicized Hollywood strike. Every labor movement also needs someone capable of defending the collective legacy of its rules with the vigor and grace of María de San José.

If your moment for unionizing has arrived, we recommend following María's strategies step by step. The first and most important lesson: The risk and strain of challenging your boss, whether now or in the sixteenth century, is faced best when backed by a network of resistance. "I saw clearly that we would be lost if we, every day, remained in the hands of those who had the power to change [the *Constitutions*]; I wrote to some prioresses I knew and told them of the danger we were in, persuading them that we should all band together." Before the London match girls' strike, before Betty Friedan, before the workers of Inditex, and before Fran Drescher, the sixteenth-century Carmelites had already sensed that preserving good working conditions always involves banding together with your colleagues and standing up to the abusive behavior of your bosses. While writing from her convent in Lisbon, María assembled in her mind a list of all the nuns who, like her, would be willing to launch a campaign to discredit the new male leadership of the order. Among them all, she chooses Ana de Jesús.

Ana had realized one of Teresa's great ambitions: the convent in Madrid, popularly known even to this day as "the convent of wishes." Both Ana and María had taken their Carmelite vows in 1570 and were well attuned to the needs of their fellow sisters, chief among them being the fact that a community of women could only thrive if it retained a degree of autonomy. They hoped that if only they could gain the approval of the pope to continue self-governing, Doria would be humiliated and their houses of friendship, prayer, poverty, and recreation would survive intact, and on June 5, 1590, Pope Sixtus V responded to their petition by approving the *Constitutions* just as Teresa had left them. We like to imagine that on that historic day for these champions of self-management and unionism, all the Carmelites let their hair down, toasted with sweet wine, beat their small drums in the cloister, and, for at least a moment, forgot about rules and constitutions, celebrating as if they had just won the right to vote. But the sense of victory did not last long—Doria, his male pride wounded, swore to himself that he would have these two interfering women publicly humiliated and punished. He wrote to King Philip II to revoke the pope's decision, and in 1592, he published a new set of regulations and had both Ana de Jesús and María de San José imprisoned. Never underestimate the dire consequences of publicly rebelling against your company's CEO.

⸗

Locked up in Lisbon, María de San José stares at the cracks of her cold cell walls, alarm fracturing her senses, as she tries to convince herself that she is not alone. She has her writing, and she writes because she knows—after so many years living in seclusion—that through writing, it's possible to feel, if only faintly, the warm comfort of your companions.

> Do not be disheartened, my dearest sisters, nor let your faith weaken, even if it seems that the Lord has left us for so long in the hands of those who persecute and afflict us. Do not think it wrong that we have worked for so many years in the service of our Faith, exiled in distant lands, enduring extreme poverty and the unbearable trials of founding and sustaining convents . . . I implore you, dear daughters, do not sorrow over my confinement here, nor grieve that all the doors of human means are closed to my freedom . . . I do not consider my words to be in vain, even though I know you may not read them. But they will serve as a testament before God and men . . . Let it be known that you remain ever present in my thoughts and will never fade from my memory, despite being confined to such a narrow prison.

There is nothing like a Counter-Reformation prison to make you cling ever tighter to worker solidarity. The death of Doria in 1594 gave her some respite, but it would prove short-lived. In 1600, one of Doria's henchmen, Father Francisco de la Madre de Dios, assumed presidency of the order and the fate of María de San José took another turn for the worse. One night in 1603, his cronies forcibly removed María from the Lisbon convent, which after so many years had finally begun to feel like home, and relocated her to Cuerva, a tiny village nestled among the *dehesa*s of Toledo. She died alone nine days later.

We hope (vain as she was) she died knowing that although

Doria and his followers had thwarted her goals in life, they could never extinguish the spirit of rebellion and resistance she had instilled in her friends, sisters, followers, and companions. She would have been right. Nearly a decade later, on September 28, 1611, Ana de Jesús wrote from her convent in Brussels to Francisca de las Llagas, prioress of a convent lost in the middle of La Mancha: "May she [Teresa] grant us the grace to be her true daughters. Here, we strive to uphold her *Constitutions* to the word. If Your Reverence has any of the copies I printed in Madrid, and they are not needed there, send them to me by a safe route so they do not get lost." Teresa's long legacy endured. The administrators and leaders of the order would continue to change—some more benevolent and understanding, others less so—but by virtue of María's persistent stewardship, the Carmelite working class had already learned something they would never forget, a lesson that we would gratefully inherit for generations: Often, discreet self-management and veiled resistance are the only ways to keep your project intact, and sometimes they are enough.

All Work and No Play Makes the Nun a Dull Girl

The first thing we discovered about each other was our shared passion for nuns; the second was that we are both pathologically accommodating creatures. The third of our mutual agonies was our inherent contradiction: We had built our identities around an iron will and bottomless capacity for work but, deep down, we were tortured by a repressed longing for hedonistic indulgence. The greatest concession we had made to our true selves was coincidentally both abandoning, at the age of eighteen, the sensible but suicidal determination to study law and politics, opting instead for the more enjoyable path of literary studies. Blessed be that day.

Even so, had it not been for the teachings of María de San José, we wouldn't have learned to neglect the academic yoke in pursuit of pleasure.

Imagine spending weeks locked away in archives and libraries, absorbing page after page of bland, restrained prose. If you're lucky, you write something that passes the vicious audit of dense academic journals that are nearly impossible to access and are read by fewer people than the least-sold book in the most sparsely populated country in the world. Then there are the months dedicated to preparing applications for precarious and unconvincing job offers at universities in cities that neither you nor anyone you know could find on a map, and even more time spent diving into the farthest chasms of the internet, desperately searching for a postdoctoral fellowship, an associate professor position, or a position at some dubious online university, all in an effort not to fall behind in the Spartan marathon of an academic career. The restorative exercise of complaining, which we had so diligently internalized from that Augustinian Recollect, kept us afloat during the first years of our doctoral studies. Then came March 2020. Trapped in an increasingly claustrophobic Providence and tormented by the devastating images assailing us from televisions and newspapers, the greatest repugnance mantra lost its power to soothe. But when the survival strategy of one nun fails you, there is always another waiting to leap to the rescue.

In addition to being a little conceited and possessive as well as resolute and rebellious, María de San José was, like us, torn between a life of confinement and a love for the finer things. In 1585, suffocated by the regime of terror that was to come with Doria's rise, María decided to write the *Book of Recreations*. An answer to the doctrines of solitude and discipline that were brewing among the order's higher echelons, the *Book of Recreations* was a playful project—a party of a book that is a celebration of delight, a bucolic dream, a communal act of resistance. It probably would have been easier to write a chronicle of the order or a dull biography of Saint Teresa, but it would also have been far more boring. To dramatize the daily struggles and pastimes of the nuns, María de San José invented five Carmelites: Gracia, Justa, Atanasia, Josefa, and Dorotea. Sister Gracia, who María clearly modeled after herself, mentions the greatest repugnance she feels at having to obey her confessor's demand to write a dense, spiritual autobiography. Stuck in our tiny rooms and forced, more than ever, to do nothing but write those dissertations in which we could hardly recognize ourselves, we completely understood Sister Gracia's anguish. We were grateful that another of María's made-up nuns, Sister Justa (who was a bit of a mischief-maker and is thus forever in our hearts), proposed a much more appealing endeavor: writing Teresa's biography together. Sister Justa convinces Sister Gracia to trade this solitary task for the much more joyful and rewarding practice of coterie writing. And so it is that by chatting with the other nuns and celebrating their shared Carmelite genealogy María de San José's alter ego, Sister Gracia, motivated by the voices of her friends, gradually composes a biography of Saint Teresa. It is from her we learned to never be deceived by the meritocratic logic that rewards solitary work—always have a Sister Justa in your life.

During that pandemic spring, inspired by Sister Justa, we gradually, almost without realizing it, shifted away from dedicating every hour of the day to our dissertations. Furtively but with increasing enthusiasm, we instead began to devote ourselves to a playful and communal task befitting María de San José: We launched a podcast about sixteenth- and seventeenth-century nuns. In each episode, we intertwined personal anecdotes, popular culture, and generational angst in an attempt to imitate the imaginative exercise that is the *Book of Recreations*. Far from the individualistic and digression-averse strictures of academic writing, the podcast was, in the words of María describing her book, "many things [that] seem irrelevant and serve only to make the work long winded, such as the quarrels between the nuns that I introduce, and other extraneous conversations that are mixed in beside the point." This was exactly what we were looking for: an irreverent, eclectic patchwork. That concession to our more fun-loving natures, that cheesy yet rigorous mélange, saved us from fading away into a monotony of no return. The cramped and grimy bathroom where we recorded the first episodes, lined with duvets and towels to muffle the sound, wasn't the bucolic, flower-filled gardens where María de San José imagined her chatty nuns. But the joy of recording and releasing our episodes, along with the thrill of knowing that we were fostering a new community, felt undeniably Carmelite. The buzz of comments each episode generated served to remind us that this diversion had not been an act of mere avoidant indulgence. We were playing, prioritizing delight and detours over discipline in the tradition of María de San José. For as she knew, an unholy amount of work will not make you any more holy.

Body

> *And suddenly, from all the wounds and lashes that afflicted her sacred body, emerged a multitude of freshly baked and sweet-smelling bread rolls and cakes.*
>
> Juana de la Cruz

Nothing Tastes as Good as Holiness Feels: How to Turn Food Neurosis into a Refectory of One's Own

In the last decade of the seventeenth century, the monastery of the Capuchin Poor Clares in Città di Castello, Umbria, played host to some truly grim gastronomy. Up until that point, the typical diet of its resident nuns could scarcely have been more austere. They consumed no meat (unless poor health demanded it) and ate two small meals a day: for lunch, a watery bean stew and a single egg, occasionally accompanied by a small piece of fruit; for dinner, an almost transparent soup diluted from the midday stew, with a slice of bread added for the hungriest diners. The more frugal Capuchin Poor Clares were satisfied with only a handful of grapes, two walnuts, or an apple. Occasionally, they would dare to liven their dinner water with a few drops of wine, and, on certain days during Lent, the lunchtime egg would be replaced with a piece of fish. But that was all. In short, following the austere diet of the Poor Clares was even more dispiriting than growing up under an almond mom.

In 1677, however, the keenly felt sense of food deprivation among all those Italian Capuchin Poor Clares would abruptly change. The year marked the arrival of Veronica Giuliani, who, with her extreme culinary mortifications, made the eating regimes of most other nuns resemble a Michelin-starred-restaurant tasting menu. Sister Ceoli, who would one day become the abbess of the convent but was still working in the kitchen at the time, could never understand why her dishes always left the stove perfectly cooked, only for Veronica's portion to arrive at the refectory where they all dined spoiled and covered in filth. But that was the reality: The daughter of Francesco Giuliani and Benedetta Mancini, who had grown up surrounded by the finest tableware in the Duchy of Urbino, would often receive her portions, somehow, miraculously topped with cat vomit, dismembered mice, balls of hair, cockroaches, worms, and leeches, whose oozing blood gave color to the broth. Clutching their napkins to stifle their nausea, and barely listening to the lesson being read by the prioress, the rest of the Capuchin Poor Clares had to chew their walnuts as they watched Veronica, her long neck held high, finish every last crumb of her repulsive feast with unwavering dignity.

Squeamish as we are, we inevitably had to choke back our gag reflexes while reading the testimonies of the Capuchin Poor Clares detailing Veronica's eating habits—but we also could not help but empathize. Anyone who has ever fallen under the dietary spell of starting the day with a shot of turmeric and ginger or cultivating their own pungent symbiotic colony of bacteria and yeast to experiment with cleansing the body through homemade kombucha tea knows that the judgment the nun faced bore an uncomfortable resemblance to the looks of disgust that contemporary diets can provoke.

⸸

Since starting the podcast, we have opened every episode by asking each other the same, simple question: "What did you eat today?" Often, the answer was something as sad and as evocative of a Capuchin Poor Clare's meal as: "a few baked parsnip slices and two soft-boiled eggs," "beet soup and a cup of yogurt," or "a plain omelet with sautéed celeriac." Providence welcomed us with exorbitant prices that ate away at our graduate student stipends, and with a local supermarket an unrealistic walking distance away. Thanks to this ominous combination of logistical resignation and a dubious ambition to merge "health" and "sustainability," we soon allowed our sustenance to depend entirely on the university-run local vegetable co-op. This choice carried with it a certain monastic inclination toward moderation and renunciation—the dietary expression of the academic and personal isolation we had embraced when we said yes to the PhD. The penury of our meals quickly became a running joke among our podcast audience. But the lighthearted way listeners discussed our peppered celery or chia-studded cups of oatmeal was far removed from the pretentious suspicions encountered by any nun who aspired to achieve sainthood through the harsh discipline of fasting.

⸸

Veronica subjected her body to far more severe practices than the consumption of proteins of dubious origin. For five years, she consumed nothing but bread and water. Only on Fridays would she allow herself to eat a few mandarins: five to be exact—one for each of Christ's wounds. Alarmed, her superiors tried to confine her to the convent's infirmary, attempting to force her to at least take some soup, but the nun would abruptly vomit up every spoonful she swallowed. It doesn't matter what century you're reading this in: Women's eating habits are always scrutinized. So it will come as no surprise to learn that Veronica's extreme mortification became the talk of Città di Castello. There was no shortage of people who dared to question whether her fasting was genuine, their speculation fed by grapevine rumors. The fact that she never witnessed Veronica indulge in a secret binge herself did not stop Abbess Ceoli from testifying that she had heard from some other Capuchin Poor Clares that the previous kitchen overseer had caught Sister Veronica crouched in the pantry, furtively gorging on the convent's provisions.

Many years later, eighty-seven years old and no longer able to distinguish the beads of her own rosary, a certain Sister Jacinta would insist on testifying, with poorly concealed resentment, that all that fasting left Veronica too weak to carry out her share of the communal duties. Perhaps to put an end to the incessant complaints of Sister Jacinta and the other nuns, Abbess Ceoli eventually turned to Bishop Antonio Eustachi for help putting Sister Veronica on the straight and narrow. Eustachi assigned Veronica's confessor, Father Giovanni Maria Crivelli, with administering the necessary discipline, though his punitive methods seem to have somewhat backfired. Crivelli himself recounts that, among the many orders he imposed on the nun to break her will:

> [...] One was that she should retire to a dark cell within the infirmary and remain there until I ordered her to leave, and, on her knees, she was to lick the floor with her own tongue, as well as the walls of her cell, and consider herself unworthy to be there. She followed my orders with such delight and

satisfaction that she even swallowed the cobwebs, and the spiders themselves, collecting them with her tongue as she licked the walls . . . I told her that was too much, that it was not my intention for her to ingest the spiders and their webs, that it truly disgusted me because it could be harmful to her. And she replied that I had done well to command her so, that I had done her a great favor, and she stayed in that cell for two months or more, only leaving to pray.

Cobwebs, rodents, leeches, hair—Veronica's cravings seemed straight out of an episode of *My Strange Addiction*, that most compelling TV show featuring people with compulsions like chewing stones until they break their teeth, drinking their own urine, or gnawing on the corners of walls. While the hypnotic power of all those cases lies in the unfathomable nature of their fixations, when it came to Sister Veronica, the opposite was true. Her contemporaries read her eating disorders through the lens of a saint's hagiography. Veronica had listened to enough stories of saints to memorize the essential boxes every girl had to tick to prove she was supernaturally sanctified. And she checked them all off: She bore her crown of thorns (mysterious punctures that appeared on her forehead), consummated her mystical marriage with Jesus, displayed an impressive amount of stigmata, and survived many years of extreme mortification. In 1839, 112 years after her death, Saint Veronica was finally canonized by Pope Gregory XVI. She is typically depicted crowned with thorns, embracing the cross, and holding her own heart in her hand—though perhaps she ought to have been portrayed clutching an image of Saint Catherine of Siena, for more than any other mystic, it was this medieval figure who inspired Veronica's severe acts of penance.

There has always been an It Girl. While figures like Kate Moss, Chloë Sevigny, and Alexa Chung (as well as their spiritual forebears Cindy Crawford, Naomi Campbell, and Linda Evangelista) set the bar for unattainably high cheekbones and an inimitable, effortless arrogance, nearly every nun born in the seventeenth century sought to model her behavior after the most charismatic influencers among the saints. For Veronica, the ultimate It Girl was always Caterina di Jacopo di Benincasa: Saint Catherine of Siena (1347–1380). On April 29, on the day the Italian mystic was (and still is) celebrated, Catherine appeared to Veronica in a vision: "I experienced a deadly pain. It felt as though a sharp lance pierced my heart, and nails drove through my hands and feet. This pain granted me a flame of love toward the divine . . . It seemed to me that the Lord wanted me to take the saint as my teacher." As a teacher, Saint Catherine was remarkably multifaceted: After joining an adventurous group of women who were unofficially dedicated to Dominican spirituality, she built a dazzling career as a mystic, composed a handful of spiritual treatises, and even persuaded Pope Gregory XI to return to Rome after the schism he had caused by moving the papal seat to Avignon. From this varied catalog of impressive achievements, Veronica chose to cling to the least healthy one.

Catherine was well known for her extreme hunger strike. Once, Christ appeared to her and invited her to drink from the succulent wound in his side, the snack seventeenth-century nuns craved most. From that moment on, her appetite miraculously satisfied forever, she could no longer consume any earthly food without vomiting. Her confessor, Raymond of Capua, an unwitting ally in Catherine's mad spiral of self-destruction, describes the agonizing eating routine of the future saint:

> Her stomach could digest nothing, and her body heat consumed no energy; therefore anything she ingested needed to exit by the same way it entered, otherwise it caused her acute pain and swelling of her entire body. The holy virgin swallowed nothing of the herbs she chewed; nevertheless, because it was impossible to avoid some crumb of food or juice descending into her stomach . . . she was constrained every day to vomit what she had eaten. To do this she regularly and with great pain inserted stalks of fennel and other plants into her stomach, otherwise being unable to vomit.

Catherine died at thirty-three, exhausted and malnourished by the severity of her fasting. The strictness of her diet and her spectacular display of heroic penance would obsess generations of nuns, all tempted by the false spiritual gifts promised by what came to be known as "holy anorexia." We had to grow up under the shadow of Kate Moss's infamous motto, "Nothing tastes as good as skinny feels," a macabre absurdity that evoked a scrawny existence sustained by little more than cigarettes. Veronica, like many other nuns, grew up under the influence of another motto with consequences proving no less dire: "Nothing tastes as good as holiness feels."

It's hard not to attribute Veronica's strict bodily practices to her blind fanaticism for the famous mystic. We're certain, however, that the nun would vehemently deny such a suggestion, insisting her descent into "holy anorexia" was simply the result of following her own instincts, and not some trend. (Who hasn't responded in the same way when accused of mindlessly copying an internet personality?) And she might have had a point. As a baby, already exhibiting signs of the stubbornness that would later define her life, Veronica would sometimes refuse to nurse from her mother. The poor Benedetta Mancini stopped worrying about her daughter once she realized that Veronica's refusal only occurred on traditional Christian fasting days. On those days, Veronica would sit perfectly still while her mother relieved her inflamed breasts by nursing another hungry infant. This preposterous tale of early, devotional fasting seemed designed to reinforce the pedigree of Veronica's spiritual gifts and refute any notion that her behavior was merely a weak imitation of the truly enlightened path taken by other religious women. She certainly had plenty of stories to refute. One of her sisters recalled an incident when, determined to reproduce the sacrifices of Saint Rose of Lima (a Peruvian Dominican who ranked highly in the seventeenth-century spiritual hierarchy), Veronica purposely placed her fingers in a doorframe and nearly lost her hand—much like Saint Rose, who had burned her hands as an act of self-imposed penance. Those who saw Veronica following so closely in the footsteps of these famous martyrs had no doubt: The Capuchin nun would continue to waste away, disciplined and famished, until she faded into as hallowed and premature a death as her beloved Catherine of Siena. Instead, Veronica's eating habits took an unexpected, slightly healthier turn that allowed her to live until the age of sixty-seven (quite impressive, for the time), eventually falling victim to a stroke.

The dizzying trajectory of the nun's life—and holy anorexia—offers a clear example of the balancing act required to navigate the clash between the discourses that discipline the body and the acts of subversion that aim to liberate it. We interpret her seemingly erratic behavior as an attempt to craft an autonomous and emancipated response to the jumble of stories and commandments that held sway over her digestive system. Some whispered that her fasting was the devil's work, while others gossiped about clandestine binges. Several confessors were ready to violently correct what they saw as mere whims and delusions of grandeur, while another, intent on championing her miraculous diet, advised her to sniff rotten fish whenever she felt hungry. Even God himself overwhelmed her with his demands: "As I sat at the dinner table, it seemed to me that our Lord was reproaching me with every bite I took. Sometimes I heard an inner voice, 'When will you fulfill My commandment and live exclusively on water and bread?' And my soul was consumed with sorrow because I could not do what my Lord had ordered me to do." The Capuchin nun found herself subjected to directives even more contradictory than those faced by readers of women's magazines attempting to choose between the artichoke diet, intermittent fasting, or the Dukan method. In the end, however, she devised a strange yet personal regimen that allowed her to regain control of her body and the narrative of her holiness, without sacrificing her health. One day, without warning, she announced she would return to the ordinary diet of her sisters—but every day she would also drink five drops of a divine liquor that would thereafter flow from her left breast. No one objected.

※

The chronicle of Veronica's tortuous journey of excess and self-regulation reached us through an account published by the abbot Filippo Maria Salvatori and its analysis by historian Rudolph M. Bell, who in his book *Holy Anorexia*, sought to answer a single question: "Is there a resemblance between the contemporary anorexic teenager counting every calorie in her single-minded pursuit of thinness, and an ascetic medieval saint examining her every desire?" Reading this during the early days of the pandemic, locked in our homes and exchanging increasingly frantic messages about our anxious flirtations with an app for intermittent fasting and daily vitamin intake, we would have liked to tell Professor Bell that there is, of course, a superficial resemblance, but that it also goes much deeper. Under a lockdown that sharpened the sense of individual powerlessness, and with the usual barrage of advice and judgments on supposedly healthy habits refusing to relent—if anything, the pandemic-inspired neuroses intensified them—who could resist the promise of regaining some control by succumbing to a little orthorexia, or the obsession with eating healthily? Who would not be drawn to the illusion of certainty inspired by practices as absurd yet comforting as consuming foods by color? Who could resist the urge to meticulously calculate, with scientific precision, the ratio of proteins, carbs, and sugars one consumed each day? And ultimately, who was in any position to judge Veronica's five drops of dubious divine liquor? We, clearly, were not.

At the beginning of 2023, a rather curious trend went viral—one that we suspect Veronica would have adored. Under the hashtag #GirlDinner, millions of women began sharing photographs of the snacks they prepared while home alone. These were not recipes; the charm lay precisely in showing off the improvised, easy, mismatched, and not traditionally appetizing creations they allowed themselves to enjoy when there were no guests or companions forcing them to spend hours in the kitchen nor, we guess, the noise of opinions about their bodies or their health. In the world of #GirlDinner, anything goes: a plate of fries with pickles and a glass of chocolate milk; a microwaved potato with ready-made garlic sauce and a can of tuna; half an avocado with a squeeze of lime and a soft-boiled egg; and yes, even Veronica's dismembered rodents. If the Capuchin nun had had access to #GirlDinner via smartphone, she might have come across the Mexican Discalced Carmelites of her century devouring chilaquiles made with bugs, or the novice Francisca de la Natividad, who swallowed a raw egg sprinkled with worms each night. The possibilities for a Girl Dinner have always been delightfully endless.

"What did you eat today?" Perhaps by asking that question at the start of each episode, we ran the risk of reviving the strict body-monitoring practices of our beloved nuns. We sensed, however, that by posing the question and sharing our answers with all our listeners, we were also partaking in another long-standing tradition. A tradition that, from convent cells to TikTok videos, has meant seeking, amid the shouts of confessors, women's magazines, nutritionists, and even the voice of God himself, a refectory of one's own: sovereign, playful, and (sometimes) a bit nasty.

"A Multitude of Freshly Baked Loaves and Rolls": How the Mystical Visions of a Franciscan Nun Explain Your Obsession with Recipe Videos

In 1671, while a still habit-less Veronica Giuliani luxuriated in the jams, fine dishes, and brocades of her home in Piacenza, a Dominican tertiary born in Peru had just achieved sainthood under the name of Saint Rose of Lima, becoming the first saint born in the Americas. When Veronica stepped through the doors of her Umbrian convent in 1677 intent on outshining the other Capuchin nuns, Catholicism had already become a mass phenomenon imposed (by force) on more than half the world. For Veronica, and indeed any Catholic girl entering adolescence in the late seventeenth century, the popularization and instrumentalization of Catholicism had its perks. If she worked hard enough, perhaps she could be the next Saint Catherine, the next Saint Rose. "Saint

Veronica Giuliani" honestly sounded incredible. She had just turned seventeen when she gave her final yes to the austere brown habit of the Capuchins, but she already sensed that beyond obedience, devotion, and having the right connections, there had to be some magical ingredient that explained why certain nuns were immortalized in engravings and holy cards, while others—the majority—were remembered only in the obituary books written by their sorrowful convent sisters. The obsession with decoding what it takes for content to go viral, then, is nothing new. Sister Veronica managed to master the sinister algorithm of the Counter-Reformation thanks to a timeless intuition: If something works, stick with it. She knew that putting food at the center of visionary rhetoric and conventual practice had helped some of her favorite nuns achieve the greatest successes in the Catholic world, so she wisely decided not to stray from that path. And it worked.

With our dark circles and sallow faces, we might have looked the part, but we were neither visionary mystics nor Capuchin nuns licking cobwebs off the floors of our tiny apartments at the behest of our thesis advisor. Ever since we arrived in Providence, however, food had become the obsessive center of our biorhythms and conversations. Every Thursday after picking up our vegetables at the co-op, we confronted the same set of mysteries, week after week. What the hell was a Jerusalem artichoke and how do you cook it? Could you make soup with that celery root that looked like a mandrake, or should it be fried instead? Or was the best course of action to give up entirely and throw everything in the trash? Was it reasonable to eat nothing but radishes and beets? And on it went, for years. All those pitiful root vegetables abandoned in the drawer of our fridge weighed on us almost as much as looming rent payments or imminently due essays on medieval epic poetry. As our eating habits became more and more like those of the seventeenth-century Discalced nuns, our long hours of procrastination, glued to our phone screens, were almost exclusively fueled by videos and reels that, in under a minute, managed to convince you that your entire life had been leading up to cooking one particular baked feta pasta dish or an inordinately creamy bowl of ramen carbonara. It is no surprise that after locking our phones' screens, we would return to our beets and bok choys, the latest online culinary trend fading like a vision of sweet milk flowing from Christ's wounds.

We knew that we were not alone in our urge to spend hours watching hypnotic videos of people chopping onions or pickling lemons. In August 2023, the *New York Times* published an article that tried to fathom what was behind the sixty-four billion views amassed by videos on TikTok under the #foodtok tag. The piece, which looked back at instructional cooking videos that flourished in the 1950s, showed how although the psychotic boredom brought on by the pandemic had sparked an era-defining (and somewhat unhealthy) obsession with cooking tutorials, fascination with culinary processes had always existed. Every article—and there are hundreds—that attempts to answer why we invest so much time watching strangers cook eventually becomes a collective exercise in reassurance: Don't feel bad for watching that video of a smiling tradwife baking twenty-five homemade croissants at seven in the morning without a hair out of place; don't worry if you only turn on the TV to lose yourself in *MasterChef* and its deceptive fantasy of the haute cuisine's democratization. We all do it. We were intimately familiar with that sense of communal relief that comes from watching outlandish food rituals. The nuns had taught us everything. The nuns, and a certain researcher. In Providence, as we built the pillars of our budding friendship on anxious groans about celery stalks and bunches of beets, the book *Holy*

Feast and Holy Fast: The Religious Significance of Food to Medieval Women by Caroline Walker Bynum fell into our hands. There they were: dozens of nuns, saints, and Beguines who, long before the TikTok tradwives, had spun fame out of their relationships with food—sometimes through obscene and fanciful demonstrations, other times by adopting the most restrictive regimens imaginable.

++

On May 3, 1497, Franciscan tertiaries abandoned their tasks to attend the profession of the latest candidate for the habit at the convent of Santa María de la Cruz. They could never have imagined that Juana Vázquez Gutiérrez, a self-assured teenager who had knocked on the community's door a year earlier disguised in a man's habit, would transform the convent into an immersive, multisensory gastronomic experience—an experience that would not be to everyone's taste. Like Veronica almost two hundred years later, and Saint Catherine a century earlier, Juana had been a virtuoso of fasting long before her first tooth appeared. "She had barely been born," her biographers claimed, "when the greatness of God's wonders began to manifest in her, and at such a tender age, she revealed this to the astonishment of the people: for, as a newborn, she fasted on Fridays, nursing only once a day."

Upon arriving at the convent, Juana Vázquez became Sister Juana de la Cruz and spared no effort distinguishing herself in the crowded race for the fame of sainthood. She fasted for up to three days straight, levitated at the most inopportune moments, and experienced elaborate visions, which, in the throes of ecstatic alienation, she insisted on describing to her fellow sisters so they could hastily copy them down. Daily life with Juana in the convent was, quite simply, chaotic. Gossip about Juana traveled from cell to cell in a constant stream of whispers. Cubas de la Sagra, the tiny village south of Madrid where the nuns resided, couldn't handle all the commotion, especially now that Emperor Charles V himself, the busiest man of the sixteenth century, had made time to drop by and listen to one of Juana's sermons.

For thirteen years, another nun from the convent, Sister Maria Evangelista, devoted herself to transcribing the sermons Juana performed each time she was overtaken by a divine revelation. The nuns, their stomachs growling in discontent from the soft-boiled egg and single bread crust of their last meal, would sit mesmerized as they watched Juana's body contort more than Pina Bausch, eyes closed with a forced serenity. In a voice we can only imagine as hoarse yet impeccably articulate, Saint Juana began:

> Now, my friends, I shall satisfy and delight you [. . .]. And at these words, suddenly the wound on her sacred side opened, and from it flowed a stream of very clear and fragrant water; and so it poured into all the chalices and cups [. . .]. And from her left hand flowed another very precious and aromatic liquid; and from the wounds on her feet emerged a multitude of delicacies. And then she flew upwards and placed herself upon the tables. And suddenly, from all the wounds and lashes that afflicted her sacred body emerged a multitude of freshly baked and sweet-smelling bread rolls and cakes.

All a Franciscan tertiary needs to momentarily ease the culinary monotony of convent life is to witness the body of Christ transform into a piñata bursting with freshly baked rolls and cakes. Sermon after sermon, Juana turned the saints into "ripened and ready-to-eat fruits," and the Communion wafers became "like little sugary cakes and rolls, white as snow and delicious." She mentally laid the tables for dozens of guests with "large golden plates" and "cups, all made of gold and precious stones." She even envisioned a celestial landscape where Christ was dismembered by the guests at the divine banquet: "One took one hand and another the other, a foot and the other foot, and each of the others took a wound from the thorns on his sacred head or from the lashes on his holy body, pressing their mouths to all those sacred wounds, and from them poured sweetness, delicacies, drinks and liquors."

One day, stirred by curiosity or perhaps driven by envy, the nun in charge of watching over Juana's cell could no longer resist the temptation to pounce on a small coffer she knew Juana guarded with special reverence. Upon opening it, the nun was "astonished" to find "some very fresh green leaves, much like precious vine leaves." She carefully prodded the leaves, glanced left and right to ensure no one was watching, and reached inside. As she unfolded the leaves, she discovered something hidden with the same care someone might take when wrapping the last sandwich in existence: a Communion wafer. She looked around again, growing anxious. She didn't want Juana to catch her rummaging through her little treasures, but before she had realized, it was too late: At that very moment, the blessed Juana de la Cruz returned from her elevation . . .

> . . . And had barely regained her senses when she saw the nun going through the coffer. And she said to her hastily, "Sister, stay your hand and do not touch that relic, for it is the Most Holy Sacrament. Instead, bring me the coffer, on your knees." With many tears, and with admirable reverence and fervor, she said, "I must do what the angels have commanded me, and receive Our Lord, though I am not worthy." She then took the most holy wafer, consumed it, and ate the leaves in which the Blessed Sacrament had been wrapped, leaving nothing

behind. Though the nun begged her to leave at least a small piece of those holy leaves as relics or to taste them herself, Juana responded, "I have not been given permission to share any part of it with anyone. I alone must take it and consume it all."

And so, oblivious to her companion's distraught gaze and at the risk of choking on a poorly chewed vine leaf, Juana reserved the pleasure of devouring that strange feast for herself. For the Franciscan tertiary, her calculated acts of dietary restriction never stopped her from keeping one foot firmly planted in a delirium of gluttony. Juana de la Cruz is, without a doubt, the friend who dines on steamed broccoli with a dash of lemon each night while simultaneously flooding your DMs with videos on how to make the perfect molten chocolate cake or replicate KFC fried chicken at home.

There is no shortage of theological and Eucharistic reasons to justify Juana de la Cruz's gastronomic spectacles, but we like to think that behind each imagined candied fruit and dreamt-up shot of liquor, there lay something more. Juana knew that to reach the pedestal of spiritual excellence, she would have to submit, like Catherine, Veronica, and so many other nuns, to unhealthy and excessive fasts. She also knew she had to feign a toxic and exclusive relationship with God, and that when a consecrated wafer fell into her hands, she had to turn herself into the convent's greediest nun. But perhaps, in the dreamlike spaces opened up by her mystical journeys, Juana allowed herself to entertain the longing for another life, one less lonely and demanding than the one she enacted through her fasts: a table full of friends, one with sugar on the corner of her smile, another tipsily humming a tune, and all of them exchanging contented glances before offering each other the last bite of sponge cake. "It turned out better this time," they say, all bursting into laughter, without quite knowing why.

Thou Shalt Not Sweat in Vain: How to Escape the Gym and Embrace the Daily Routine of Microfitness

It is hot in the convent of San José in Ávila. It's just after two in the afternoon and the heavy August heat is starting to burn beneath the habits of the thirteen Discalced Carmelites singing the vespers hymn. By the time they reach the psalms, Isabel de Santo Domingo can barely maintain her composure. She shakes her shoulders, trying to suppress the tickling sensation of sweat trickling down her cleavage. The voices fall silent. A sudden hush fills the room. Isabel's cheeks flush, thinking that her awkward fidgeting has caused the interruption. She soon notices, however, the eyes of her fellow sisters fixed on Teresa. It is happening again: The Carmelite founder is levitating.

Everyone knew that Teresa levitated. The rumor had spread from the cells of San José to the farthest reaches of the clerical and secular world, both within Spain and beyond. But hearing about the spectacle was one thing; witnessing it was something else entirely. Years later, in 1610, during Teresa's beatification process, Isabel would testify before a crowd of ecclesiastical officials, recounting every detail of the enigmatic aerial acrobatics with which the founder astonished the Carmelites during some of her raptures, ecstasies, or whatever it was that suddenly catapulted the future saint's body through wild gymnastic feats.

> As an eyewitness, and one of those who most regularly accompanied the holy Mother [. . .] the force of the divine spirit by which the Lord communicated with her was so great, and the

devotion with which she surrendered to God was so strong, that not only was her spirit elevated to Him, but her body was also lifted from the ground. And because the holy Mother was very humble and greatly desired not to be regarded as a saint, she earnestly begged this witness and her other daughters that, when they saw her rising, they pull strongly on her clothing to bring her back down. And when she began to feel that the Lord wanted to lift her, she would grasp at the mats on the floor and the choir's grilles.

Upon reading Isabel's testimony, we were expected, as academics, to analyze the framework of persecution surrounding a construction of sainthood established during the Counter-Reformation, or to study the subtle theological nuances of each of Teresa's spiritual raptures. The truth is, languid and lacking in muscle tone as we were, we could only picture the choir stalls of the San José convent as the stage for an unexpected session of cloistered calisthenics: twelve nuns bending their knees and using the full power of their biceps to pull on Teresa's skirt, while the future saint herself manically engaged her core in order to cling to the choir grilles for some upside-down pull-ups. With the platonic sports obsession of those who spend fourteen hours a day tied to a chair, it was hard not to view Teresa's mystical levitations as a form of anachronistic fitness.

Of course, not a single page from all the historiography we consulted supported our suspicion that the famous trances of the Carmelite nun required athletic training. In fact, even the most respected voices of the time saw no signs of a fitness regime in the conventual landscape. In 1713, an Italian doctor named Bernardino Ramazzini added a brief essay, entitled "On Protecting the Health of Nuns," to the new edition of his treatise *On the Diseases of Workers* and raised the alarm. According to him, the life of nuns was abominably sedentary, devoted to nothing but prayer, sewing, and singing. "While I should not be ready to deny that singing and psalmody count as exercise," he wrote, "I maintain that they do not suffice if they do not exercise the whole body also with some suitable physical activity . . . Mere reading and singing exercise the lungs, but not the whole body." It is possible that during his conventual investigations, Ramazzini encountered more than one nun who disagreed and defended the aerobic routine of her order, because a few lines later, the doctor felt compelled to add: "The nuns will urge that they exercise the whole body daily, in ringing the church bells, in the early hours, in the morning and in the evening, a type of exercise heavy enough to warm the whole body and frequently induce perspiration." Knowing the size and weight of certain bells, Ramazzini's skepticism always seemed unfair to us. If tug-of-war was an Olympic sport until 1920, and air pistol shooting has made the cut since 1998, nuns ringing the bells for matins—who surely boasted hardened quadriceps, calloused hands, and biceps as tough as steel from maintaining the continuous rhythm of monumental bells—deserve a place in the Olympic roster.

We do not know how many convents the Italian doctor visited before deciding he had gathered enough demographic data for his little essay, but perhaps he should have supplemented his fieldwork by reading a spiritual autobiography or two. Anyone who reads, for example, certain passages of *The Life* written by Teresa cannot dismiss the physical demands of spiritual elevation. We, who took exactly six days to abandon a promising fitness program with a personal trainer, find it impossible to read chapter 20 of the saint's autobiography without feeling that God's physical demands bear an uncanny resemblance to the motivational shouts of a sadistic gym instructor, and that Teresa's exhaustion mirrors our own as we collapse in the locker room after a session we know will leave us incapacitated for the rest of the week.

> The Lord seizes the soul (let us now imagine it as clouds drawing up the vapors of the earth) and lifts it completely away, and the cloud rises to the Heavens . . . A sudden and powerful force comes upon you, so strong that you see and feel this cloud, or this massive eagle, rising, grabbing you in its wings, and taking you, even as you resist, to such an extreme that many times I wished to fight it . . . Sometimes I could manage it with great strain, like someone battling a fierce giant, and afterward, I would be exhausted. At other times, it was impossible, and it would take my soul, and almost always my head too, and sometimes my whole body would be lifted . . . I begged the Lord many times not to give me these external signs anymore, for I was already so tired . . . It felt as though, when I wanted to resist, an immense force was lifting me from under my feet, a force I could not compare to anything, far more intense than any other spiritual sensation, leaving me shattered; for it was a fierce struggle, and ultimately, when the Lord willed it, no power could stand against His.

There is no denying that Teresa had a regular and hardcore ecstatic fitness regime, although, judging from her resistance to movement, it doesn't seem she was the most athletic member of the convent. But the motivation for exercise, as we well know, is very fickle.

┽┾

It's nine at night, and we're both perched atop stationary bikes. We are pedaling at a good pace, with the resistance level set to something just shy of reckless. Sweat burns our faces, and our breath is becoming increasingly ragged, but we don't care; we want the effort to show. We're not in a spin class nor are we shielded by the anonymity of a gym. Instead, four spotlights are trained on us, and 150 people are watching. We are onstage at an arts center, and this is a live episode of our podcast, which has now morphed into a performance. Once we started releasing our first episodes, it wasn't long before we began receiving proposals to do live recordings in the most unexpected places: a deconsecrated baroque church, a festival of digital culture, or, like tonight, an art installation that connects fitness and climate adaptability in disturbingly dark ways. We are exhausted. At some indeterminate point, our magical plan to balance academic research, the demands of a podcast, the writing of a book, showbiz, and life itself simply spun out of control. Stubborn like the most persistent founding mother, however, we continued our mad race forward at a cruising speed not far removed from what we are managing to achieve now on these bikes, under the somewhat incredulous gaze of our audience.

The truth is that, in recent years, as our horizon of obligations expanded, so too did a blind and absurd faith grow within us: We believed that establishing a fitness routine and following it with Carmelite discipline would be enough for us to handle anything. If our minds could no longer cope, then our bodies would have to rescue us. Of course, neither boxing three times a week, nor Pilates, nor spin classes complete with music so deafening that it almost succeeded in banishing everything from our minds except its pounding beat could save us from our overwhelming fatigue and the toll our overloaded schedules inflicted on our battered bodies. On these two stationary bikes sit two PhD candidates, three muscle strains, a more or less controlled hypothyroidism condition, and two all-too-recent vascular surgeries. And yet, here we are, because true to our time, we have been swept up by a vision of fitness that has become largely theatrical and aspirational. Fitness routines are recorded, Pilates is performed against the backdrop of bizarre machinery, and the mental and physical transformation one undergoes before entering a gym is akin to method acting: the very specific attire, the motivational sentences echoing in your head. We had agreed to participate in this setup because, burdened by the weight of academic tradition, we wanted to contribute a premodern perspective to this artistic initiative addressing the climate crisis through the lens of adaptability. However, we have to confess that it was the idea of being two bookish types unexpectedly flaunting toned abs and muscled shoulders that beguiled us, even if behind that pretense of fitness lie two rather broken bodies. Perhaps what we all really need is a seventeenth-century nun to come along and tame this unhealthy sense of spectacle that shapes our relationship with our bodies and their acrobatic exertions.

María de Jesús de Ágreda wouldn't have had a moment's patience for facial fitness videos, televised sports, or the widespread obsession with isometric exercises. Among the countless occupations to which this Conceptionist nun dedicated her life—she was a master of geopolitics, an adviser to King Philip IV, and a practitioner of bilocation (though she never left her convent in a tiny village in Soria, she claimed to have teleported herself to the farthest reaches of New Mexico to catechize indigenous populations)—she was also blessed with the gift of levitation. In *The Life of the Venerable Mother Sor María de Jesús* (1687), Bishop José Jiménez Samaniego recounts how, during her mystical raptures, the nun went unconscious while her body "rose slightly, without touching the ground, and became as light as if it had no natural weight. So

much so, that like a leaf from a tree or a light feather, even the slightest breath from afar could move her." And that was not all. In her ecstasies, María de Jesús achieved a remarkable level of aerobic excellence: Her feat sparked a veritable Super Bowl that soon got out of hand. Between 1620 and 1623, the Conceptionist convent of Ágreda became an arena, drawing hundreds of spectators who also took part in this unusual mystical spectacle.

The devotion of some, perhaps stirred by curiosity, made such strong entreaties to the Foundresses to let them witness this wonder that they eventually gave their permission, and while the Servant of God was in her trance, having received Communion as she always did, they opened the Communion gate to allow a view of her. As they did so, the nuns removed the veil from her face so that everyone could see her extraordinary beauty, and the lay-people experimented with blowing on her from outside to move her. These witnesses would then spread the word about what they had seen, and anyone of their standing who heard of it would request the same privilege. As a result, with one request leading to another, and no one daring to refuse what had already been granted, the situation descended into an imprudent and dangerous disorder.

The nun, floating unconscious from one person to the next, blown along by a series of breaths, was completely unaware of the public and the shameless pandemonium into which her sisters, the promoters of this conventual entertainment, had turned her levitations. When she finally found out via whistleblower, her displeasure was legendary. In a letter written years later, she said: "If secular justice had found me guilty of some great crime and paraded me on a donkey to shame me in public, it would not have grieved me as much as knowing that I was observed having those ecstasies and levitations of mine." María de Jesús de Ágreda renounced her Olympian, crowd-pleasing levitations forever. From then on, she exercised her body with genuflections, the crossed arms of prayer, and all the bodily rhetoric that accompanied her devotions, forgoing sweaty and performative exertions in favor of a more discreet and sustainable microfitness routine.

Love

Let's not speak of how much we love each other because it's endless.
Ana de Jesús to Beatriz de la Concepción

How Two Nuns and a Jesuit Might Persuade You to Finally Download that Dating App

"That you're a woman far away / is no hindrance to my love: / for the soul, as you well know, / distance and sex don't count." It might sound like a queer collab between Billie Eilish and Phoebe Bridgers, but this isn't the chorus of a yearnful pop song currently topping the charts. Instead, these rather daring verses were composed by a Hieronymite nun for her beloved vicereine, the wife of the Spanish king's representative in New Spain. Sor Juana Inés de la Cruz and María Luisa Manrique de Lara y Gonzaga (a rather pompous name that encompassed two major hereditary estates, a principality, a county, a marquisate, and, for a time, a viceroyalty) met in 1680 in Mexico City. We would be lying if we said we haven't fantasized that the encounters between the nun and the countess carried the electric charge of the scenes that the 2016 Netflix series *Juana Inés* imagines for them, but, sadly, the cruel limits of the archive prevent us from reliably fleshing out the details of this hypothetical love affair. Of course, that hasn't stopped us from whiling away entire nights eating pizza and turning over the slightest hint that might sustain our hope that the much-talked-about "close friendship" between the Hieronymite nun and the countess was, in fact, disguising an intense love story.

※

On November 30, 1680, a procession of new viceroys made their triumphant entry into Mexico City. María Luisa knew that the appointment of her husband as viceroy, an honor bestowed by King Charles II, would signal a meteoric rise for the couple, elevating them to a sought-after position in New Spain and allowing them to sharpen the blades of their lineage with political influence. Accustomed as she was to the discreet goings-on of the Madrid court where she performed her duties as lady-in-waiting to the queen, it is unlikely María could have predicted the extravagance with which their new city would receive them. Not even modern Pride parades enliven cities with as much glittering delirium as that triumphant procession. Every street became part of a vast urban stage designed to dazzle the viceroys: facades and other surfaces were draped in expensive decorations, hordes of horses and riders rounded every bedecked bend, and for the entire duration of the proceedings, artillery salutes thundered at regular intervals, accompanied by the icy blast of trumpets. By the time María Luisa and her husband reached the cathedral square, she had no doubt that the local dignitaries would treat them with all the refinement that protocol demanded during their six-year stint as viceroyalty. But what truly enraptured the vicereine, and what ultimately convinced her that this new post would prove to be a blessing she would find hard to part with, was a sight that would leave her nostalgic until the end of her life: the spectacular triumphal arch awaiting them by the cathedral.

That towering piece of ephemeral architecture, almost ninety-eight feet high, was an intricate, three-tiered temporary structure, expertly painted to mimic jasper and bronze. The arch framed eight panels adorned with inscriptions and images steeped in obscure mythological references, designed to portray the newly arrived viceroy as a modern-day Neptune of Mexico, and the vicereine as his Minerva. We imagine the arch so hysterically overloaded with columns and figures that it produced the same kitschy shock as the gaudy sight of Disney's Cinderella Castle. If at any point María Luisa hesitated, doubtful about the tastefulness of this colossus, those doubts vanished the moment a representative of the city council delivered a witty and audacious explanation of the arch. María Luisa almost felt compelled to get down on her knees as she passed beneath its columns. She immediately wanted to know who had conceived this spectacular piece of architecture and crafted its verses. The final grand surprise of her first day in Mexico came when someone informed her that the creation was the work of a single nun living in the seclusion of the Hieronymite convent of Santa Paula, just a few miles away.

María Luisa was eager to meet Sor Juana, and meet they did. On December 30, 1682, two years after their initial encounter, the vicereine wrote a letter to her cousin, the Duchess of Aveiro, containing her only surviving words about Sor Juana. She could have chosen to write about the strangeness of featherwork art, the cloying sweetness of pineapple, or any other novelty she encountered in the Americas, but instead María Luisa was consumed by one single obsession: "There is nothing more pleasing than the visit of a nun from San Jerónimo. She is an unusual woman, there is no one like her," and "I tend to go there from time to time. I always have a delightful time, and we spend many hours talking about you." What exactly happened between them we will never know, though we suspect it involved much more than spending long hours discussing the vicereine's cousin. What we do know is that from the day they met, Sor Juana devoted herself to writing ardent lyrical poems dedicated to María Luisa—authentic hits, worthy of any entangled situationship.

In Sor Juana's verses, the vicereine is a cruel creature who never reciprocates. Hopelessly devoted, the nun claims that the harsh treatment she receives from the vicereine is so enjoyable that it manages to "make pain lovable and torment glorious," and she cries out, kneeling, "let no one pity me for being bound, for I would trade being Queen to become a Slave." Even when her verses boldly wander into blush-inducing territory—"Your fingers are alabaster dates / springing in abundance from your palms, / frigid if the eye beholds them, / torrid if the soul should touch them"—critics and historians have insisted on extinguishing their glaring passion and denying any romantic involvement, arguing that the Hieronymite nun was merely appropriating the literary codes of courtly love as a gesture of vassalage toward the vicereine. This argument has never quite convinced us. We know full well, as will any girl who grew up following the antics of Carrie Bradshaw or Hannah Horvath, that love is sometimes nothing more than the performative game of reproducing the plots and tropes of a TV show to feel like the main character in your own life. But the truth is, even we sometimes struggle to imagine Sor Juana truly consumed by the pangs of love—not because we believe she was simply adhering to an innocent courtly rhetoric that, according to critics, wouldn't have raised any eyebrows among her contemporaries. (A fact often forgotten is that her publishers had to include a disclaimer in the compilation of these poems to reassure readers that the relationship between the writer and the vicereine was "pure" and free of any untoward behaviors.) If we ever doubt a consummated romance between the nun and the vicereine, it is because we think Sor Juana, perpetually absorbed by the highest philosophical pursuits and always engaged in composing her next, more convoluted hyperbaton, was quite capable of rejecting a night of passion to retreat to her cell and tinker with her astrolabe. Still, the stubborn insistence of so many to deny the possibility that a seventeenth-century nun could have been a lesbian has always baffled us, and the vehemence with which they defend their stance quickly began to affect us as well.

In the summer of 2022, the Prado Museum asked us to live stream a video from their Instagram account so that we could comment on some of our favorite paintings. Within minutes, we were deluged in an avalanche of furious comments. None of them had anything to do with a chronological slip or a mistaken attribution—the hostility was reserved for our brief references to the existence of lesbianism in sixteenth- and seventeenth-century convents (the fact that one of us was wearing a T-shirt emblazoned with the message I WAS A LESBIAN CHILD on the day of the recording probably didn't help much either). More than 110,000 people have watched that video so far, and to this day, a stray commenter still occasionally sees fit to leave a snide remark. We have been accused of twisting history, fabricating scandalous facts to suit our own agenda, and we even received a threat of legal action from the Association of Christian Lawyers. The conservative backlash isn't surprising, but we were still left genuinely puzzled by the unshakable belief that a lesbian nun is as far-fetched a notion as a flying elephant. In fact, our otherwise beloved Saint Teresa already acknowledged the dangerous possibility of "particular friendships" emerging among her nuns back in 1567, warning of the issues that arose when nuns were allowed to visit each other from cell to cell. In her *Constitutions*, Teresa is very explicit in her prohibition: "No sister may enter another's cell without the prioress's permission, under the penalty of a grave fault." She goes on to say that the tranquility and very life of the convents depended on ensuring that "no sister embraces another, nor touches her face or hands, nor forms private friendships, but that they all love each other generally... This loving each other generally and not in particular is very important." In 1567, Teresa understood the risks of intimacy better than that friend of yours who is convinced she can maturely handle a close friendship with her emotionally unavailable crush.

When we met in 2016, one of us already knew absolutely everything about the havoc that going from cell to cell inevitably spawns and could stroll around Brown's main green with the poise of a veteran, wearing the I WAS A LESBIAN CHILD T-shirt that would cause us problems later. The other, however, was still pretending to live oblivious to "particular friendships," silently restless within her young heterosexual marriage. That her friends, coincidentally, were increasingly lesbians, that the stories of their passionate ups and downs enthralled her infinitely more than her own life, and that the few hours of freedom granted by her PhD were spent secretly binge-watching episodes of *The L Word* were all pretty clear signs of the inevitable outcome, but a willful blindness prolonged that ordeal for a few more years. Fortunately, when you are in the throes of self-deception, there will always be a seventeenth-century religious treatise that can rescue you.

⊹

In 2021, with the podcast already underway, we decided to record what is probably our most cherished episode to date: "What's a

Lesbian Like You Doing in a Convent Like This?" While we were researching our script, we came across *The Bride of Christ* (1635), a didactic treatise for nuns in which a Jesuit moralist, Bernardino de Villegas, included a chapter that immediately caught our attention: "On the Seven Inconveniences of Particular Friendships Between Women." With such a heading, one might think they were about to read a list of conventual disturbances caused by a failed group dynamic, but what Villegas actually gives us are the seven infallible clues for detecting a lesbian in the convent—or, for that matter, anywhere else. We like to imagine the seventeenth-century novices reading Villegas's treatise with open palms and hearts pounding, ready to put their fingers down as they recognized themselves in each of the Jesuit's clues, much like someone today might open TikTok and have the epiphany of their life in a video that says: "Put a finger down if you often dream about your best friend. Put a finger down if you've always thought that all women are attracted to other women. Put a finger down if..." At least one of us read Villegas's seven infallible clues this way (and perhaps now you will do the same). The clues are as follows:

1. **The Perpetual Meta-Chat** or, in Jesuit terms: "the conversations between those who are fond of each other, which are filled entirely with little stories, jokes and laughter, with the main course of their discussions always being how much they love one another."
2. **The Suspiciously Clingy Friendship** or, in Jesuit terms: "the affection with which those who love each other gaze at one another on every occasion. They always want to be together, one leaning on the other, unable to part even for a moment."
3. **The Toxic Anxious Attachment** or, in Jesuit terms: "the

restless mind and the heart's unease when one does not know what the loved person is doing... the nun may be in the choir praying with her body here, but her soul is in her friend's cell, eagerly waiting for the prayer to end so they can be together."

4. **The Jealousy Attack** or, in Jesuit terms: "the impatience that overtakes the person who loves deeply when they see their friend gazing at someone else."
5. **The Big Couple Argument** or, in Jesuit terms: "the anger and turmoil that sometimes occur between those who love each other, when the slightest offense causes them to hate each other with the same disorder they once had in loving each other."
6. **The Affective Bribery** or, in Jesuit terms: "the improper presents and trinkets, childish things, and sweet nothings shared between them."
7. **The Amorous Nepotism** or, in Jesuit terms: "the improper concealment with which one covers the faults of the other, each exonerating their friend from offenses that are harmful to the community."

Perhaps Villegas's assessment more accurately describes a toxic relationship than a true lesbian romance, but we know his list was the catalyst for at least one belated coming-out. In the twenty-first century, the Jesuit moralist's identification protocol is a paradoxical exercise in normalization. Villegas's hunch—shared by Teresa and even the Inquisition itself—that, without proper vigilance, a female community would inevitably lead to romantic bonds between women, inverts the presumption of heterosexuality that weighs just as heavily today on those of us living outside the convent as it does on those who lived within it during the sixteenth and seventeenth centuries. The gaydar of a founding mother and a Jesuit moralist will always be far more attuned than the intuition of a mob of reactionary haters.

⸙

Of course, the path to a particular friendship is never easy. Sor Juana's verses confirm that venturing into the dating pool is always like stepping into a dark abyss.

> *Love begins with unease,*
> *longing, burning desire and sleeplessness;*
> *it grows with encounters, risks and suspicion,*
> *and is sustained by weeping and begging.*
> *It learns coldness and indifference,*
> *and persists under deceitful veils,*
> *until, with grievances or jealousy,*
> *it extinguishes its fire with its own tears.*

Her love verses to Luisa are the only ones in which you can sense some calm. For the most part, Sor Juana comes across like that friend who, destroyed after a catastrophic stint on a dating app, drinks half the bar dry, and writes a ballad entitled "In Which the Irrational Effects of Love Are Rationally Described," only to mumble, with the clarity that comes in the lowest moments: "To make fancy come true / my poor heart strains / but, thwarting desire, / only gloom remains." When the viceroys finished their six-year term, they resisted leaving Mexico for two more years, but in 1688 Sor Juana and Luisa finally had to say goodbye forever. During our nighttime emotional assemblies, whenever Sor Juana's pessimism about love seemed to lead us by the hand toward a vow of chastity, we would cling to the fact that when Luisa set foot in

Madrid again in 1688, she carried Sor Juana's manuscript under her arm, ready to publish it and transform her "special friend" into the most famous nun of the seventeenth century. The path could be tortuous and deceitful, but the situationship between Sor Juana and the vicereine convinced us—even if they themselves wavered—that the *encounters*, *risks*, and *suspicions* of love are among the best ways to keep life interesting.

How the Emotional Ups and Downs of Two Lesbians Persecuted by the Inquisition Can Put Your Romantic Misfortunes into Perspective

As she idly walks toward her final interrogation, Inés de Santa Cruz considers when she first felt a surge of jealousy. We picture her weighed down by regret, thinking that she would do anything to erase even one of the many toxic dramas with which, for years, she has tried to secure the exclusive closeness of Catalina de Ledesma. This is not the first time Inés has been asked to unpack the comings and goings of her relationship before a group of wide-eyed officials and scribes. It doesn't feel fair that she must once again air her personal matters before these ecclesiastical bureaucrats, but Inés knows (because it's been three years since this hell began) that silence is a luxury she cannot afford.

Before she can gather her wits, Inés is bombarded by the first round of questions: "How long has it been since you met Catalina de Ledesma? Under what circumstances did you meet, and where?" No corner of that gloomy room, dominated by a crucifix, invites romantic reveries, but Inés cannot help it. Apparently there's nothing like the tension of a summary trial by the Inquisition to make you remember those first vivid kisses that spiraled out of control. Sweat drips from the scribe's forehead, who barely manages to record Inés's testimony without flinching. Determined not to fade further behind her own implausible ellipses and lies, Inés begins to speak, pacing herself to match the frenzied rhythm of the scribe's pen:

> It's been about four years since this confessor [Inés] was in charge of a house of penance for women in the city of Valladolid, where they brought the aforementioned Catalina de Ledesma, and since she had no bed, this confessor let her sleep in hers. A few days later, which would be more than four months, this confessor lay with the aforementioned woman, and they began to caress and kiss and say loving words to each other, inflamed by lust. Catalina said to this confessor [Inés], "My soul, my life, do you want to fuck?" And with that, this confessor climbed on top of Catalina like a man, opening the said woman's private parts and shame, and this confessor pressed her body against hers until she discharged her seed into Catalina's body. At this time, this confessor used her hands to open Catalina's parts as described.

Inés is that friend of yours who goes into a little too much detail when you innocently ask, "So, how was last night?" But when your listener is the Tribunal of the Holy Office, the risks of conjuring such graphic imagery to describe your nocturnal activities go far beyond provoking a few uncomfortable grimaces.

Even with the threat of your standard inquisitorial punishments (like lashes or exile) looming, Inés couldn't help but enjoy the pleasurable aftertaste of remembering her early encounters with Catalina. She did find a few seconds to worry about what really unsettled her: Catalina's testimony. Their years together had not been free of possessive spasms, raised voices, and complicated polyamorous liaisons, but Inés trusted that when Catalina had to testify before that same tribunal, she would cling to their shared love as she had.

╬

Catalina was five years younger than Inés, had previously abandoned a husband, and possessed far fewer institutional connections than her girlfriend with which to help escape the Inquisition's wrath. Since they had first met at the *beaterio*—a kind of convent without official recognition set up by Inés in Salamanca to house women preparing for religious life—their relationship had survived joint exile, a death sentence (that was later revoked), and several dalliances in nonmonogamy. (It doesn't matter what century you're reading this in: No long-term relationship can escape that uncomfortable conversation about the meaning of the word "fidelity.") In front of the same dilapidated crucifix that witnessed Inés's testimony, Catalina will try to offer an honest confession of their relationship—but one sweetened just enough so she avoids ending her days in agony at the gallows:

> For the past three years, this confessor [Catalina] and the said Inés have carnally known each other like man and woman, with this confessor beneath the said Inés and Inés on top, and Inés discharging her seed into this confessor's body. They kissed and embraced, speaking loving words like man and woman, and this occurred about 30 times, give or take, but since they were exiled, they have not had said carnal relations . . .

Discretion isn't the couple's strong suit. Catalina is aware of the swirl of gossip that finds them in every city where they've lived, neighbors who comment on their public displays of affection and a cohabitation that was often more tumultuous than a picture of honeymoon bliss. She barely has time to collect herself before hearing the next questions: Were the said Inés de Santa Cruz and this confessor jealous of each other? Did the said Inés forbid this confessor from standing by the window, wearing makeup, or speaking with men? Did they quarrel frequently about it? Catalina hates to admit it, but she ends up conceding that, "Yes, she and the said Inés sometimes fought over telling one another not to go to the window or put on makeup." Why chance a flirtation with someone outside the walls of their happy home when they are already in a committed relationship? It's tempting to judge Catalina's and Inés's controlling tendencies but let anyone raise their hand who feels their conscience is clear enough to submit their own relationship dynamics to the judgment of the Holy Inquisition.

When the stack of over one hundred pages of documentation about the trial of Inés de Santa Cruz and Catalina Ledesma reached us, we had, between us, survived a divorce, more than a dozen relationships and their corresponding breakups, two coming-outs—one early and discreet, the other late and dramatic—and a fair share of infidelities, sometimes committed, sometimes suffered. In short, life. We had experienced enough emotional wreckage to look at the twists and turns of Catalina's and Inés's lives the same way someone might devour the pages of *Hello* magazine or binge-watch *Keeping Up with the Kardashians*, hoping to find some relatable comfort in the romantic disasters of distant figures like Khloé Kardashian or Drew Barrymore. But there was something more. It was 2021, and academic constraints, which required us to assume professional responsibility and provided us with a source of income, had become a refuge from our increasingly chaotic personal lives. The vortex of messages on our WhatsApps would have driven mad even the most unflappable emotional expert. Sometimes we tried hard to fake a nonexistent calm that the other, paralyzed in her own inaction, only served to reinforce.

—Carmen, I truly believe that when I see her again, everything will be fine.
—Of course it will. Remember what Saint John of the Cross used to say: "The sickness of love / is not cured / except by presence and image."
—That's true, you're right.

We were in such a bad place that seeking advice from a sixteenth-century Carmelite friar actually helped. At other times, we turned to new romantic theoretical frameworks and the rash of relationship neologisms besieging our algorithm, trying to find some support for our sentimental crises. First it was conscious uncoupling ("Ana, I've been reading a book called *Conscious Uncoupling: 5 Steps to Living Happily* Even *After*"), then it was agamy ("Reading *Agamy: Program for Collective Relational Emancipation* has helped me so much"), and then the possibilities of polyamory ("When you read *Monogamous Mind, Polyamorous Terror*, you really start to understand a lot of things"). But the truth is, none of these books managed to placate our anxiety.

That summer, we were invited to collaborate on a radio program providing sensational stories about the sixteenth and seventeenth centuries. As reluctant then as we are now to indulge in the lurid tales of sexual dissidence preserved in the disciplinary records of the Inquisition, we nonetheless decided to explore them, hoping to find a juicy story to fill the five minutes of airtime they were offering us on that Saturday morning in August. We dove into a book entitled *The Reeds: A Trial for Lesbianism in the*

Early 17th Century. There they were, Inés and Catalina, fused into a single term, the Reeds, a nickname they had earned thanks to "a reed shaped like a virile member" that they used in their sexual encounters. They also had "a woolen contraption resembling a man's private parts," "another somewhat thick pointed reed," and "a thick broken piece of reed." It seemed that the Reeds had come straight from the seventeenth century to debunk the myth of lesbian bed death—the urban legend that claims lesbians in stable relationships have a prematurely withered sex life. The details of the trial revealed that, in 1606, Catalina and Inés had also opened their relationship to include a certain Ángela Jerónima, who was herself involved in an affair with a woman named María de la Paz. It seems your polycule might not be quite as groundbreaking as you thought.

Devouring the trial of Inés and Catalina distracted us from the tomes on relationship models that had been occupying any time not dedicated to the construction of the Royal Monastery of El Escorial or the most intricate verses of poet Luis de Góngora. We knew that the documents cataloging the Reeds' persecution carried with them the sticky residue of pornographic motivation in the punitive rhetoric of the Inquisition. Still, we had found the sentimental and lesbian archaeology we had been looking for, just when we needed it the most. Knowing that, four hundred years ago, two women in their thirties, deeply in love, had been able to deal with the pressure of routine, the strain of numerous relocations, the homophobic rumor mill, and the risk of falling for other women—not to mention a hostile and public persecution—soothed us. It isn't that discovering the Reeds magically fixed our own romantic debacles, but knowing that Inés and Catalina had been tormented by sentimental struggles so familiar to us today—overwhelming desire, snowballing resentments, jealousy, the quest for the perfect sex toy, and the effort required to choose tenderness against all odds—helped us navigate our own discomfort with much more ease and determination. If Inés, Catalina, and their arsenal of dildos had made it through, maybe we could too.

After the ill-fated summer of 2021, *Benedetta* hit theaters. Paul Verhoeven, the director of *Basic Instinct*, had brought the lesbian escapades of a Theatine nun in seventeenth-century Pescia to the big screen. We were intimately familiar with the relationship between Benedetta Carlini and Bartolomea Crivelli, so we went to the cinema two jaded know-it-alls, convinced we knew more about the film we were about to see than any other audience member—or even the people who had made it. In 1619, church authorities tried Benedetta because her mystical visions had ultimately revealed something far worse than a pair of stigmata or a fanciful vision of Mary: a two-year relationship, at times nonconsensual, between Benedetta, the convent's prioress, and Bartolomea, her assistant. The official scribe present in Bartolomea's declaration wrote that

> For two continuous years, two or three times a week, in the evening, after disrobing and going to bed waiting for her companion, who serves her, to disrobe also, she would force her into the bed and kissing her as if she were a man she would stir on top of her so much that both of them corrupted themselves because she held her by force sometimes for one, sometimes for two, sometimes for three hours. And [she did these things] during the most solemn hours, especially in the morning, at dawn . . . Benedetta, in order to have greater pleasure, put her face between the other's breasts and kissed them, and wanted to be thus on her.

In contrast with Bartolomea's testimony, Verhoeven's torrid, unproblematic portrayal repulsed us. Upon leaving the cinema, we indignantly noted how Verhoeven's camera was a carbon copy of the pornographic gaze that the inquisitorial trials represented. That was when we decided to seek refuge in much more comforting conventual romances.

How the Rhetoric of a Codependent Carmelite Might Save Your Long-Distance Relationship

"Believe that we are enchanted with one another, for on the days I do not speak with Your Reverence, I cannot live." We do not know how Beatriz de la Concepción felt when, on January 16, 1608, she discovered these words at the top of the latest letter from the Discalced Carmelite convent of Mons, Belgium. We can picture Beatriz walking eagerly toward the turnstile upon hearing news of the messenger's arrival, her quick yet measured stride communicating a calm that comes from knowing your messages will always be answered. She was right to be confident—since Ana de Jesús had left the Discalced Carmelite convent in Brussels to found another in Mons forty-five miles farther south, not a week had gone by without Beatriz receiving a letter from the woman with whom she had lived for fourteen years. Though both women were long past the impatient fervor of youth—Beatriz was thirty-nine and Ana had just turned sixty-three—the letters they exchanged during their barely three months of enforced long-distance love were an invitation for us to contemplate more tranquil and intimate possibilities of conventual love than those which set alarm bells ringing among seventeenth-century Inquisition henchmen. The sighs and "I love yous" of Ana de Jesús and Beatriz de la Concepción, our conventual Sarah Paulson and Holland Taylor, would be of no use to the prying lens of Paul Verhoeven's camera. And it is precisely for that reason that they are of such use to us.

When Ana de Jesús took the Carmelite habit in 1570, she left the name Ana de Lobera y Torres behind at the gates of the convent of San José in Ávila. She was twenty-four at the time and could never have imagined that the vow of enclosure would involve a whirlwind of relocations—Granada, Madrid, Paris, Dijon, Amiens, Brussels, Leuven, Mons—and exhausting upheavals, not the least of which was being imprisoned in Madrid on the orders of Nicolás Doria, the Genovese friar who had been the nightmare of María de San José's Carmelite union. When she was finally released from that arbitrary isolation, Ana had only enough strength left to retreat to the convent that had always felt like home to her: the Discalced Carmelite monastery in Salamanca. Her few companions remaining were, like her, now old and frail, but some younger faces (with far more agile kneelings) had joined the convent to secure the continuation of the community. Of all these, none would captivate Ana de Jesús as much as Beatriz de la Concepción.

When they met in 1594, both Beatriz and Ana could recite entire passages by heart from the book every girl must master if she is to excel as a Discalced Carmelite: *The Way of Perfection*. It had been almost thirty years since Saint Teresa had composed this manual to guide her nuns through the most remote and barren reaches of religious life. As we already know, there was something more grave than melancholic flare-ups, visions of dubious divine inspiration, or the advances of lustful confessors that kept the Carmelite founder up at night. The true agent of chaos in the convent's harmony was "particular friendships."

Here, all must be friends, all must love each other, all must cherish one another, all must help one another; and beware of these particular attachments, for the love of the Lord, no matter how holy they may seem, for even among siblings they can be poisonous, and I see no benefit in them . . . In curbing these attachments, great care is needed from the very beginning of friendship; this must be done more with kindness and love than with harshness. To prevent this, it is best not to be together except at the appointed hours, nor to speak, following the custom we now practice, which is not to be together . . . but each one apart in her cell . . . and if the will leans more toward one than another . . . let us take great care not to let that affection gain mastery over us.

In our darkest days, we too attempted to adhere to this Carmelite emotional detachment, but time and time again we failed: There was always a glance, a word, a few caresses that mercilessly dragged us back into subjugation.

Perhaps these passages from *The Way of Perfection* echoed in Ana de Jesús's mind as she wrote with the intensity of a lovestruck teenager to Beatriz de la Concepción during the brief months they were forced to live apart. Or perhaps Ana felt that she had already made enough sacrifices for the order, and that Beatriz's affection and companionship were the only worldly privileges she was unwilling to give up. "Let's not speak of how much we love each other," she would write on January 24, 1608, "because it's endless. These six weeks have felt like six years, and each day I feel it more." Like everyone, Ana soon flouted her own boundaries, writing in a letter to Beatriz, "Asleep or awake, your absence torments me, and the effect it has on me feels like a temptation. If what you feel for me causes you the same, I pity you." After three agonizing months,

Ana de Jesús returned to her convent in Brussels, swearing to never again part from her beloved Beatriz. When, in 1612, Beatriz's talent and good standing positioned her as the leading candidate to head the foundation of the Discalced Carmelites in Krakow, Poland, Ana de Jesús flatly refused to bear another separation. Her biographer, the Cistercian Ángel Manrique, recounts that when Beatriz de la Concepción showed even the slightest interest in joining the Carmelite venture in Poland, Ana did not hesitate to roll up her habit sleeves, set her pen to work, and write urgently to Spain: "Mother Superior [Beatriz de la Concepción], in her good spirit, wants to exile herself again [to Krakow]. God forbid that we part until He [God] takes me with Him." And so it was. Ana de Jesús would pass away on March 4, 1621, in Brussels, with Beatriz de la Concepción by her side. Without social media on hand to offer small tributes that might ease the weight of grief, Beatriz channeled all her sorrow into writing a biography of Ana, aiming to accelerate her beatification and canonization. And she did so in a beautiful way: meticulously gathering information from all the nuns who had lived with Ana, keeping her memory alive through a polyphonic and entirely feminine chronicle.

In May 2024, Bumble, a well-known dating app that both of us have turned to on more than one occasion, launched a multimillion-dollar campaign in the hopes of reigniting its waning popularity, which had been increasingly eroded by mounting critiques of online dating's fundamental premises. In the ad, a twentysomething exhausted by a string of romantic failures makes the decision to join a convent and embrace celibacy with admirable nonchalance. Under the watchful gaze of the prioress and the other nuns (who rather implausibly wear yellow habits), the young woman fails miserably at every conventual task: She's late to the refectory, neglects her calisthenics routines, and cannot resist the allure of a shirtless gardener with slick, overly defined abs. The onslaught did not stop there: Across the United States, billboards warned in a tone more menacing than counseling, "Thou Shalt Not Give Up on Online Dating and Become a Nun." The response was so immediate, so virulent, and so widespread that by the following week, not a single billboard remained. Hundreds of internet users, including Julia Fox, Kate Hudson, and Khloé Kardashian, claimed that the ill-fated campaign delegitimized women's emotional and sexual freedom. They were right. We quickly joined the wave of indignation, but we did so knowing there was also a colossal error in the ad's assumptions: While Bumble's creative director had turned to the convent as a symbol of emotional constraint, forced celibacy, and romantic abstinence, those of us who had the letters of Ana de Jesús on our bedside tables knew that what Julia Fox and others like us seek by fleeing an increasingly catastrophic, commodified dating culture is precisely the loving refuge that nuns like Ana and Beatriz knew how to cultivate in their conventual life together.

Like the *Reeds*, Ana and Beatriz entered our lives at a fortuitous moment. Every other Sunday, our iMessages read something like this:

> —Ana, was I too drunk or did you really make out with X in front of Y?
> —Carmen, did you really run into your ex-in-laws with your girlfriend? Well, I guess they know you're a lesbian now.
> —Ana, you broke up with her before signing the apartment lease, right?
> —Carmen, tell me you're not looking at U-Haul rates. You met her two weeks ago.

After a series of emotional disasters that would have alarmed even the most seasoned Inquisition tribunal, the two of us found some peace in loving partners who—unfortunately for everyone involved—resided on the other side of the Atlantic. The letters of Ana de Jesús helped soothe the restlessness of our long nights of longing in an increasingly inhospitable Providence, the fire of the codependent Carmelite's pining a pillar of any long-distance relationship's prosperity.

Money

> *I assure you that had the money been sent for my own food, I should not have felt more grateful.*
>
> Saint Teresa to María Bautista

Out with Girl Math: In with Convent Math

"God save us from money," begs Rosalía in her 2019 single of the same name. Had Saint Teresa heard the singer's plea, we're certain she wouldn't have hesitated to make it her own, given that in January 1570, the Carmelite nun lamented that although she "despised money and matters of business, the Lord has decided for me to deal with nothing else, which is no small cross for me to bear." Nearly a decade had passed since she decided to found a religious order, and Teresa had already accepted that her dream of sustaining her convents without patronage and living solely on alms was nothing more than a naive fantasy. Almost two years earlier, at the end of 1568, she received word that her elder brother, Lorenzo de Cepeda, had sent enough money from Peru either to pay for the establishment of a new house or to undertake the extensive and urgent repairs of the leaks and cracks plaguing nearly all her existing convents. In the absence of a more efficient system than the cumbersome *Casa de la Contratación*—a kind of premodern Western Union—the more than two thousand silver pesos had become stuck in Seville. By mid-January, Teresa had finally managed to navigate the labyrinth of paperwork and intermediaries, and it seemed that within days, the money would be in her hands. "I have become such a trafficker and tradeswoman, with all these houses of God and the Order, that I am knowing in everything," she wrote, with the same smug satisfaction as a colleague flaunting the ridiculously low interest rate on their mortgage—while refusing to reveal any of their negotiation tactics. In short, the nun had declared herself a thrifty negotiator with the same shamelessness as Rosalía, who, in the EP where she first begged God to save her from money, then prophesied that, "I know I was born to be a millionaire," just five years before launching her real estate empire, Tresmamis S. L. The Discalced Carmelites weren't real estate developers, nor was Saint Teresa an artist-entrepreneur-model who had managed to push Spain to the front row of every major fashion week, but she came close. Teresa quickly realized that managing her spiritual reform would have less to do with memorizing spiritual treatises, amassing biblical knowledge, or spending hours embroidering scapulars and more with handling mortgages, signing loans, and tracking down patrons.

╬

It is 1576 and Teresa is about to turn sixty-five. She senses that time is running out, and although she has successfully founded more than a dozen convents and monasteries, her ambitions aren't yet satisfied. More than anything in the world, she does not want to die without first being certain that she has succeeded in making her religious order, the Discalced Carmelites, an independent organization, free from the oversight and regulations of their main adversaries: the Calced Carmelites. It was a bureaucratic nightmare akin to determining which city taxes you need to pay for permission to extend the terrace of a small restaurant or which government office you need to visit with that mystifying form that somehow confers on you permission to work as a freelancer. But, if you were a Catholic nun in the sixteenth century, the solution to almost any problem could be found at the feet of a single person—the pope. The administrative work involved in setting up a meeting with the pope, however, is especially overwhelming for a community of nuns who, as Teresa grumbles, "have neither wheat nor money but a world of debts." Exhausted, she mentally reviews the accounts; the thought of paying for the friars' trips to Rome to handle negotiations is daunting, and the vast sums needed for international correspondence would be beyond the means of any convent. The only way out, Teresa knows, is collectivization.

Drawing on a complex operation of spiritual economics, in which God acted as a rather convenient universal guarantor, Teresa first appealed to the nuns of Valladolid for the money she needed, reassuring them that any money lent to her would later be repaid in full by God—with interest—in the kingdom of heaven. (A year and a half before this the Valladolid convent had enthusiastically welcomed a novice so well-connected that, upon her arrival, she handed over a lavish dowry paid by none other than King Philip II himself to the convent's treasurer.) When Teresa received the two hundred gold ducats, a favor as monumental as sending a stack of hundred-dollar bills, Teresa inevitably forgot about detachment, rhetorical discretion, and her vow of poverty.

> May the Holy Spirit be with your reverence and repay you, and all those sisters, for the Easter joy they gave me by so willingly granting the letter of payment . . . I assure you that had

the money been sent for my own food, I should not have felt more grateful. They acted with generosity and great delight. May the Holy Spirit repay them. I tell you, may God give them much more in return.

With a wad of cash in hand, even the humblest of girls will morph into a rapper in a music video, lasciviously pressing bills to their lips while sprawled across a four-poster bed.

Unfortunately, the two hundred ducats from Valladolid were not enough. With the same persuasive, borderline extortionate negotiating skills of a friend trying to convince you to invest in their natural cosmetics start-up, Teresa then turned to the nuns of Seville, who complied, but not so charitably. "You have been generous in what you have given to the Order. May God reward you," Teresa wrote in thanks, noting pointedly that "No house has given so much, save Valladolid, which has given fifty [ducats] more." Compared to the pile of gold from Valladolid, 150 ducats seemed but a pittance, and it felt wrong not to mention the discrepancy in the name of her righteous campaign. When in August 1580, news that Pope Gregory XIII had finally approved the independent province of the Discalced Carmelites threw the convent of Medina del Campo into a frenzy, Teresa must have felt vindicated in her petitions. Sometimes, even the novice in her worn-out sandals or the exhausted nun most attached to her wooden board for sleeping had to roll up her sleeves, seek out an interest-free loan, and master the intricacies of mortgages. As Teresa would remind her nuns, "as long as there's money, anything can be done," even amassing enough cash flow to fund the diplomatic mission of two friars in Rome. We're certain that as she managed inheritances and formed ever more ambitious plans for real estate acquisition, nothing would have soothed Saint Teresa more than humming along (perhaps a little off-beat) to the rhythms of Rosalía: "But all this, I know I can't do / Until the day I have plenty of money."

—⊹—

Every founding nun in the sixteenth century knew that it was impossible to undertake a spiritual reform without delving into the mysteries of debt, but not every twenty-first-century girl is as clear on how to navigate the dubious privilege of having a credit card in her name. By the end of our first week in Providence in 2016, the two of us went to the only on-campus bank we could find with the simple intention of opening an account to receive our PhD stipends. To our amazement (an amazement only understandable to those, like us, who did not grow up with American banking culture), we left dazed, holding the debit cards we had expected, but also the credit cards we had not, which immediately began burning holes in our pockets with the same stinging mix of torment and desire as a cilice. We now had credit. But did we have even the faintest shadow of Saint Teresa's thriftiness? We did not. That fall, we embarked on a pattern of poor financial hygiene that would have drained even the healthiest of the Vatican's bank accounts.

A revealing exchange we had early on:

> —Ana, I think having a credit card gives you a lot of flexibility. I need to pay off a $250 credit card debt, and I also have a $250 bill to pay. But if I pay off the $250 credit card balance, I can use the card to cover the $250 bill. It's like having two bills for the price of one, right?
> —Seems like a foolproof plan to me.

Years before the convoluted and sneaky logic of Girl Math enabled so many cringeworthy examples of spectacularly misguided financial reasoning, we were already faithful practitioners of questionably justifying our expenses. If the department reimbursed us $200 for books, that meant we didn't have to worry about splurging on a pair of $200 boots that season, because they would essentially be free. Passing up any 2-for-1 deal meant hemorrhaging money. And if we bought a suitcase originally priced at $150 that was marked down to $100, it wasn't an expense—it was, in fact, a gain of $50. Our first season with credit cards ended in considerable disappointment and, inevitably, the purchase—always the purchase—of a Kakeibo budget book. No disrespect to the ingenious Japanese savings method, but we are convinced that all of us would have a much better chance of escaping the trap of Girl Math by turning to the letters of Saint Teresa.

+++

To no one's surprise, the genealogy of Girl Math seems to have had its inaugural episode in the Carmelite reform. On September 1, 1582, just a month before her death, Saint Teresa wrote a letter to her friend and ally Jerónimo Gracián bemoaning the questionable equations with which her nuns in Salamanca were balancing the convent's finances. Word had reached Teresa that the Carmelites in Salamanca, especially their prioress, Ana de la Encarnación, had become fixated on a terrible real estate deal. They were determined to move their convent to the house of Cristóbal Suárez de Solís, a distinguished gentleman of the city who, according to the nuns' determination to close the purchase, must have had an aesthetic taste rivaling the most dazzling property ever featured in *Architectural Digest*. We, who frittered away valuable work hours in our student dorms perusing laughably unaffordable apartments on real estate websites, never dared to judge the Carmelites' misstep. Saint Teresa, however, saw no reason to indulge them. "There's much to be said about the Salamanca affair," she warns Jerónimo, who she hopes will be the bearer of her reprimand to those nuns so devout in their overspending. While her sisters dream big and put the convent's hard-earned assets in peril, Teresa sweats with the anxiety of someone forced to balance an Excel sheet with a mind of its own: "I tell you, Your Reverence, it's given me no small amount of grief."

The Carmelites' math simply did not add up. In taxes alone, the property deal would mean they had to pay six thousand ducats, an outrageous amount for such a humble community. "How can these poor nuns," Teresa grumbled, "throw away so much money?" She knows that the whole town is gossiping about the situation with as much bewilderment as she feels: "Where will they find the money now to pay the interest? This whole business leaves me stupefied." The Carmelites' thought process was certainly perplexing, if familiar. Since they had settled other pending transactions by giving money to the Carmelite friar Antonio de Jesús and a local man named Antonio de la Fuente, they were convinced that they could ask the owner of their coveted house, Cristóbal Suárez himself, to collect that same money from them. The money wasn't theirs anymore, but it had been at some point, so why not have those coins find their way into the hands of the seller and secure the house once and for all? Girl Math. Teresa explains to Jerónimo that, of course, she immediately wrote to those men, ordering them not to part with any money that did not belong to her scatterbrained nuns. But she is unable to move past their incoherent logic. "It's a demonic mess, and I don't know what it's based on [other than] the overwhelming desire [the prioress] has for this wretched house that's made her lose her senses."

The next time you fall victim to disastrous Girl Math, you might be tempted to blame it on demons, but Teresa's exasperated final words on the matter may be the antidote you need to quit hiding behind the opacity of numbers and get your affairs in order. "Don't believe the nuns," she informed Jerónimo, "for I tell you that if they want something they will make you believe a thousand things. [. . .] And it is better for them to find a little house like poor nuns and enter with humility (for afterward they can find something better), than to be left with many debts." Determined to put an end to the nonsense, Teresa secretly contacts the nuns' current landlord and rents the house for another year "so the prioress can be at peace." We don't know how the Carmelites of Salamanca reacted to the news, but we imagine Ana de la Encarnación gazing forlornly at the damp spots on the walls of the parlor, forever doomed to yearn for the soaring ceilings of Cristóbal Suárez de Solís's house, whispering softly to herself, "God save us from money."

Teresa's financial advice is sound, but her warnings can occasionally, as we know from her censure of "particular friendships," be too severe to provide the comfort we seek when, like blind chicks, we stumble through her words. In coming down so harshly on the Carmelites of Salamanca, Teresa was not far from replicating the backlash that the Girl Math phenomenon received across the media, where its practitioners were accused of perpetuating gender stereotypes and bimbo-fying spending habits into satire without thinking of the consequences. While genuinely reckless Girl Math can be disastrous, verbalizing the inescapable feeling of financial chaos through self-parody can be an effective coping mechanism in an undeniable reality: No matter how many financial skills one tries to develop, the individual scope for monetary maneuvering is often as stiflingly modest as a Carmelite cell. That's why, quite wisely, a good number of women began to push back against this biased reception of Girl Math, holding a mirror up to the economic gurus and crypto bros of our time who have also fallen prey to mathematical miscalculations. "Boy math is paying $44 billion for a $25 billion company and, through business smarts and entrepreneurial know-how, turning it into an $8.8 billion company," wrote one woman on Twitter, referring to "the demonic mess" orchestrated by Elon Musk with his 2022 purchase of the app. Or, as Democratic Party Congresswoman Ilhan Omar tweeted, "Boy math is never raising the minimum wage but still expecting Americans to keep up with the cost of living." Even Saint Teresa acknowledged the good-humored mirroring nature of Girl Math in a 1577 letter to her brother Lorenzo de Cepeda: "I am laughing to myself to think how you send me sweets, presents, and money, and I send you hairshirts." No matter what century you are reading this in, and no matter the vow of poverty you may have taken, an illogical exchange that works in your favor will always be a reason for joy.

╬

If we can use conventual know-how to glean any lesson from the phenomenon of Girl Math, perhaps it has to do precisely with the urgency of reclaiming—whether thoughtfully, metaphorically, or playfully—the discourse of finance and the rhetoric of economics and credit. Luckily for us, as always, a nun did it first. Sor Juana—the most famous nun of seventeenth-century New Spain, a writer of unfathomable intelligence, an epistemological adventurer, possible lover of the vicereine, and an absolute master of job quitting—expanded her multihyphenate identity by signing an autograph in 1691 as "Juana Inés de la Cruz, accountant." Thanks to her numerical aptitude, the Hieronymite nun was for years the treasurer of her convent. The task was no small one, but neither were the means. While Saint Teresa had to wrestle with scarcity, Sor Juana oversaw the accounts of a wealthy convent, enriched by real estate and the investment capital that novices brought with them upon taking their vows. She calculated profits, managed the community's expenses, operated the petty cash for daily needs, oversaw the yearly earnings, and even litigated when necessary. The tools that the rest of us mere mortals can inherit from Sor Juana have little to do with her brilliance at the helm of the convent's economic operations. (Thankfully, neither of us are a wealthy Hieronymite nun with a duplex cell attended by slaves, though we wouldn't mind enjoying liquidity akin to Rosalía's real estate empire.) What's more within our reach is the skill with which Sor Juana absorbed the language of credit and money that saturated a Mexico City already transformed into a commercial industry, appropriating its masculine semantics into the most unexpected corners of her writing. "Affection, how often, / as sweet amusement, / feigns carats to grow / to half its rightful price?" In another poem, she adopts language used by the crypto bros of her day to boldly discuss the tragedy of marriages of convenience: "Love does not seek the payment / of willing hearts aligned, / for such low interest would be / unworthy usury for the gods." By the late seventeenth century, Sor Juana, who was also an avid reader of Saint Teresa, knew full well that it wasn't worth the effort to pretend her spiritual life as a "convent girl" clashed with claiming her place in the great economic abstraction that already ran everything. Explaining the imbalances of carnal and spiritual love as financial operations—being clear-eyed about the cycles and systems that impact all parts of life—is just one clue as to where, perhaps, we should be steering our own troubled math. When Rosalía implores, "God save us from money," an echo replies, "by having, having, having it." Perhaps the conventual response should be "God save us from money (by naming, naming, naming it)."

How the Nepo Nuns of the Seventeenth Century Will Remind You that Meritocracy Is a Myth

The habit of the Colettine Poor Clares is not particularly flattering. The neutral brown of the oversize tunic clashes horribly with the black veil, and the coif, always too tight, only serves to accentuate the worst of one's features. And yet, no nun's portrait dazzles as much as that of the seventeenth-century Colettine Poor Clare Sor Ana Dorotea de la Concepción. Sharp cheekbones, a flawless complexion, lips slightly plump and perfectly defined, her face looks like it has undergone a canthoplasty by the most exclusive plastic surgeon in LA. Despite the minimalist modesty the habit attempts to enforce, everything about Sor Ana Dorotea screams of a purely patrician pedigree.

Sor Ana Dorotea de la Concepción was, in her earlier life, Ana Dorotea of Austria, the illegitimate daughter of Rudolf II, emperor of the Holy Roman Empire, cousin to King Philip III of Spain, granddaughter of Emperor Maximilian II, and niece to Archdukes Maximilian and Albert of Austria. Today, she would be one of those exquisitely placed, multimillionaire teenagers making her debut at the famous Le Bal des Débutantes in Paris but, as she was born in 1611, her lineage led her to a place with fewer photographers but a similar degree of exclusivity. In 1622, at the age of eleven and after weeks braving the jostle of her velvet-cushioned carriage and one near-deadly pirate attack in the Mediterranean (debutantes today have a much more comfortable time of it), Sor Ana left behind the rigid aristocracy of Vienna to settle at the Convent of the Royal Discalced in Madrid. There, her aunt Sor Margarita de la Cruz, otherwise known as Archduchess Margaret of Austria, awaited her, along with more than a dozen nuns who, behind the humble names they had chosen upon taking their vows, concealed more titles belonging to duchies, marquessates, and principalities than those held by the guests of the Rose Ball in Monaco.

The nuns of the Royal Discalced knew nothing of mortgages or haggling with moneylenders. Had they been able to get a gel manicure in those days, they would never have suffered a single chipped nail. They had no idea what it was like to write a letter in ever-shrinking, cramped handwriting, squeezing words into every last millimeter of the margins because the convent's accountant had declared there was no more money for paper that month. Nor were they privy to the hardship of soups made from the previous day's vegetable scraps, because each week the same "fresh fish, fruits, vegetables and other provisions" that supplied the Royal House arrived at the convent. Amid Rubens tapestries, marble staircases, Japanese lacquered reliquaries, and little lapdogs with gleaming coats sporting "collars stitched in thick yellow silk," the premises of the Royal Discalced bore more of a resemblance to the mansion of an art-loving Russian oligarch than a convent of cloistered nuns.

Since its founding in 1559 by Juana of Austria, sister of King Philip II, the Poor Clare nuns of the Royal Discalced inhabited the convent with that liberal nonchalance and vain eccentricity that only comes from growing up cushioned by inexhaustible wealth. Sor Margarita de la Cruz, for example, spent her years in the convent obsessed with its collection of small polychrome sculptures of Baby Jesus, which arrived at the convent's parlor from the world's most prestigious artistic workshops. The nuns, who managed to amass nearly three hundred sculptures, lived in close (and rather eerie) coexistence with this horde of reborn dolls. Each was given a nickname—the Firstborn, the German, the Handsome, the Poor Little One—and they dressed them in the finest fabrics. Cradling them in exquisite bassinets, the nuns would entertain the dolls during the best hours of the day "with the sweetest words that the heart dictated to the tongue." But it was the archduchess-turned-nun Sor Margarita who maintained a uniquely startling relationship with the reborn dolls. "Her ailments required doctors to order her to eat meat," writes her biographer, the Franciscan Juan de Palma, in 1653.

> Since this could not be done in the refectory...Her Highness was given meals in a different room, at a small table, served by the nun who accompanied her . . . Upon finishing, she gave thanks with great devotion and asked for a Christ Child to be

brought to her and placed on the table. Sometimes, she had him with her throughout the meal, saying he was her guest, offering him what she ate, and gratefully acknowledging the generous hand that provided for her sustenance. She kissed his feet, uttered many tender words, and thus, in the presence of the Divine Child, she would remain a while atop the table.

We sympathize with the nun in the shadows tasked with feeding a mesmerized Margarita. Like a personal assistant scandalized by the latest whim of her despotic boss three economic tiers above her, we imagine the nun nodding and smiling in feigned deference to yet another bizarre demand.

When it comes to hobbies and eccentricities, daughters of fortune tend to specialize. Every heiress has her quirk: When she's not riding in the Olympics, Charlotte Casiraghi runs a literary rendezvous sponsored by Chanel, and Prince Andrew, Duke of York, loses his wits if his collection of teddy bears isn't arranged in a specific order. While Sor Margarita de la Cruz spent fifty years in the convent basing her entire personality around caring for Baby Jesus figurines, her niece, Sor Ana Dorotea, channeled all her religious fervor toward the Immaculate Conception. Sor Ana entered the convent not only shielded by the privilege of the archduchy but also by a sizable inheritance of her own—an inheritance that, like any true nepo baby, she would dispatch in service of her most lavish desires. No private islands or vegan beauty empires for Sor Ana; in the seventeenth century, nepo nuns' extravagant caprices always involved flashy devotional objects and swoonworthy sacred relics. For Ana Dorotea, that meant squandering her cash on the construction of the Altarpiece of Our Lady of Guadalupe by the artist Sebastián de Herrera Barnuevo—seventy-three oil-painted mirrors depicting scenes of female biblical fandom surrounded by golden cherubs, sculpted plants and flowers, and, at the center, a huge bronze altar supporting a Virgin Mary dressed in pink and blue. She made sure to include an inscription that would remind all the nuns to stop and admire her commissioned splendor: "The altar you behold in beautiful ceremonies, an honor to the mind, a dedication of the soul, and a labor of love, describes the triumph of the sacred heroines executed in praise of Mary. Dorotea, versed in art, daughter of Rodolfo, who was distinguished in piety and notable in war in the service of Christ, dedicates this."

We wonder what the lay servants who cleaned the convent thought as they stood in front of the altarpiece. Or the nuns who, despite also hailing from aristocratic families, had to watch the ostentations of their royal-blooded sisters from behind the barrier of class disparity. Soon after her profession of vows, Sor Ana Dorotea obtained a special license from the Order of Saint Francis to have, among many other perks, however many nuns at her beck and call as she desired. Whenever we pass by the doors of the Convent of the Royal Discalced, we think of those anonymous nuns exiled from the memory of the archives. Lacking the privileges that softened convent life and perpetually condemned them to live at the mercy of those above them—digging their nails into their palms every time they heard Sor Ana whine, like any A-list Hollywood nepo baby, that she too had struggled to make her way in the convent.

As a child attending a private school for rich girls, one of us learned that a uniform, like the habit, never fully disguises the truth of one's family lineage. As a twentysomething in a master's program at Oxford, the other of us gaped in shock when she saw tanks with live sharks at one of the university's wild, nepo-baby-run parties. With all this in our past, it was impossible to read about the social hierarchy of the Discalced without thinking of those other Poor Clares—aristocratic but less so, wealthy but less so, fortunate but always just a little less so. Not every nun of the Discalced, and certainly not every maid, has had her story treated with the archival care granted to the letters of Sor Margarita de la Cruz or Sor Ana Dorotea. As these nuns gazed at the altarpiece's dazzling cherubs on their way to prepare the day's fish ration, or as they observed from a distance the cozy way Ana Dorotea treated the future wife of Louis XIV during her long vacation stays at the convent, did they realize that no merit of theirs could ever elevate them to the esteemed ranks of the convent's gentry? The gleam of the Discalced's reliquary room was as blinding as the light from your phone when, in the darkness of your room, you strain your pupils and drain your spirit devouring the Instagram stories of people who have been worth millions since birth. Perhaps it is in our attention to the gaps and silences of the most exclusive convent of the sixteenth century that we might find the key to transforming envy into ire, rather than shame. God save us from money (by dreaming, dreaming, dreaming of it). May we be spared from resigning ourselves to being mere spectators of wealth, from fantasizing about unattainable inheritances designed to make us forget that we belong.

Put Your Friends to Work: How to Launch Your Convent Company

In 2020, a group of Dominican nuns from the Santa Clara convent in Manresa, a town near Barcelona, participated in one of the many viral challenges flooding TikTok. Wrapped in their black veils and white habits, the four nuns attempted with stiff, slightly arthritic moves to replicate the viral choreography of the hit song of the moment: Jason Derulo's "Savage Love." Behind their awkward smiles and hit-or-miss coordination with the reggae beat, there pulsed a pointed motive—the nuns needed to raise funds to cover the maintenance costs of their crumbling fourteenth-century convent so that they could continue to live there. If seeing these Dominicans subject their time-ravaged bodies to the pop rhythms of "Savage Love" yielded sympathy for their plight, it was also an unsettling reminder that no vocation exempts one from the capitalist tyranny of productivity and the exhausting rituals of self-promotion. The Dominicans of Manresa haven't been the only modern nuns to submit to the attention economy of today. In Argentina, a very young nun went viral with her irresistibly nun-core rendition of "Tusa," the 2019 number-one smash hit on the *Hot Latin Songs* chart by Karol G and Nicki Minaj. After all, who wants to sing the heartbroken line, "but when they play the song / she gets a silly sadness / crying, she starts to call him," when one could be singing, "but give your heart to God / and you'll see how He transforms / your tears into pearls of the sea"? Around the same time, the famous Episcopal nun from New Jersey, Sister Monica Clare, starred in a TikTok ad, praising the social network as a tool in the service of God and, in passing, defending it from the political voices threatening its survival in the United States. We weren't surprised to learn that these nuns had found their way into the most unlikely corners of the internet. Instead, it confirmed for us that when it comes to securing the material subsistence and popularity of one's convent—whether you are reading this in the thirteenth century or the twenty-first—almost anything goes.

The article "Entrepreneurship and Faith: What a 12th-Century Nun Has to Say to 21st-Century Entrepreneurs" did surprise us. It was published in the *Journal of Biblical Integration in Business* and was dedicated to the medieval saint Hildegard of Bingen, a nun who lay outside our usual historical scope (she was born in 1098) but was famous enough for us to feel a kind of affectionate, simulated proximity to her. A biopic by Margarethe von Trotta—*Vision: From the Life of Hildegard von Bingen*—and a song by Devendra Banhart—"Für Hildegard von Bingen"—had taught us everything we knew about the German Benedictine: her harrowing entry into the convent at age eight; her attachment to her mentor Jutta, with whom she lived in seclusion for nearly a decade; her supposed invention of hoppy beer; her work as abbess; her musical gifts; her visionary charisma; and her tireless dedication to writing treatises on medicine and natural philosophy. What we didn't know was that Hildegard had been a late-blooming, thrifty negotiator centuries before Saint Teresa and Sor Juana.

In a Europe that was slowly abandoning the feudal system to embrace global mercantilism, Hildegard was shrewd enough to realize that her influence, and that of her nuns, could extend far beyond the tiny German village that housed the mixed monastery of Disibodenberg, where at just fourteen, she had accepted the thick black habit of the Benedictines. Despite fierce opposition from Abbot Kuno and the male elite running the monastery—who by then must have suspected that she was destined to monopolize the social capital of medieval Christendom—Hildegard managed, through a long list of connections, to raise enough funds to establish a monastery at Rupertsberg exclusively for herself and her nuns. It was there, cocooned by the peace that only a monastery of one's own can provide, that she finally completed the treatise she had been working on for nearly a decade, one that would propel her to stardom in her later years: *Scivias*. Twenty-six mystical visions. Thirty-five miniature illustrations. Two hundred thirty-five parchment pages. A psychedelic journey more intense than your worst LSD experience. A book that two solitary hands could never have produced. Without the advantage of a printing press to speed production, Hildegard—exuding the calm resolve typical of someone who has dodged death for over fifty years in the Middle Ages—supervised a meticulous chain of mass production composed of her nuns and her mentor Volmar that enabled copies of *Scivias* to reach the major spiritual centers of France and Germany. Hildegard's collective bestseller earned her the blessing of Pope Eugene III, empowered her to embark on no less than four liturgical tours, and earned her enough money to buy yet another monastery, accommodating all the nuns who flocked to her.

There's no doubt that Hildegard was the ultimate medieval master of entrepreneurship and faith. What is less clear, however, is which specific teachings from her business model should be revived. Take, for instance, that article in the *Journal of Biblical Integration in Business*, which encourages a readership keen on reconciling deep faith with entrepreneurial ambition to emulate the Benedictine's "passion," "risk-taking," and "craving for autonomy." Yet amid all this Business 101 advice, the article fails to acknowledge the collaborative framework that supported Hildegard's enterprise. This insistence on preaching individualistic risk-taking reminded us of the discipline reinforced at every stage of our scholarly journey in humanities: Stake everything on your love for literature; permit your emotional stability to hang by a thread; do your research in hermetic solitude; only then, perhaps, will you reach the pinnacle of your academic career. Our daily struggle to envision a future of economic stability within the university certainly colored our reading. Fortunately, our discovery of Hildegard and her publishing operation converged with a video call that would forever change our view on money and work.

In November 2021, our podcast had built a modest yet

enthusiastic audience. It was enough to catch the attention of the curator of a small festival on digital culture, who invited us to participate by recording a live episode. We were more or less prepared to face an audience—for better or worse, the path of academia is dotted with conferences where, after much begging for university funds to cover at least the basic travel expenses, you finally get to read your paper in front of ten or fifteen people who share your peculiar interest. What we weren't prepared for was the curator's final question: "What's your fee?" We met his inquiry with a too-long silence. When we finally saw our stunned faces in the small video call window, we tried to recover and act naturally with little success. Today, we still haven't come to terms with the fact that we are now not only reimbursed for travel expenses but also paid a well-deserved fee for the same research, writing, and dissemination work that we once did within academic boundaries for free (or even at the cost of going into debt). In every small moment of doubt, when insecurity jeopardizes our sense of the value of our own work, there is a nun—always a nun—we cling to like a lifeline: Arcangela Tarabotti.

Like any self-respecting multibrand conglomerate, the Venetian nun had many names. Baptized Elena Cassandra Tarabotti in 1604, she later professed her vows as Arcangela in the Benedictine convent of Sant'Anna, but she was also known as Galerana Barcitotti and Galerana Baratotti, the pseudonyms under which she published a number of incendiary texts with titles reminiscent of low-budget soap operas, including *Paternal Tyranny, Conventual Hell,* and *Innocence Betrayed.* Under her religious name, Arcangela, she ran a true industry leader in the textile sector of her time and, most importantly, she cultivated the supportive environment that should guide any enterprise worthy of being considered a Convent Company. When her parents confined her against her will to that Benedictine convent at just eleven years of age, Arcangela could scarcely imagine that in just a few years' time, those walls—seemingly impenetrable save for the wafting stench of the Venetian canals—would transform into a boundary as elastic as the size of her orders. In 1615, five years before professing her vows, it was still too soon to foresee the episodes her convent life had in store for her. But perhaps even then, she was beginning to devise strategies that would allow her to sidestep the sartorial austerity observed by the Rule of Saint Benedict and to skew the order's motto—"Ora et labora"—in its more lucrative direction.

It is no coincidence that Arcangela found a way to fill her convent's coffers by delving into the world of fashion. Inspired by Dante Alighieri's *Divine Comedy* to outline the nine circles of her own monastic hell in *Convent Life as Inferno*, the nun recalls a childhood drama that—no matter the century—every little sister has to endure: the eternal fate of never having new clothes to wear. Arcangela was actually the eldest of seven sisters, but her parents, believing her congenital limp precluded marriage, deposited twelve hundred ducats at the convent of Sant'Anna so she could profess with the Benedictines, leaving the rest of their wealth for the dowries (and wardrobes) of her sisters. Remembering the softness of her sisters' shirts trimmed with Dutch linen stung like a penance, especially because the trunk Arcangela brought to the convent contained only a humble woolen habit and a couple of stiff shirts. "The condemned in the tomb of a cloister," Arcangela reflects with the dejection of a fashionista limited to T.J.Maxx, "are forced to cover their legs with coarse cloth and to wear on their feet wooden clogs badly lined with leather. Many times," she adds, as though this detail invites no further argument about the dire nature of her circumstances, "[the poor nuns' blouses] aren't long enough, and sometimes the sleeves don't even match the rest." Confronted with this aesthetic catastrophe, there were only three possible solutions. First, one could debase oneself with a plea like that of fellow Venetian Laura Acerbi, who in 1715 sent her father a tearful letter regarding her clothing deficiency: "The moment of my church profession is nearing and I am without any sort of cell furnishings or linens and in great need of these things . . . it is necessary to hurry dear Father, You can only imagine how ashamed I am because I cannot appear alongside the other nuns. I then beg you Dear Father to be good to me." The less depressing, far more entertaining option was to customize the few rags one had to create an outfit as daring as the ensemble a Venetian official encountered in 1597 at the convent of Sant'Andrea della Zirada, where the nuns wore "silk veils that leave the curled hair visible and generous necklines with great scandal." The final, and most enticing option was to monetize the sewing skills of one's companions—rally them to work, as Arcangela did, and capitalize on the insatiable demand for the fashionable fabrics, laces, and silks that the city's female population coveted.

Venetian nuns were the crème de la crème of DIY, renowned for their skills in painting, music, and, most notably, their needlework. While ecclesiastical inspectors generally praised these handiworks, they couldn't resist occasionally introducing regulations. After a convent visit in 1521, one of these spoilsports concluded that "it is great disorder, and many evil thoughts are born from the fact that nuns do not work together in the workshop." He decreed that all should work in a shared space, "and never in their own cells . . . The works executed in the workshop need to be approved by the Mother Superior, and only commissions coming from honest people of good name and reputation are to be accepted." The powers that be feared that, sheltered in the privacy of their cells, the nuns might apply their sewing skills to frivolous tasks lacking spiritual direction and, above all, that they might learn to turn their art into a commodity, weaving social and commercial networks beyond the church's watchful eye. Yet in what was meant to be a check on the nuns' autonomy, Arcangela could sense an attractive new business opportunity. Seeing all her Benedictine sisters gathered together, teaching one another the intricacies of drawn thread work, lace loops, reticella, and other details of convent lacemaking, Arcangela realized the church inspectors had gifted her a golden opportunity to manage the human resources of her budding initiative. Why not consolidate the powers of her skilled sisters for all their benefit? Similarly, once our podcast was up and running, it quickly became clear to us that our quirky, diminutive venture didn't end with just the two of us. Soon, we roped in our talented friends to create all those things we couldn't ourselves: a jingle, artwork, a few promotional photos. It doesn't matter what century you're reading this in, nor how eccentric your friends' strengths may be, if you gather them in one room and telegraph a piercing entrepreneurial vision, you can pull off your own Convent Company. With a thrifty and negotiating spirit, there is almost always a business model to match your freak.

Under the baton of Arcangela, the convent of Sant'Anna began functioning at an impressive pace. Through her provocative prose and tireless letter-writing, the nun had cultivated connections with the wealthiest circles of the city and, when the time came, she knew how to mint all that social capital. She primed her extensive web of acquaintances to place lacework orders with her convent, and even engaged in a bit of industrial espionage, closely observing the garments worn by visiting guests in the convent parlor, ensuring she kept up with external fashions and identified which new patterns her nuns should start producing. In her letters—an instructive lesson in business know-how, comparable to the inbox of Miuccia Prada—Arcangela dexterously managed the demands of this collective enterprise. In a letter to one Isabetta Piccolomini Scarpi, Arcangela gave the assurance that her order, though it was driving the nuns "crazy," would be ready on time. In another letter, she notified the Marchioness Renata di Cleramonte that there would be a delay because "the nuns that committed themselves to the work are [. . .] sick," and she had granted them a kind of sick leave. With the wife of the French ambassador, Arcangela high-pitched her trafficker and tradeswoman's tone, informing her that the lace she ordered would cost "no less than 60 ducats per braccio," but promised to personally oversee the lace's execution and shipment. Arcangela was all logistics and networking. She and her Benedictine sisters were, to put it simply, a seventeenth-century Prada infused with the convent's redemptive and equitable reputation.

To be honest, we only dare to read Arcangela's busy letters in tiny doses, so as not to inflame the now-chronic PTSD embedded in our bones after years spent juggling flooded university inboxes with our own fledgling Convent Company. But in the right measure, the Venetian nuns—like those in Manresa or Hildegard herself—are always good reminders that the rewards of communal passion and pleasure are endless, even when you least expect it.

Soul

And I came to think that it all came from the devil.

Jeanne des Anges

The Rewards of Sadfishing: How to Harness Your Woes by Serving *Mater Dolorosa*

In the *beaterio* of Santa Catalina in Ávila, sleep was impossible. During the coldest, darkest hours of the night, when the tertiary Dominican sisters were finally snuggled up and lost in dreams of Christ's wounds and forbidden sweets, the keening sound of inconsolable weeping would shatter their hard-earned peace. The oldest, more patient sisters usually dismissed the matter with a soft sigh as they shifted position on their straw mattresses. But for the less forgiving among them, every disruptive sob was yet another reason to expel that young girl, the culprit of every missed stitch, the one they blamed when they nodded off gracelessly during confession after another sleepless night. She was barely twenty, but it wasn't the first time María de Santo Domingo had turned a *beaterio* upside down with her tears. She had come to Ávila after a rather tumultuous exit from another religious house in Piedrahíta and would soon be forced to leave this second house, too, when her most insomniac and (perhaps) envious sisters managed in 1507 to have her transferred back to Ávila, this time to the Dominican convent of Santo Tomás. It wasn't melancholy or mania that seized her at night—María's crying was, in fact, the damp complement to her fantastic mystical raptures. In scenes charged with drama, she would either stiffen like a tree trunk or converse directly with the Virgin (who she addressed as "mother-in-law," for she had wedded Christ). No matter how varied María's performance might be, her mystical pyrotechnics leaned heavily on one flourish: the gift of tears.

If everything that happens to us already happened to a nun in the sixteenth or seventeenth centuries, then almost everything that happened to those nuns had already happened to a medieval religious woman. In the twelfth century, long before María de Santo Domingo was born in Castile and blessed with a flair for blubbering, the thirty-year-old Belgian mystic Marie of Oignies had already left her husband to join a community of Beguines, finally able to devote herself entirely to the grace of the stigmata and incessant weeping. Judging by her words, she enjoyed it immensely: "These tears are my food, they are my bread day and night. They do not afflict my head, but nourish my mind; they torture me with no pain, but refresh my soul with deep peacefulness. They don't empty my head but fill my soul with plenty, relaxing it with a sweet kind of anointing, as long as they are not compelled to come forth through violence but are freely given by the Lord as a healing potion." Is Marie of Oignies a self-justifying crybaby, or do her tears call to mind the tears one seeks swaddled in a blanket, ready to watch *Titanic* for the umpteenth time? Are those tears not also a sweet kind of anointing? A kind of healing potion? It doesn't matter what century you're reading this in: Every girl knows that when the soul is tormented, nothing is as soothing as a couple of hours spent bawling. If you were lucky enough to be a Holy Weeper in the Middle Ages, you had, beyond the logic of release, the somatic framework of medieval spirituality—the conviction that when holiness lodged itself in the body, it did so in the form of effusions like blood or tears, treasured hagiographic marks and undeniable signs that your own flesh was embracing Christ's pain. For this reason, women like Marie of Oignies could thoroughly savor their tears without shame. Others, like Beatrice of Ornacieux, could take their tearful devotion nearly to the point of blindness, and some, like Margery Kempe, punctuated their sobbing with such extravagant contortions that a well-meaning friar once whispered to her, "Woman, Jesus died a very long time ago," with the compassionate honesty of that friend who bids you to get over your ex. By the early sixteenth century, however, the spiritual temperature on waterworks had evolved dramatically. When María de Santo Domingo's gift of tears began to reveal itself, it was no longer a simple matter for women to dabble in stigmata and other corporal stunts. Now, they had to deal with the Holy Inquisition breathing down their necks.

The scandal that María de Santo Domingo's impassioned tears unleashed in the convent and *beaterio* was tied up in the reservations of fellow mystics, nuns, and ecclesiastical officials: Were María's wails the closest they would ever come to glimpsing the sweetness of divinity, or was it all the work of the devil, nothing more than an attention-seeking stunt? It was a legitimate doubt, one that had even gnawed at the medieval Italian mystic Angela of Foligno, a great pioneer of ecstatic weeping who nonetheless alleged that the tears of others indicated a devotion to the spotlight rather than a higher power: "And in the instant that the world adores and watches her, the tears, the sweetness, the trembling and the screeching that arise from this impure spiritual love grow even greater. And though impure spiritual love may have tears and sweetness, they do not originate in the soul but rather in the body, and the love itself does not reach the soul." In other words, Angela was accusing other religious women of sadfishing. It is with several centuries' distance the very same accusation that was leveled against supermodel Bella Hadid when she posted for her fifty million followers a brief text revealing the depths of her sadness, accompanied by a few photos in which, naturally, she appeared beautiful, her striking eyes swollen and red as tears slid down her breathtaking cheekbones.

☩

As well as being devoted scholars of sixteenth-century concepts—from the transubstantiation of the Eucharist to the holy radioactivity of relics—we are also avid students of more contemporary coinage—be it Girl Math, revenge bedtime procrastination, or lesbian bed death. So we felt a jolt of personal interest upon encountering the 2019 article in which British journalist Rebecca Reid first made use of the term *sadfishing*. The article described the affection-chasing antics of celebrities like Kendall Jenner, who appeared on social media professing emotional devastation brought on by the ups and downs of her battle with acne. As Reid recalled, Kendall's confessional turned out to be nothing more than a millionaire's marketing ploy for the skincare brand Proactiv. Our Convent Company had no corporate sponsorship, yet we couldn't claim that, with each complaint aired in our episodes, we weren't crossing the line from harmless venting into exaggerating our roles as pitiful PhD students in order to squeeze every drop of emotional currency from our tears. We had already developed a habit of beginning each episode whining about the New England cold, the toughness of our mattresses, the distance from our friends and girlfriends, or the end of daylight saving time. We were embodying, we realized, two cardinal sins of the modern age: podcasting and sadfishing, a chilling combination worthy of at least one hundred inquisitorial lashes.

Perhaps we were becoming, like those celebrities transmuted into twenty-first-century incarnations of *Our Lady of Sorrows*, exactly what Saint Teresa criticized when she warned in *The Interior Castle* against nuns of "bodily weakness," or "people of sensitive characters who cry over every trifling trouble." Maybe those commentators who seize on any media opportunity to decry the "snowflake generation" and its fragile desire for safe spaces and trigger warnings were right. Were we like those Carmelites Teresa complained about, who "would never stop crying: believing that tears are beneficial, they do not try to check them nor to distract their minds from the subject, but encourage them as much as possible"? More than likely, we are. Fortunately, just as we were on the verge of flagellating ourselves with seven ropes of penance for succumbing to embarrassing emotional displays, we discovered María de Santo Domingo. Thanks to her scripted, tearful demonstrations, we learned to avoid guilt and shame and accept that sometimes, if done well, harnessing the power of your woes for high drama is a media strategy as valid and effective as any other.

☩

No one ever served *Mater Dolorosa* with as much virtuosity as María de Santo Domingo. The poet Heather Christle noted in *The Crying Book* that after "a real cry, most people are hideous, as if they've grown a spare and diseased face beneath the one you know, leaving very little room for the eyes." This was not the case for Bella Hadid, nor was it for María. Far from surrendering to her visions in any random attire, the mystic took great care to time her ecstasies to when her exceptionally long mane had been recently lightened (apparently dyed with a kind of bleach) and, taking advantage of the fact that Dominican tertiaries were not obliged to wear habits, when she donned her best crimson tunic and coral jewelry. What María de Santo Domingo wanted was that adulterated tear-streaked beauty that the crying filter on Snapchat gives you, or the innocent puffiness faked with one of those postcry makeup effects that, believe it or not, are trending in the depths of YouTube. To the dismay of the skeptical, sleepless nuns tormented by María's histrionics, her tearful beauty captivated a circle powerful enough to free her from the serious accusations questioning her orthodoxy that closed in around her between 1508 and 1510.

In the winter of 1508, King Ferdinand summoned María to Burgos, the court's residence at the time. The provincial responsible for María was sowing suspicion about her now-famous raptures, but the king elected to investigate the matter himself. A girl always knows how to prepare for that one day when everything is on the line; that is why, when María arrives at the castle in Burgos, she no longer has to passively wait for one of her ecstasies to overtake her—her tearful fits can now conveniently burst forth upon request. Awaiting her trance are, among other notable figures, the king, the queen, Juana of Aragon, and Cardinal Cisneros. All eyes are on the mystic, and it is best not to keep them waiting.

María closes her eyes, raises her arms, and clears her throat to prepare her voice before setting the machinery of rapture in motion with a prayer.

> Grant me, then, some of that love and warmth that you gave to your pious Magdalene. Grant me those streams and tears

that never tired in her but have dried up in me . . . Grant me, O pious queen, a small share of your sorrows and loves so I may cry, grant me that my eyes may not tire . . . Grant me, most gracious Father, that knowledge and those tears that you gave your precious Magdalene, for Heaven and Earth seemed but little to her to give all for you.

And the tears are not slow to come. From here, María descends into a delirium of sobbing during which she becomes the ventriloquist for the weeping of the Virgin, Mary Magdalene, the apostles, and even Christ himself. Through tear-filled eyes, María—the actor, scriptwriter, and producer of her own ecstasy—peeks at the tears that begin to slip down the moved faces of her audience, securing her reign as the ultimate sadfisher of the sixteenth century.

Is it really so bad, after all, to be one of those "people of sensitive characters who cry over every trifling trouble"? Reading the *Book of Prayer* by María de Santo Domingo, an anonymous compilation of her doctrine that includes a detailed account of her raptures, we resolved that the rhetoric of weeping is not a sign of weakness but rather an eloquent and theatrical maneuver to elevate one's sorrows onto the stage they deserve. Without the spectacle of her tears, María might never have left the *beaterio* in Piedrahíta, just as, without their constant collective lament, the "snowflake generation" might never have managed to bring public attention to issues that for decades were ignored. It is possible, too, that without our plaintive sadfishing, we might never have kindled an affection between the two of us that, in those years of grief and loneliness, truly was a "sweet unction . . . a healing potion" capable of soothing us at our lowest point.

How to Find the Comfort You Need in a Fourteenth-Century Dominican Nun's Taxonomy of Tears

"You beg knowledge of the reasons and fruits of tears, and I have not despised your desire," God told Saint Catherine of Siena one ordinary day in 1378. Or so she claimed. In the time saved by skipping meals in the refectory, the most inspiring It Girl of medieval sainthood set out to become an outspoken visionary with an uncompromising edge. Over the course of Catherine's long conversations with God—which she dictated to her confessor, Raymond of Capua—one gets the sense that even God was growing a tad weary of her constant demands, which had lately morphed in tenor from those of a charmingly fervent follower to that of a hostile stalker, unable to stand having her messages go unanswered. "You are the one who puts this desire in my heart," Catherine would tell God, driven by an assertiveness from which, maybe, we could all learn, "therefore you must fulfill this desire of mine, which is nothing but the fulfillment of what you ask me to want." (With these manipulative syllogisms, Catherine always had God cornered.) Hungering to probe the breadth of fourteenth-century spirituality, the Italian Dominican guessed that splitting her voice to disguise it with the full garb of divine authority was the only way to let her creative juices flow and theological insights flourish. And so she did. It was an avant-garde writing exercise: five hundred pages of questions and answers with God, united under the concise title *The Dialogue*, an encyclopedia of the torments and obsessions that Catherine dictated to her confessor.

Catherine cried a lot. She cried almost as much as she fasted. She cried so loudly and so unremittingly that one day, her first confessor, Friar Tommasso, begged her to please "try to control yourself" because her pathetic display interrupted Mass, causing the priest to stumble so significantly that the congregation could not even tell when they were supposed to murmur "Amen." Lying on her straw mattress, staring up at the ceiling of her cell, Catherine was no longer sure if her crying was a form of spiritual purification or simply due to the pain of yet another aggravated cilice sore. With eyes so swollen that she could barely make out the overhead beams she counted each night before sleep, she tossed in the rough fabric of her habit and asked God once again: Why do I keep crying? (For Catherine, God was like that friend you bombard with voice notes and messages in the middle of the night but before they can offer even a hint of consolation, you're already off on a tangent of self-reflection.) One night, Catherine dried her tears on the worn taffeta she kept beside her pillow and began to submit her cries and sobs to a rigorous, dissecting analysis that would make up *The Dialogue*—because we all know that no crying is worse than the one that has no known cause. The nun quickly set in motion her little performance of divine doubling, and in her daily dictation session, she presented Raymond of Capua with her taxonomy of tears.

There were five types:

1. "The tears of the wicked men of the world. These are the tears of damnation." These are the tears brought forth by those men you wisely banished from your life: the only tears unworthy of your attention.
2. "The second are those of fear, and belong to those who abandon sin from fear of punishment and weep for fear." Much like, we imagine, the tearful regret that overwhelms you in bed on a hungover morning, afraid to unlock your phone and face the irreparable mistakes of the night before.
3. "The third are the tears of those who, having abandoned

sin, are beginning to serve and taste [God], and weep for every sweetness, but since their love is imperfect so also is their weeping." This must have been Catherine's signature tear.

4. "The fourth are the tears of those who have arrived at the perfect love of their neighbor, loving [God] without any regard whatsoever for themselves. These weep, and their weeping is perfect." Is this the innocent, almost childlike crying that overcomes us when our mirror neurons light up while watching a TV contest where someone wins a beach apartment, or a video of a baby getting glasses and seeing for the first time? It could be.

5. "The fifth are joined to the fourth and are tears of sweetness let fall with great peace." It doesn't matter what century you're reading this in: These are the tears we all wish for, the most aspirational kind of weeping.

We confess that Catherine's five types of tears left us a little disappointed. By this point, even if Saint Catherine of Siena herself—doctor of the church, patron saint of Italy, and co-patron of Europe—begged us, we were not about to rise from sin, and no one was going to convince us that the imperfections and impurities of love, hard-won as they were, deserved our tears. But, in truth, the Dominican nun had done as much for us, if not more, than our therapists: She had given us the introspective nudge we needed to sit down, scalpel in hand, and carefully examine our sadness.

╬

We had spent nearly a year away from Providence, thanks to a research fellowship that freed us from teaching duties, and our return—though we knew we only had two more semesters of inclement weather, root vegetables, and office hours spent grappling with student arrogance—had plunged us into an unfamiliar unease. It was 2022, and those two twentysomethings who had arrived in Rhode Island six years earlier, determined to do whatever it took to secure a place in the tyrannical Ivy League job market, felt as foreign to us as the new students who arrived at the department each year with their smooth faces, intellectual nonchalance,

and eyes sparkling with hope. We were like novices who had managed to dodge the dowry and enter the wealthiest convent, aiming to climb to the prioress position, only to find ourselves paralyzed along the way by a lack of vocation. Every morning, our inboxes overflowed with emails for grueling preparatory seminars: "How to write the perfect cover letter"; "What to do with your PhD outside academia"; "Five strategies for publishing in top-tier journals." When we closed our laptops and curled up in bed, seeking solace in some cute animal video, our phones would start vibrating with messages from friends and colleagues forwarding job offers. The professors in our department looked at us with the disapproval reserved for wayward teenagers who, for cryptic reasons, had gone from straight-A students to skipping exams altogether. We were numbed by sadness, paralyzed by uncertainty. Our obscure, half-finished dissertations on economic crisis and alchemy and architecture and language in the seventeenth century weighed on our shoulders more heavily than the cross of Calvary. The passing months counted down the days to freedom, but also marked an agonizing race against the clock toward a future where the Brown University paycheck that supported us would vanish. Almost without noticing, the charismatic strategy of complaint, for which we had long advocated, had taken over everything and, behind closed doors, we had become two lamenting wrecks, feeding on each other's misery. It was then that Saint Catherine appeared, offering us her doctrine of tears.

Determined to put an end to our emotional aphasia, we embraced Catherine's example and set out to develop a taxonomy of tears that had less to do with spiritual fervors and mystical renunciations, and more to do with the psychosomatic ruptures common to almost everyone who has reached their thirties. We came up with six categories (some borrowed from Saint Catherine), but we suspect there may be as many kinds of tears as there are tearful souls in the world:

1. **Tears for self-fulfilling prophecies.** The kind of weeping spurred on by a review of every possible catastrophic scenario, conducted with the precision of a miniaturist. Although these tears might seem unnecessary, sometimes a girl just needs to imagine the worst, licking at nonexistent wounds, to achieve a tearful release from her terrible knot of anxiety.
2. **Tears of exhaustion.** When "the greatest repugnance" overwhelms you, there is a spontaneous kind of crying that possesses you, suspending your unsustainable race toward peak productivity.
3. **Tears of guilt.** In *Way of Perfection*, Saint Teresa wrote that "thus, even if it isn't precisely what they blame us for, we are never completely without fault." Though we are strong believers in eliminating excessive guilt, in a therapy-saturated culture that is increasingly inclined to validate our own perspective, perhaps tears of guilt are the prerequisite for embodying the famous concept of emotional responsibility.
4. **Hormonal tears fueled by premenstrual syndrome.** Irrational, merciless, yet deeply vital.
5. **Tears of vulnerability.** The ones you shed while compulsively unlocking your phone, waiting for that message you know will never come.
6. **Tears of sweetness.** When the nine circles of hell calm down and life offers a sudden reprieve, sometimes an almost ecstatic weeping emerges, the kind every girl should experience at least once a year. If tears of sweetness are not forthcoming, your place is elsewhere.

That night, as we devoured two greasy pizzas in the least welcoming restaurant in Rhode Island and chatted about how to fit our tearful torrents into the sterile framework of classification, life suddenly felt a little less bleak. We had found a way to socialize our weeping. Relieved to have found a comforting after-dinner conversation, we became addicted to theorizing about tears. We might have abandoned our rigorous investigative dissertations on seventeenth-century linguistics, but nothing stopped us from spending long hours eagerly searching for tear-related monographs on the shelves of Brown's Rockefeller Library: *Holy Tears: Weeping in the Religious Imagination*, *Telling Tears in the English Renaissance*, *Crying: The Natural and Cultural History of Tears*. We learned that some doctors contemporary to Catherine, Bolognese physician Mondino de Liuzzi, for example, conceived of the body's fluids as part of an infinite circular economy—breasts produce milk from warm, refined blood; eyes shed tears, which are a type of milk that nourishes the heart, which in turn produces blood that becomes milk. A charming physiological notion. That is why Catherine's God assures her, "I wish thee to know that every tear proceeds from the heart, for there is no member of the body that will satisfy the heart so much as the eye." For us, who knew just enough about natural sciences to keep up appearances of basic schooling, this whimsical fluid circuit was a comfort.

We wrote our taxonomy of tears on Post-it notes and stuck them in a corner of the whiteboards where, each day, we recorded the tasks we knew we would not be able to complete. As we anxiously reviewed our lists, snow falling outside the window, each of us surrounded by the deafening silence of our empty houses, the tears welled up ready to spill from our nearsighted eyes. We asked ourselves: Are these tears of exhaustion because it's 6 a.m. again? Do they stem from the guilt we feel for the three episodes of *The*

Real Housewives of Beverly Hills that kept us up until 2 a.m. last night? Are our periods about to start? We thought of each other's tears, imagining a community of weeping friends. And suddenly Saint Catherine's voice broke through to disrupt our whimpering, consoling us with the tenderness of a demanding and doting mother superior: "I have already told thee how tears come from the heart, and how the heart distributes them to the eyes, having gathered them in its own fiery desire."

Don't Let Them Name Your Demons: How a Seventeenth-Century Ursuline Nun Can Help You Process the Thousand Faces of Your Anguish

It is a spring morning in 1634 in the small French town of Loudun. A line of seventeen Ursuline nuns crosses through the convent gate, moving down the cobbled street at a brisk pace. No words pass their lips, but the morning silence is broken by the rustle of their black twill habits and the gentle hush of their collective breathing, reminiscent of a murmured prayer. The abbess, Jeanne des Anges, is barely thirty and has a limp that causes her to sway with each step, yet she leads the procession with the speed and certainty of someone who knows she is responsible for what is about to happen. The time has come: The seventeen Ursulines are walking purposefully toward their own exorcism.

They will all endure the same torment, though not together. Some will go to the Church of Sainte-Croix, others to Saint-Pierre-du-Martray, and the rest to the chapel of Notre-Dame de Château. As they near the crossroads where they must part ways, they barely meet one another's eyes, fearful of revealing the terror within. Jeanne arrives at the Church of Sainte-Croix, flanked by five Ursuline sisters. None of them expect the scene that awaits them. Before the main altar, on wooden planks, a stage has been built high enough so that even those sitting in the farthest row will be able to see what is about to unfold. The sisters barely have time to process this tableau before they are shackled and led to a bench, where two ropes bind each of them—one securing their legs, the other pressing their stomachs and spines tightly against the wooden backrest. When no one else can fit into the church, Father Mignon and Father Pierre Barre approach the Ursulines, who understand that it is all about to begin. In just a few minutes, under the insatiable gaze of the entire town, these pale, trembling nuns will begin to bark, sweat, convulse, and howl blasphemies, bellowing like billy goats and exposing their genitals in macabre contortions fit for Angélica Liddell.

Up to this point, no detail deviates from the standard script of any nunsploitation movie. From *Mother Joan of the Angels* (1961) by Jerzy Kawalerowicz to *Prey for the Devil* (2022) by Daniel Stamm, and from *Agnes* (2021) by Mickey Reece to *The Devils* (1971) by Ken Russell, cinemas and our own screens at home have for decades featured nuns writhing in unimaginable poses, hollering in the hellish voices of their demonic invaders. We ourselves have been ardent fans of the genre because few things are as cinematographically satisfying as shots that let us peer into the deranged intimacy of a cloister overtaken by the devil's misdeeds—or, more implausibly, by supposed group hysteria. Even as we succumb like that spellbound audience in the church of Sainte-Croix to the undeniable allure of demonic-conventual cinematography, we have never once managed to finish one of these movies without exchanging a whisper or a text expressing our impatience about how demonic possession is portrayed as an external, purely physical phenomenon. The nunsploitation canon foregrounds weak and disoriented nuns at the mercy of their ever-more-prudent exorcists.

It seems these directors and screenwriters would have agreed wholeheartedly with the French demonologist Jean Bodin. In *On the Demon-Mania of Witches*, a 1580 treatise obsessed with conceiving new ways to torture witches and sorcerers—especially witches, because Bodin claimed, with the kind of magical statistics conjured by a defensive incel, that "there are 50 witches and possessed women for every man"—the jurist staunchly defended the idea that, no matter how hard they tried, neither the devil nor any of his demons could ever access the intellectual or spiritual faculties of their human victim. In other words: Only the body could truly be possessed. His theory was certainly flattering for the human soul, but it left little room for the will of the nuns.

—⧾—

Jeanne des Anges was never willing to let herself be manipulated by demonological discourse. In the opening pages of her 1644 spiritual autobiography, the Ursuline nun depicts herself as the worst of demons, a creature of inherent wickedness, deserving of more tears of guilt and repentance than all those shed by Catherine of Siena and María de Santo Domingo combined. "When I think of the life I have led, I find that I have great reason to blush before God and men, for the debaucheries of spirit to which I let myself be drawn. If obedience would allow me, I would describe with singular pleasure and in detail all my malice, hypocrisies, duplicities, arrogance . . ." And indeed, she does not hesitate to investigate all her perversities. With her autobiography, Jeanne inaugurated a brief period during which France saw the emergence of a series of texts sharing certain unusual characteristics. After decades of priests, exorcists, and theologians speculating about, for instance, the demons' favorite point of entry (according to Bodin, the preferred entrance into the body was undoubtedly "the shameful parts" of the nuns), these new manuscripts finally described the phenomenon of demonic possession from the personal experience of the women who endured it within the convent.

Jeanne was not alone in performing an almost psychoanalytical examination of her own conscience. In September 1634, just a few months after those unsuccessful exorcisms, the Jesuit Jean-Joseph Surin arrived in Loudun to take on the spiritual guidance of Jeanne, who was only a couple of years younger. In *The Triumph of Divine Love over the Powers of Hell in the Possession of the Mother Superior of the Ursulines of Loudun* (1636) and, three decades later, in *The Experimental Science of the Afterlife Acquired in the Possession of the Ursulines of Loudun* (1663), Surin surgically examined the time he spent diagnosing Jeanne's troubles. For the Jesuit, that period concluded with a few certainties. First, that more than one of the demons he battled was particularly averse to the Discalced Carmelites, and thus the relic of Saint Teresa that Surin used proved very effective in driving many of them out. Second, that Jeanne des Anges's demons were not only those spectral, sinuous figures capable of twisting the nun's spine as if it were made of clay but were also mental darknesses and deeply embedded traumas. "As soon as he saw me," Jeanne herself writes, "he knew that my affliction was as great within me as it was upon me." Surin quickly detected the demonic afflictions of his spiritual daughter, but he found that ridding himself of them was not as easy. In 1645, he attempted to end his life by throwing himself from a second-story window, and he spent the rest of his days plagued by a depressive state that he never managed to exorcise.

The truth is that, once we dismantled the projection of possession's cinematic treatment, everything we can reconstruct about the case of Loudun from contemporaneous texts suggests that those nuns inhabited a profoundly inhospitable environment. It all began in 1632, when Jeanne declared that Father Urbain Grandier, the seductive priest of a nearby church, had appeared in her cell to take "that which she had vowed to keep for her heavenly husband, Jesus Christ." She was not the only one. Soon, many more nuns claimed to have been possessed (in every sense) by Grandier, by the convent's spiritual director, and by other figures in the local ecclesiastical hierarchy. Where we see an entire convent terrorized by a self-aggrandizing priest, history sees, to the surprise of nobody, an outbreak of hysteria. Although Grandier—who was not wanting in influential friends and had already been embroiled in other scandals of a sexual nature—wasn't the only one accused by the nuns, the historiographical coverage of the case often clings to a later retraction by the Ursulines and the irremediable gaps in the archives to conclude that this man had, in fact, never been there at all. Instead, it was all a hysterical delusion provoked by Jeanne's resentful obsession with the priest who had refused to be her spiritual director. No matter how much authoritative voices like Michel de Certeau or Aldous Huxley have written and reflected on the Loudun possessions, we fear we may never fully understand what really happened inside that convent. We do know, however, that historiography has consistently preferred to support the idea of the nuns as victims of collective hysteria, or as victims of opportunistic superiors set on turning them into a spectacular instrument of Catholicism against Protestantism, rather than assuming for one moment that Jeanne and her Ursulines might have been the catalysts of an early #MeToo movement, couched in the trompe l'oeil of demonological phenomenology.

✢

That the Ursulines of Loudun appropriated the vocabulary of witchcraft and possession to name the trauma of their abuse is, for now, only a hypothesis. What we do know is that Jeanne des Anges reclaimed the internalization of demons that Surin offered her to create a complex map of her toxicities and mental health. It was a much-needed course of action, since at that point she had entered "a great worry, sadness, despair, remorse, so that I did not know what to do." If categorizing tears is an infallible convent remedy to analyze and share your sorrows, then classifying the thousand faces of your anguish and your guilt is a good way to exorcize them. According to Jeanne's inventory, her inner self housed seven demons, and she baptized each of them by way of an assertive introspection our therapists would commend. It doesn't matter whether you anatomize yourself in front of your twenty-first-century psychologist or your seventeenth-century exorcist: Every girl aspires to ace the nonexistent report card of a well-examined soul. That is why Jeanne carefully deconstructs every angle of her turbulent personality.

> Leviathan, the chief of the demons that possessed me, made use of my tendency towards indulgence, which led me to want to please everyone and to be esteemed; he strengthened my pride and pushed me to hold myself in high regard. I harbored desires within me to achieve something great, even fantasizing about leaving my order to attain other dignities. He made me see all others as beneath me.

If Leviathan was her heightened narcissism, Behemoth aligned with Jeanne's laziness, though he also moved "me to pronounce blasphemies against God's majesty, provoked my anger and my hatred towards my sisters [. . .] when this evil spirit took me . . . I ripped with my teeth every veil I encountered." But Balaam's operations "were all the more dangerous as they appeared less bad: He only disturbed my imagination a little and then he let my nature act, for there he found great advantages to maintain himself." Grésil and Aman embodied the most impenetrable corners of the Ursuline's constant inner anguish, so opaque that she "could not distinguish their inner workings." Every disorder has its demon.

We discovered Jeanne des Anges early on, even before meeting each other in Providence. But we didn't feel a real closeness to her until, immersed in the emotional shipwreck of our PhD program, we both decided barely a year apart that staying afloat would require a therapy life jacket. We, who had become so accustomed to letting words pour forth, to accompanying any triviality with four times the amount of adjectives, to coining phantom terminology as needed, suddenly found ourselves near mute, unable to name our demons. Little by little, we learned that the gears of therapy crank slowly into action over time, at an almost unbearable pace that often made us wish for something akin to a convenient contemporary exorcism manual to help us assign names to our fears. But if Jeanne des Anges's greatest feat was to make the nomenclature and symptomatology of demons her own—demons all her superiors except Surin insisted were external—perhaps now the true feat lies in externalizing the demons that a tangle of media voices insists on divorcing from the structural forces that abet them. It's easier to blame "postvacation syndrome" than the precarity of a tyrannical job; more common to speak of ADHD medication than of a lifestyle that overwhelms us all; and much easier to label ourselves as "highly sensitive persons (HSP)" than to point out the saturation of stimuli that suffocates us every waking moment. Fortunately, Jeanne des Anges's autobiography reminds us that no matter what century you're reading this in: You should never let others name your demons.

How a Nun Who Took the Habit at Seventy-Five Years Old Can Help Ease Your Chronophobia

It was cold in Puebla on October 10, 1679, and the whole Mexican city smelled of flowers and molten wax. The chill of autumn was beginning to set in but nothing could keep the masses from venturing out into the early morning to the convent of the Discalced Carmelites. It was crucial to arrive at the convent gates ahead of schedule and elbow one's way through the crowd to procure a prize. Many would retrace their steps home, satisfied to be leaving with a memento tucked under their arm or delicately holding "the flowers that adorned her body." The luckiest among them managed to persuade the nun at the turnstile to gift them "something of Sister Esperanza's" and would rush home with the adrenaline of someone who had managed to snag a selfie with Beyoncé, carrying "the bowls she ate from and the small pitchers she drank water from." Though it had been barely "a year minus nine days" since Juana Esperanza de San Alberto had reluctantly donned the Carmelite habit, her death turned the city into an unprecedentedly riotous procession. The flower-laden, candlelit coffin was, for the whole of that cool October, the talk of Puebla.

Juana Esperanza de San Alberto was born in Guinea-Bissau at the beginning of the seventeenth century. When a slave ship threw her onto the docks of Veracruz at the age of five or six, she was purchased by María Fajardo, a Spanish woman who had also arrived in Mexico as a child, though her journey had been distinctly more comfortable than that of her enslaved companion. After becoming a widow, María withdrew from the world to join the Discalced Carmelites in Puebla, donating all her belongings to the convent—including the two women she enslaved. María died soon after taking her vows and, although the nuns and church officials resisted the idea of Juana Esperanza remaining in the convent, she eventually softened their hearts: "Daughters of Jerusalem, brides of Jesus Christ, though I am black, I am beautiful, and the mighty King loved me and brought me to His Church." Thanks to the dedication of one of her companions, Juana's life was unexpectedly spared the fate of obscurity in the form of a biographical account that eventually circulated, sweetened and likely abridged, in the printed chronicle of the convent penned in the eighteenth century by Mexican cleric José de la Parra.

Juana Esperanza de San Alberto rarely spoke. While the other Carmelite nuns spent their days indulging in eccentric pastimes like passing "a tiny piece of flesh the size of a fingernail . . . from our Holy Mother Teresa of Jesus" from cell to cell, each one competing to outdo the other with the most spectacular mystical vision, Juana Esperanza—who was never invited to partake in this macabre game—wandered alone. After finishing her duties in the kitchen, she would take a jug out to the courtyard fountain under the pretense of fetching water and instead remain there, gazing at the stars, deep in prayer, until three or four in the morning. Whether she was truly praying, or instead deliberating under the vast night sky, lost in thought about the nun who had accused her of ruining that day's meal, or the one who had blamed her for breaking a clay pot, or the disdainful Carmelites who hurried her to serve their supper, we do not know. Nor do we know if, during the long hours she spent "sitting on the ledge of a window, staring at the heavens," Juana Esperanza murmured Our Fathers and Hail Marys through clenched teeth or if she contemplated over the tragic fate of all those women with whom she had shared her agonizing journey across the Atlantic. She disliked confessing her troubles to the priests, deans, and friars who constantly fluttered around her adjusting their silly hats and clutching their habit cords, pestering her with questions about the state of her soul. Juana Esperanza always remained silent.

—+|+—

There came a time when Juana Esperanza could no longer keep track of how old she was, though she realized the years were piling up behind her. For many of these years, she had handled the convent without fully accepting the role of a Discalced Carmelite. Maybe the offer of the habit seemed, to someone who had never been able to raise the required dowry, like an act of charity she did not want to deign to accept. Or maybe she just did what many of us would like to do: live like a nun without the full lifestyle commitment. But in 1678, sick and dependent on the women around her, she changed her mind. Perhaps the desire to embrace a sense of belonging, one that her future sisters had always questioned and that she herself had resisted, finally outweighed her reservations. One year before her death, at nearly seventy-five years old, Juana Esperanza de San Alberto finally took her vows as a Discalced Carmelite.

It had been a long time since she could walk without her ever-present cane, and, were it not for the assistance and care of the other nuns, she wouldn't have even been able to drag herself to Communion. She, who not so long ago could distinguish Mariana del Sacramento from Mother Nicolasa by the sound of their sandals scurrying through the cloister, now mixed up their faces and voices. Yet, prompted by the sensory isolation of old age, she could still gauge the importance of the convent's visitors by the stir their arrival caused. And much to her misfortune, there was not a single marchioness, vicereine, or high-ranking church official who would take their leave without meeting that "beautiful Black woman" who had lived among the Carmelites for the past thirty years. On the day Don Diego de Malpartida Centeno, dean of Mexico's cathedral, called on the convent, we're sure that the nuns pinched their cheeks to appear a little rosier, but we know Juana Esperanza did not. She endured his questions with her head bowed, utterly silent. When the irritated dean said, "Look, Esperanza, don't fail to tell the father all that's in your soul and all that has happened to you in prayer," Juana could not hold back—she was too close to death and too protective of the dignity she had preserved, carving out, against all odds, a respectable place in that convent. "Am I supposed to do now what I haven't done in all my life?" she retorted—a seventeenth-century comeback that we suspect Juana had been mulling over for decades.

The passage of time, silent reflection, and the challenges of communal life had granted Juana Esperanza the authority and composure that every woman needs to welcome old age. We confess that it's hard to form a clear image of Juana Esperanza, buried as she is under the weight of condescension that veils the few accounts of her life that we managed to unearth. Yet, in every "terrible fall" followed by the aid of the other nuns (always with a "little chair" to help her get back on her feet), in the determination with which she clung to her cane to keep attending community rituals, and in her stubborn fidelity to her mysterious reserve, we find a Juana Esperanza who achieved what we all long for: to grow old well.

The end of our PhDs coincided with hitting our mid thirties. Almost without noticing, our conversations began to fill with words we would not have known how to spell just months before: *retinol*, *hyaluronic*, *collagen*, *pelvic floor*, *perimenopause*. As we journeyed toward our forties, our idea of aging gracefully involved managing aesthetic neuroses and soothing anxieties about a frail future where independence simply stops being an option. We wanted to prevent crow's-feet, find a way to guarantee lifelong autonomy, and, hard as it may be to admit, ensure our bodies would not fail to meet the demands of productivity. Convents had always seemed to us like spaces from which we could learn about aging well; it seemed like in every cloister corner there was a nun with immaculate skin and another who boasted record-breaking longevity. But Juana Esperanza's life taught us that perhaps the lesson the convent had to offer on growing old well is not so much about finding a magic formula, a substance that would provide us, like Demi Moore in Coralie Fargeat's movie, a smoother, stronger, more flexible version of ourselves, but rather about living within a cultural paradigm that practices acceptance over control and interdependence over individualism.

When we are besieged by the unease brought on by the rapidly passing years, each time we find ourselves gaping, terrified, at a wrinkle that materialized mere minutes ago, we turn to some anecdote from Juana Esperanza's old age to soothe the chronophobia that torments us. José de la Parra tells us that "in her later years, her eyesight became so poor" that a nun "left the gallery one winter's night to go to the upper choir and found Esperanza in one of the cloisters, leaning against the wall, holding onto her cane, frozen through, because she could not find her cell after coming up from the kitchen and had spent most of the night standing there until someone could help her." The nun "put her to bed, bundled her up, then went down to the kitchen to get some embers to warm her." We've comforted each other through enough premenstrual syndromes, neck contractures, and sciatica attacks to know that it doesn't matter what century you are reading this in: Fill your golden years with friends ready to warm you up when you need it most.

Fame

Do you see the noise Mother Luisa makes in the world?
                                          Petronila de San Lorenzo

You Can Try, but You Will Rarely Succeed: How to Quell Your Craving for Relevance with the Help of a Canceled Seventeenth-Century Poor Clare Nun

Imagine an international organization that has the power to subject your life to an opaque bureaucratic process that will decide whether or not you are worthy of everlasting ovations and public adoration. A group of men who gather together to scrutinize every detail of your life and work, and might ultimately declare your career so dazzling that your creations deserve to be hawked around the world. Stacks of stamped documents decree that your face has become so iconic that having a tattoo of its likeness is neither alarming nor absurd. A committee of experts that proclaim to the world that you are now a verified celebrity.

It was the Italian Franciscan Pope Sixtus V who, in 1588, established the pompously named "Sacred Congregation of Rites," an organization designed to substantiate the fame of sanctity with undeniable proof. Scandalized by the medieval proliferation of saints with dubious credentials, the pope decided to tighten the process required to earn the posthumous blue checkmark of canonization. Though the coveted flavor of authorized fame could only be savored after death, by the late sixteenth century, every Catholic nun aspiring to join the exclusive ranks of the martyrology knew that much of her success lay in the daily performance of calculated rituals: eating little, suffering greatly, and performing just the right number of miracles. Few nuns of the sixteenth and seventeenth centuries escaped the guiding mantra of Counter-Reformation religiosity: *Fake it till you make it*.

Today, there is still no refuge from a relentless media salvo—the merciless demands of advertising, algorithms, and Instagram stories urging you to internalize the pursuit of fame and social recognition as a guiding light of your existence. From the academic catacombs, buried in the social irrelevance we thought was guaranteed by our devotion to the most neglected corners of the sixteenth and seventeenth centuries, we believed ourselves immune to the infectious hunger for notoriety that eclipses our era. But then, we started a podcast, and thus our morning conversations began to look like this:

—Ana, we're not on the Spotify rankings this week. Do you think people are already getting bored of us?
—Don't say that, Carmen. Maybe we should post a reel about the last episode?
—Reels usually work, but we'll have to post it at night; otherwise, no one will see it, right?
—I'm not so sure. Maybe more people will see it early in the morning. Should we tag someone? Upload a photo too? We always get more views when we show our faces.
—Ana, do you think people don't love us anymore?

We came to understand that even a semblance of media repute can poison one with a blindness that not even holy water can cure. We felt an affinity for those would-be saints who, kneeling during prayer, likely lost focus as they debated whether to spend the rest of that morning putting on a show of levitation or tumbling into ecstasy in the parlor. Fretful that failing to sustain our public performance would doom us to a deeper oblivion than the fluorescent-lit basement library where our most-consulted books were kept, and stunned by the erratic whims of the algorithm—exalting us to the ranks of the most listened-to one day and dumping us among forgotten content creators the next—we fortunately found a nun who taught us everything that we (and you) need to know about curbing the dangerous craving for relevance.

✢

When in 1623 the future King of England went out of his way to stop by a tiny village in northern Spain to speak with Luisa de la Ascensión, the sixty-year-old Poor Clare nun knew her performance of sanctity had gone too far. It was one thing for the entire Spanish royal family and aristocracy to parade through her convent, for Pope Gregory XV to find moments in his busy schedule to write her letters, for some of the thousands of wooden crosses bearing her name to spread to the remotest reaches of the Americas, or for half of Spain to seek her out so she could cure cysts and pneumonias with a simple laying on of her hands—it was quite another for the future supreme head of the Anglican Church, so often an enemy of Spain, to fall under her spell. Luisa enjoyed that improbable encounter with the satisfaction of someone who had successfully positioned her corporate identity in the most exclusive and inaccessible of markets. Yet, a decade later, when a delegation of English diplomats visited her in 1635 and requested "two small paintings or miniatures of herself" to deliver to the now-crowned King of England, that sensation of triumph had all but vanished. Her fifteen minutes of fame had already come to an end. Luisa had gone from exchanging personal letters with the Queen and freely managing the vast donations that poured into her village of Carrión de los Condes, to being confined—by order of the Inquisition—to a cell in an Augustinian convent hundreds of miles away from the Poor Clare convent that had been her home since the age of nineteen.

Isolated in her room and cut off from communication with the outside world, Luisa—who had only recently bilocated to Japan, Flanders, and Rome and been consulted on the marriage of King Philip IV's sister—tries to stifle the anguished sighs of someone who knows that the very gifts that catapulted her to fame are the ones that have triggered her merciless cancellation. She strives, then, to erase from her memory all the times she had flaunted her fasting, every time she had shouted to the heavens that she survived (according to the defense of Luisa's public persona written by the Franciscan Pedro de Balbas) on nothing but "a dozen chickpeas" or "a hazelnut-sized piece of bread." It had worked for Catherine of Siena, canonized two centuries earlier, so why had it not worked for Luisa? Because cracking the Counter-Reformation's algorithm was as improbable as finding the fail-safe formula for success in the chaotic labyrinths of social media. Much like how the number of Bulgarian split squats one does each day won't ensure the life nor the body of Instagram superstar and bodybuilder Jen Selter ("the queen of squats"), it doesn't matter how many days the Luisas of the world survived on bread dipped in water—they might not get to stride confidently onto the sainthood highway. You can follow every tip from the Glucose Goddess, the guru with five million followers who preaches mastery over your blood sugar levels, but you still will not have her energy or her oblique abs; you can pose for every portrait mimicking the gestures of Saint Teresa, but that doesn't promise you a private party in St. Peter's Square. Perhaps it would be easier if there was a regulatory codification of the poses, filters, and outfits we use in social media photos—much like what Pope Urban VIII decreed in 1642 when he decided to cancel anyone who, sans sainthood, allowed themselves to be portrayed with glamorous halos, rays, and aureoles.

Like a celebrity who, overnight, finds themselves on the precipice of a tarnished empire, Luisa de la Ascensión casts the blame for her fall from grace elsewhere. There are all those envious nuns she has never taken seriously, like Petronila de San Lorenzo, who goes around ranting like a true hater to the other nuns in her convent: "Do you see the noise Mother Luisa makes in the world? Well, she has great sufferings coming her way. I won't live to see it, but you will." Frightened at the thought of dying a fraud, Luisa not only obsessively replays every remark she had once dismissed as petty envy from irrelevant young women, but also begins to distrust the behavior of even her most loyal followers. Why should she take responsibility for those fervent devotees who "cut her veils with scissors while she was in a trance" and then distributed them across Spain and the Americas, claiming they were relics? She now feels ridiculous, forced to invent excuses on the fly to avoid the Inquisition accusing her of "grave presumption." "The veils? I gave them to clean quills," she bluffs. Of course, no one believes her: "There couldn't possibly be so many veils needed for quills," one witness scoffs in front of the Inquisition. Was it her fault that the nuns interpret as a "miracle" what was merely a "whimsy"? She now regrets that one St. John's Day when, hoping to delight her sisters, she decorated the refectory with "some branches, and on one, cherries and oranges," only for the nuns to spread word that "the branch had suddenly produced cherries and oranges." Brainless fools. Has she ever allowed herself to be portrayed as the *vera effigies* (the true likeness) of a saint? Absolutely not. It's the fault of those fanatics who insist on tampering with images of Saint Clare and pawning them off as depictions of Luisa. Useless idiots. Holding the prints in her hands, she observes archly, "I've heard it said that they're of a saint." Would the Inquisition not gain more by pursuing those who had nonconsensually printed a list of the "virtues and graces that Our Lord has bestowed on the beads and crosses of Mother Luisa"? What she has long known is coming to a head—these so-called devotees only want to profit at her expense.

Anguish quickly turns to anger when Luisa wonders where the then-eager signers of her "Confraternity of Defenders of the Immaculate Conception" were now. She had embraced fame to proselytize her favorite cause: staunchly defending the belief that Jesus's grandmother, Saint Anne, had conceived the Virgin Mary without needing to resort to her husband, Saint Joachim—one of the great controversies of Catholic dogma. (After all, no celebrity is complete without a philanthropic action, political cause, conspiracy theory, or spiritual eccentricity to their name.) Preserved in a 237-page manuscript are the signatures of all those who, before the fateful date of March 15, 1635, when the Inquisition ordered Luisa to be removed from her convent, had no problem declaring themselves enthusiastic supporters of the Poor Clare's confraternity. Like someone scrolling through the follower list of an Instagram account to gauge social relevance, the manuscript is an explosion of verified accounts: "I, the King," "I, the Prince," "I, the Princess," "The Count-Duke," alongside Margarita de la Cruz, Ana Dorotea, and all the nepo nuns of the Royal Discalced Monastery, Sister Jerónima de la Asunción, founder of the first

Catholic convent in the Philippines, countless Discalced Carmelites, abbots, friars, bishops, and even a portrait of Saint Teresa (because no one doubts she would have signed if she were alive). Where were all those people now, those who had drooled over her crosses, her beads, and her portraits?

When Luisa came to terms with the fact that the Inquisition's punitive methods would always triumph over logic, she indulged in the memory of her stardom. Within the four walls of her Augustinian cell, she recalled how, "upon opening the door of the cloister" to leave for her imprisonment, "the entire crowd of people outside began calling her Mother and Queen," the roar crescendoing when she let the crowd kiss the holy crucifix she wore around her neck. She smiled as she remembered "the cries of the people who, without regard for the danger of being trampled, all followed after [her]." She laughed out loud, recalling the inquisitor's dumbfounded face upon witnessing the masses' applause when she arrived in Valladolid. He attempted to persuade his secretary to put a stop to it, but the young assistant could only respond, "Sir, if [Luisa] is performing miracles along the way and God is making them known, let the entire Inquisition come to stop it, because I cannot."

In the end, Luisa died alone in a cell-turned-prison in 1636, waiting for her Inquisition trial to be resolved. It would be settled much later, in 1648, when after endless deliberations the inquisitors concluded that Luisa's spectacle of sanctity concealed nothing worthy of reproach. That grand celebration in St. Peter's Square never came to pass, but over the course of her life Luisa managed to elicit far more hysterical screams and devoted sighs from her fandom than nearly any other seventeenth-century nun who went on to posthumously collect halos. Two small prints of Luisa de la Ascensión watch over each of our desks. Almost daily, whenever we get stuck while scripting an episode or lose the thread while writing this book, Luisa's gaze reminds us that it is time to stop obsessing over rankings and compulsively googling ourselves. No matter how much effort it took, every nun knew that finding fame as a "living saint" did not secure canonization after death—just as living in total anonymity did not rule out the very real possibility of being added to the list of saints two or three centuries later. Luisa taught us that you can try, but you will rarely succeed. If the mysteries of the algorithm are as cryptic as the decisions of the Sacred Congregation of Rites, then perhaps it's better to abandon the treacherous race for celebrity altogether. Better, surely, to focus on letting levitations bring you joy, allowing moments of rapture to fulfill you, and ensuring that each small, everyday miracle becomes a source of peace and wonder for those who walk alongside you.

Swifties, Beliebers, and Devotees of Saint Juana's Rosary Beads: How Extreme Fandoms Can Be Your Best Tool for Building Community

Leonora de San Buenaventura had never experienced pain quite like this. Like any seventeenth-century nun, she could recall bouts of raging fevers, the occasional urinary infection, every imaginable intestinal upset, and even muscle strains from hauling reliquaries and chests around the convent. But this particular agony was terrifyingly new. Everyone had warned her about the "great harshness of the journey": the "relentless waves," the "unbearable heat," the "paths as narrow as a brick," and the "intolerable hordes of mosquitoes." Yet no one had had the decency to warn her that, after weeks astride that wretched mule, she would find herself overcome by a discomfort so relentlessly unpleasant and, above all, so intimate. Leonora longed to dismount and continue on foot, but she knew that Acapulco—the place where she and her fellow Poor Clare nuns would finally board the ship to take them to Manila (or to their graves, as they all grimly repeated)—was so far away that the damned mule, padded with a "traveling saddle," was her only option. Dotted with mosquito bites and masking other, more embarrassing itches, she felt nostalgic for the months spent crammed in the ship that had carried them from the Spanish coast to Veracruz. It was not until the day when her pain felt as if she was straddling the roughest of cilices that she decided to seek help through tears. In a strangled whisper, she revealed to the other adventurous Poor Clares that the cause of her grimaces and bodily spasms atop the mule was an acute attack of hemorrhoids. We don't know Leonora's exact words. Perhaps she found some lexical circumlocution to avoid uttering such an unseemly term, as her confession, we suspect, embarrassed her—perched in 1620 on that bony mule en route from Mexico City to Acapulco—as much as it embarrasses you now, seated in your home office's Herman Miller chair.

In an instant, the other nine nuns surged forward to encircle a pale and increasingly sweat-drenched Leonora. If anyone could ease her suffering, it was Sister María de los Ángeles, a nurse who had joined their peculiar transoceanic entourage from the convent of La Visitación in Mexico City. Although well trained in restraint and the tyranny of wellness, something in the nurse—a dramatic swat at the mosquitoes, a reply delivered with excessive sharpness—betrayed a glimmer of alarm, the very kind you don't want to see on the face of your least hypochondriac friend when you ask: Do you think I should go to the emergency room? If Sister María de los Ángeles, who knew every natural remedy sprouting along the Mexican paths and crags by heart, couldn't find a way to ease poor Leonora's pain, the Poor Clares all knew there was but one remaining alternative: "a ground bead of Saint Juana dissolved in a glass of water." Naturally, the concoction worked. Ana de Cristo, the nun tasked with recording every hardship and surprise of their odyssey, would later recount the incident in the dispassionate tone of someone who's seen a hangover cured by ibuprofen a thousand times over: "Having done this, [Leonora] was fully well."

When Leonora was finally able to mount her mule the next day without writhing like a contortionist, the mastermind behind the entire unprecedented expedition—an elderly Poor Clare named Jerónima de la Asunción—could confirm that her idea of stuffing the luggage trunks with rosary beads blessed by a nun who had been dead for nearly a century had been a stroke of genius. Jerónima, born in 1555, had never met Saint Juana, otherwise known as Juana de la Cruz, the Franciscan tertiary who had captivated Emperor Charles V with her excessive fasting, visionary performances, improbable levitations, and heavenly banquets. Juana, who until her death in 1534 had devoted all her energy and leadership skills to transforming her convent into a multidisciplinary art residency, knew full well that her fame was so widespread that men and women across the world whispered that she was not merely a nun but "a living saint." This nun, who had inspired the sternest men of her era to behave like tearful groupies when they heard her preach, was keen to capitalize on her influence like any enterprising star of today. So she launched a global merchandising empire. Long before Harry Styles's ubiquitous tote bags or the friendship bracelets exchanged by Taylor Swift fans, there were the miraculous beads of Saint Juana.

How does one decide which objects deserve to be in circulation as official merch? Even though we had only published a modest batch of podcast episodes by the end of 2021, we had already amassed a fiercely loyal audience of modest proportions that awaited our releases with the euphoric impatience of a pilgrim hoping to witness a miracle at Lourdes. It never ceased to amaze us, but there were indeed people excited to immerse themselves for hours in complex theological debates over the consumption of chocolate, the conventual craze for lactating Christs, and the dissecting talents accumulated by a handful of anatomically inclined Italian nuns. It was around this time that we recorded what is possibly our most beloved and extreme episode to date: three hours of impassioned conversation about the gruesome universe of relics—bodily or textile fragments that can function as miraculous mediators, objects of holy greed, or marks of prestige, but which are, above all, banners of communal identity. That was when people started asking us to create some kind of merchandise, to add relics of our own making into the marketplace. With limited resources at our disposal, we simply printed stickers featuring our cover art and mailed them to anyone who asked (completely free of charge, because the spirit of Girl Math still outweighed the desire to be thrifty negotiators). But lacking stickers, what relics could a sixteenth-century nun have devised with her own hands?

The Franciscan biographer of Juana de la Cruz, Antonio Daza, recounts how one day, at the insistence of the nuns who lived with her, Juana satisfied their divine trinket desires en masse. She told her sisters to gather all the rosary beads they owned so that her guardian angel could carry them up to heaven, have them blessed, and then return the now hallowed pieces. The nuns duly rummaged the convent for all the rosaries they could find and handed them to Juana. Upon seeing the assembled beads, explains the biographer, Juana ordered them placed in a small chest and entrusted one of the oldest nuns to lock it and keep the key with her. Once this was done, Juana began to pray, and when the nuns saw her in a state of rapture, they were certain that this was the very moment when the Angel had ascended to bless the rosaries in heaven. Driven by curiosity, they hurried to the nun holding the key, unlocked the chest, and found it empty. Not a single bead remained, confirming what they had imagined.

When Saint Juana emerged from her ecstasy, "a great fragrance and sweetness of scent filled the entire convent." All the nuns rushed to open the chest and, wide-eyed, discovered that "the very same rosaries and beads they had placed inside were there, with none missing, for the Angel who had carried them to heaven had already returned them blessed . . . and Juana said that the fragrance and sweetness came from the rosaries, having absorbed it from being held in the most sacred hands of Our Lord Jesus Christ." Compared to the grandeur of rosary beads that had ascended to heaven and been blessed personally by Jesus, our humble stickers (though signed, of course, with our names and a small heart on the back) paled in significance. Perhaps the only thing today that might approach such a near-tangible encounter with the divine would be a cameo sent from Lana Del Rey.

It is easy to judge the delusions of sixteenth-century nuns who were ostensibly so ready to believe any outlandish narrative. But let us not forget that in 2020, Gwyneth Paltrow's *This Smells Like My Vagina* candle—priced at a not-so-humble $75—sold out within hours, leaving hundreds of people adrift in waiting list limbo. It's possible that this rush wasn't fueled by genuine reverence for the actress but rather by the same ironic enthusiasm that led us to buy Real Housewife Lisa Vanderpump's rosé wine. What now inspires a bemused chuckle at the commercial absurdities of fame was once

the irresistible thaumaturgic logic of relics. Juana's blessed beads, of course, had miraculous powers: They could calm storms, banish demons, cure illness, ward off temptation, and even extinguish fires. More impressively, their powers could transfer to other rosaries simply by being in contact with them. Fortified by such unbeatable product branding, the fandom of Saint Juana only grew.

When the bell that called the nuns of the Toledo convent of Santa Isabel de los Reyes to matins rang that morning in 1599, not a single Poor Clare could have guessed that within just a few hours, the promise of seclusion and enclosure they had embraced in their vows would vanish. By the end of the day, some Poor Clares griped in the halls about how you should never let a Dominican friar spend too much time in your parlor if you wish to preserve the tranquil stillness of convent life, while others spent a sleepless night, nervously imagining what the sea might smell like or how all those enormous fruits they had seen in the engravings of the New World chronicles might taste. The man responsible for all this commotion was Fray Diego de Soria, a Dominican missionary who had just returned from the Philippines, determined to find a capable nun bold enough to establish the first convent of religious women in Manila. When he saw Jerónima de la Asunción, at that time a robust forty-four-year-old Poor Clare, he knew she was the one he was looking for. Jerónima, who had longed since childhood to "know something about everything that existed," accepted the challenge with enthusiasm, unaware that papal bureaucracy would plunge her into an agonizing twenty-year wait. It doesn't matter what century you're reading this in: If you are about to embark on an administrative battle to extend your visa, update your residency permit, or obtain your order's permission to found a new convent in the Philippines, start the first step at least three months earlier than you think necessary. That way you might finish only three years later than planned.

Fortunately, Jerónima's fervor was rooted in an extraordinary patience, and she knew how to wait. Jerónima was a committed Poor Clare nun but, first and foremost, she was a Juana de la Cruz fan. So when she finally learned that she had been chosen to lead that mission—a role much coveted by other nuns—her sole obsession became finding a way to carry a fragment of that remarkable nun with her to those far-flung islands. It wasn't difficult. Jerónima might not have been able to binge-watch videos of her favorite pop star or endlessly replay the demo she recorded just before her death, but the elderly nun had access to something far better: miraculous visions, an imaginative paradigm perfectly suited for cultivating parasocial relationships. In this way, "when the Venerable Mother [Jerónima], along with her companions, was in the new Veracruz, the Lord presented her with fevers that were a great affliction; yet she did not fail to attend Mass every day. And on the last of the three [days] she spent there, the glorious Saint Juana favored her with a loving embrace." In the words of Jerónima's biographer:

> While immersed in affectionate laments and sweet colloquies with Saint Juana de la Cruz, asking for her support and intercession in this endeavor we are about to undertake (and which I have often felt she accompanies us in), I sensed her beside me . . . Saint Juana, in the manner of one person walking and talking joyfully with another . . . and as I asked the glorious Saint to obtain from God the success of this foundation, she gave me a great embrace.

Are you truly a fan of Taylor Swift if she does not appear around every corner of your home ready to offer a loving embrace and comfort you in your feverish nights? Does it even make sense to keep longing for Rihanna if you cannot hold sweet colloquies with her? Think about it.

Jerónima couldn't trade her habit for a hoodie emblazoned with the face of her favorite diva, but she could, until her palms blistered, caress the beads of Saint Juana's rosary. She had secured this prize after pulling all her ecclesiastical strings and sobbing at countless convent doors during the two decades she had to pack for the most important trip of her life. If, in the summer of 2024, millions of young women carefully examined the wrists of other passersby in search of a beaded bracelet that might reveal their shared belonging to the vast, transnational community of Swifties, then in the summer of 1620, owning, flaunting, and in the most extreme cases, ingesting the original (or at least blessed) beads of Saint Juana provided the same instant kinship we all find in a shared devotion to someone. Whenever we hear someone mock extreme fandoms and their promotional knickknacks—as though feverish fascination with someone or something were a sign of naivety or of being brainwashed—we immediately think of the barrage of videos our listeners sent us from streets, theaters, universities, bars, and supermarkets as they stuck our stickers on any surface in an apostolic mission to entice new disciples. We think, too, of the communal comfort that Saint Juana's beads provided to Jerónima and her Poor Clare nuns.

Faced with all the uncertainties and threats of an epic overseas expedition, Jerónima brought along every beacon of closeness and surety she could muster—including two nuns from the Madrid monastery where Saint Juana had performed her feverish miracle-working. In this way, Sor María Magdalena de Cristo and Sor María Magdalena de la Cruz became custodians of countless beads that could be cast into the raging sea or transformed into lifesaving concoctions in the passage's most desperate moments. They also brought with them a charismatic devotion to Juana that instantly made them the close friends that the "squadron of Poor Clares" needed to face their trek to Manila.

Although turning sixty-five today means nothing more than the potential for a new experiential, aesthetic, and romantic era (see Madonna), it's hard to believe that in 1620 a woman of that age could survive a journey lasting one year, three months, and nine days. When she finally landed in Manila, Jerónima was convinced that she owed her safe arrival to the extraordinary merchandise that Juana de la Cruz had so presciently distributed before her death. We suspect it had more to do with the love of those who, like her, considered themselves shy imitators and proud acolytes of that nun who had shone so brightly from her tiny convent a century before. If the all-consuming fandom of Saint Juana gave Jerónima the drive she needed to participate, against all odds, in the violent logistical arena of colonial expansion, it taught us something far gentler: Whether you're a Swiftie, a Directioner, a Belieber, part of the ARMY, the Beyhive, or an avid devotee of sixteenth-century nuns, the bonds of a worshipful community can be the warmest and most powerful of all.

How to Overcome FOMO: A Bilocation for Every Plan You Missed

Spring in the small town of Ágreda is cold and monotonous. The barred windows of the Concepcionist convent, founded by Catalina de Arana, look out on the reddish horizon of the plateau, and invite in treacherous winds from the looming mountains of Moncayo. Not long ago, Catalina's daughter, María Coronel y Arana, took her vows under the name Sister María de Jesús. The stone building that shelters María and a community of Conceptionist nuns had once been her family home—until one morning in 1618, when her mother awakened suddenly, shouting about a nocturnal vision. According to her revelation, the house would be transformed into a monastery for Discalced nuns of the Immaculate Conception, she and her two daughters would enter it after taking the Conceptionist habit, and her husband and two sons would move to the convent of San Antonio in Nalda. And so it came to be. Neither her husband's protests—he had no desire to suddenly become a Franciscan monk—nor the neighbors' complaints, who saw in this familial dissolution an outright "affront to holy matrimony," could alter the course of Catalina's vision. After all, who in the seventeenth century would dare defy the will of God? The divine revelation was, truth be told, very convenient for María's mother. Not only did she manage to escape an intolerable marriage, but she also put an end to her daughter's dream of joining the Discalced Carmelites of Tarazona, a childhood fantasy that would have separated them forever.

Now, five years later, María squints through her myopia to catch glimpses of the distant townspeople through the grilles of her cell and sighs. Yes, the sky-blue habit of the Conceptionists suits her well and sometimes she feels both exalted and tormented by dramatic levitations, but what good is any of it if no one, apart from her mother, her sister, and three or four other nuns, can witness it? Yes, now that she's a nun, she is supposedly part of a vast project that extends far beyond the borders of her small town, but she ended up with the Conceptionists, under the direction of the Franciscans, and not with the Discalced Carmelites and their revolutionary Teresian rule as she had dreamed. News of the unprecedented multiple canonization ceremony Pope Gregory XV recently held in Rome has reached Ágreda. Five Catholic icons—Saint Isidore the Laborer, Saint Ignatius of Loyola, Saint Francis Xavier, Saint Philip Neri, and Saint Teresa of Jesus—were elevated to sainthood. When word begins to spread in the convent's parlor as nuns read aloud letters describing the processions, extravagant festivities, sermons, poetry competitions, and ephemeral architecture enlivening the streets of Rome, María sighs again. Secretly, she dares to imagine what it would have been like to travel to Rome and celebrate the five new saints with all those people. She also, with a blush, fantasizes about being one of those saints herself. She tries to purify her pangs of envy into admiration, but alas, she cannot; she, too, would like to make a pilgrimage to Jerusalem like Saint Ignatius, die as a missionary in China like Saint Francis Xavier, or travel across Castile founding convents like Saint Teresa. But she knows she will never leave the convent, that she will die in the same house where she was born. If the Vatican ever decided to beatify her, María de Jesús de Ágreda would undoubtedly become the patron saint of FOMO, the holy intercessor for all of us who cannot help but succumb to the fear of missing out.

—╬—

The anxiety of feeling as though life is happening somewhere else is, people often say, an endemic affliction of the twenty-first century, a nasty by-product of our addiction to social media. For a long time, we were convinced that no FOMO was stronger than the one the bleak biorhythms of university life nurtured. Many a Friday night our feeds paralyzed us with proof that everyone else's lives were moving forward, while ours remained anchored to perpetually open Word documents. That is, however, until we discovered the gift of bilocation. Despite its scarce presence in the Bible and its sporadic occurrence in the Middle Ages, reports of bilocation began to multiply from the sixteenth century onward. These accounts claimed to have witnessed someone (almost always a monk or nun) appearing miles away from their usual place of residence, even as other witnesses could confirm that the same person was simultaneously praying, eating, or scrubbing the tiles of a chapel. While theologians rushed to write about this strange gift with more questions than answers—If the body was in two places at once, where was the soul? Was the second body some kind of hologram? Could that bilocated presence be a shell operated from within by an angel, or perhaps the Virgin Mary herself?—the occurrences of bilocation increased at a dizzying pace.

Sometimes, bilocation was a discreet, logistical exercise that helped skirt the inconveniences of a packed schedule. Thanks to the gift of bilocation, for example, Saint Anthony of Padua was able to continue delivering his Maundy Thursday sermon in a church in Limoges, France, without breaking his promise to teach a lesson at his monastery sixteen miles away at the same time. In more mundane moments, bilocation is the exact superpower you wish you had when faced with the nagging suspicion you've left the gas on at home but cannot teleport yourself back to check. Such was the case of Saint Teresa, who, while in the convent of Ávila, sensed that the Carmelites in Malagón had forgotten their duty to keep the chapel's candle perpetually lit. She bilocated to the cell of Ana de Jesús to warn her of their oversight. For nuns like the Carmelite Juana de Jesús María (who, without leaving her convent in Burgos, claimed to have traveled to the Americas and even dodged arrows from the natives) or the Dominican Martina de los Ángeles (who swore she bilocated between her convent in Zaragoza and the Battle of Lützen, where she supposedly killed King Gustavus Adolphus of Sweden with her own hands), bilocation was a passport to geographical emancipation that would have otherwise been unthinkable. It was also an unimpeachable way to place themselves at the forefront of the Catholic Church's frenzied evangelizing mission, even at its most far-off frontiers. For María de Jesús de Ágreda, bilocation was a double-edged sword. Her mysterious appearances on the other side of the Atlantic subjected her to the unbearable scrutiny of the Inquisition and the imaginative rumors that distorted her accounts; but even so, we suspect that when María died in her cell in Ágreda on May 24, 1665, she did so without regretting her supernatural missionary work in New Mexico and Texas.

+++

The (many) hours we spent reading the *Account of the Life of the Venerable Mother María de Jesús* (1687), written by Bishop José Jiménez Samaniego, *The Mystical City of God* (1670), a biography of the Virgin Mary written by María herself, and the testimonies collected during the inquisitorial process against the Conceptionist nun in 1649 and 1650, were invariably interrupted by periods of ten minutes to two hours of curling up on our mattresses with our phones in hand, and inevitably surrendering to the acute anguish of FOMO. The ritual of this self-inflicted martyrdom usually played out like so:

First, we would open every app that allowed us to monitor, in real time, the fun being had by our closest friends, friends of friends, or celebrities we had never met but who were without exception enjoying life to the fullest far away from us.

Then, as our bitterness mounted, we couldn't resist checking the tags of every photo, tracking the new connections materializing between groups that were once distant, and noting how the bars we used to frequent were now being replaced by new haunts we had never even set foot in.

The final phase of this terrifying confirmation of our own ghostly irrelevance always included some sad exchange of screenshots to share a revelation: your ex drunk with your friends, the bar with those amazing pickles now shuttered, selfies with tiled backgrounds we couldn't recognize. Afterward, all that remained was the silence of our rooms as we blinked back to the present, bewildered and still confined to the same sad apartment in New England.

Fortunately, when this self-imposed suffering ended, María's books were still there. And we soon realized that she too often submitted herself to the penance of FOMO. Rarely did a day go by when she wasn't up late reading *Cosmographia* (1548) by Petrus Apianus, *Treatise on the Matters of Astronomy and Cosmography* (1573) by Juan Pérez de Moya, or *Book and Treatise on Terrestrial and Flying Animals, Including Their History and Properties* (1615) by Jerónimo de Cortés—books that intoxicated her with the endless variety of everything that existed in the world beyond her walls. What she found hardest to bear—the visionary stalking that caused her the most suffering and sent her speeding down the convent corridors in despair—were Franciscan missionaries' accounts of their evangelizing journeys through the Americas. María stored every new detail in a mental archive, which she later broadcast via an intricate epistolary network. With a remarkable knack for networking, the nun managed to correspond with numerous prominent figures including the Viceroy of Aragón, the chaplain of the Royal Discalced in Madrid, and even King Philip IV himself, from whom, in exchange for her advice, she obtained even more information about all that was going on in the places she could never reach. She liked to think that every little piece of counsel she wrote was a way of extending herself beyond the convent walls. But when María let her pen drop onto the desk after signing each letter farewell, she would find herself overcome by the same despondency that gripped us when we finally dropped our phones, their muffled thud on the mattress putting a definitive end to our virtual excursions.

It doesn't matter what century you're reading this in: Every girl has only two options to choose between when seeking to tame FOMO. You can always fall back on the unbeatable response Lindsay Lohan gave in January 2019 when she was asked why she hadn't been invited to participate in Ariana Grande's "Thank U, Next" music video—a tribute to cult classics like *Mean Girls* (2004) that featured a procession of Hollywood cameos, minus Lohan, a glaring absence. "They probably couldn't get in touch with me, I guess. I don't know. It's not that easy to just fly in from Dubai," she said. María de Jesús de Ágreda could have followed Lohan's method and embraced the inevitability of her exclusion: The ecclesiastical hierarchy did not recruit her for far-flung missions because she was a woman, tucked away in Castile. We, too, could have spared ourselves the heartache of every missed birthday invitation by reminding ourselves that, in the end, everyone knew it wasn't that easy to just fly in from Providence. There is, however, a second way: exercising the gift of bilocation.

One day in 1620, channeling the disorientation of someone waking up in an unfamiliar place with the worst hangover of their life, María confessed to Bishop Samaniego that

> having been suddenly raptured into ecstasy by the Lord without perceiving how, it seemed to her that she was in another region, with a very different climate, and among a people whose appearance, customs and disposition matched those who had been shown to her abstractly as the Indians. It seemed to her that she saw them with her own eyes, that she physically felt

the warmer climate of the land, and that her other senses experienced that diversity.

In other words, without knowing how or why, María confessed to having bilocated to the American continent. It would not prove an isolated incident. Though it is difficult to determine the exact number, later accounts claim she eventually undertook no fewer than five hundred transatlantic journeys—a figure that might seem small compared to Taylor Swift's use of her private jet, but was unheard of for a seventeenth-century nun. In her account of this first bilocation, María still seems somewhat perplexed about the mechanics of miraculous teleportation. Eventually, however, she was able to explain it in great detail. Her mode of transportation? Saint Michael and other "Guardian Angels" who "came for her personally, by command of God our Lord," to carry her through the air to "the provinces of New Mexico, Quivira and jumanas." There, María devoted herself to converting the local Jumano people to Catholicism. Language, of course, posed no obstacle. Who needs Duolingo when you can work wonders? María claimed that "she preached in Spanish and that the Indians understood her as perfectly as if it were their own language." While the gift of bilocation, utilized in the service of the church's aggressive and cruel missionary agenda, wasn't new, the scale of María's outings quickly captured everyone's attention. Especially after July 22, 1629, when something happened that made it nearly impossible to doubt María's angelic flights.

The Franciscan mission known as San Agustín de la Isleta was established in 1613 in what is now Bernalillo County, New Mexico. From time to time, a group of Jumano people would visit the mission, traveling from other areas of Texas and northern Mexico to trade buffalo hides. One day, they arrived with an entirely different purpose. If we are to believe the missionaries' accounts (and we probably shouldn't), the Jumanos begged, with tears in their eyes, to be converted to Catholicism to fulfill a promise they had made to a beautiful woman clad in a sky-blue mantle who had visited them some time before. Upon hearing this, the Franciscans of San Agustín identified the nun as Luisa de la Ascensión, who also claimed to have bilocated to Mexican lands (it seems that, at a certain point in the seventeenth century, the traffic of bilocating nuns was denser than California's US-101). But when the Jumanos were shown a portrait of Luisa, they noted that their "lady in blue" was much younger—even four centuries ago, there was always someone ready to assess your tally of wrinkles—and the Franciscans immediately recalled a letter sent to the Archbishopric of Mexico from Burgos, describing the miracles and journeys attributed to María. The pieces fell into place: The lady in blue must have been the nun from Ágreda.

From that moment on, María began to feel that the narrative of her bilocations was slipping out of her control. In 1630, just a few months after the Jumanos' astonishing revelation, the Franciscan Alonso de Benavides, with the speed and opportunism of a true crime hack, published a *Memorial* on the miraculous missions of the lady in blue. A year later, with little concern for the threat of overexposure that could turn María into a pawn of the Catholic expansionist project, Benavides traveled to Ágreda to compel the nun to write a letter confirming that she was indeed the woman who had evangelized the Jumanos. Many years later, when the killjoy bureaucrats of the Inquisition cornered her with their grim questions, María would downplay Benavides's account and maintain that she had not spoken with the Jumanos beyond 1623 (while Benavides, perhaps envisioning an entire saga, spoke of eight years of bilocations). María's retraction was undoubtedly driven by the fear of ending up like the Franciscan Francisco de la Fuente, who in 1632 was sentenced to four years of galley service for falsely claiming he had bilocated to the Americas to convert native populations. She was by now an exhausted witness to men amplifying her story solely to promote the missionary efforts of the Franciscan order, while the narrative she truly longed to be a part of, the story that ignited her FOMO and for which she had first orchestrated these remote hikes, was something entirely different.

It's no easy task to choose the iconographic scheme by which you would like to be remembered, and even more difficult to control it. Britney Spears, for instance, may never escape the enduring infamy of that iconic photograph of her menacingly wielding an umbrella with a freshly shaved head, much as Mexican singer Paulina Rubio may never live down her apparent drug-fueled social media video during the COVID-19 lockdown. María, too, had no say in the art direction of her own image. The iconography traditionally used to represent her depicts the nun either accompanied by the Virgin Mary and sheltered under the Immaculate Conception or surrounded by Native Americans amid a scattering of exotic vegetation. Had she been charged with her own posthumous portrayal, perhaps we would now have paintings of the Conceptionist nun surrounded not by saints and natives, but by the trappings of cosmographers and naturalists: a table strewn with maps, quills, compasses, pieces of coral, measuring instruments, minerals, and a globe. In her *Treatise on the Roundness of the Earth*—an intricate mystical text on cosmography and geography that, to us, reads as the lost gateway to Ursula K. Le Guin—María describes how she came to know "the wonders of the Lord, so that I might know the entire Earth and its roundness, the sea, certain great kingdoms and their animals, their inhabitants, the cities and realms, and the variety of creatures." From a worn-out desk in Ágreda, with the meager light filtering through the barred window of her cell, María made the most of the logistical apparatus of missionary bilocation. Elevated by the clarifying heights of her journeys—where, lest we forget, she was ferried on celestial cruises by angels—she justified her descriptions of each orb, her explanations of the moon's mysteries, and her visions of the earth's most remote peoples. For María, bilocation became the key to soothing the gnawing FOMO that arose each time she read the literature published by scientific pioneers in the service of the voracious imperialist project. Sometimes a girl has to turn to the mystical phenomenology of bilocation if she really wants to bridge the STEM gap.

※

Not all of us, of course, can count on the assistance of mystical grace to secure a shred of relevance in the world we yearn to belong to. In the absence of the gift of bilocation, we have the internet, which (minus the angelic contribution and divine intervention) is practically the same thing. At least that is what the devotees of San Pedro Regalado believe. This fifteenth-century Franciscan friar accumulated so much bilocational experience that his followers now petition the Vatican to declare him the patron saint of the internet, even suggesting his name be officially spelled as S@n Pedro Reg@l@do. María's *Treatise on the Roundness of the Earth* and the stories of her fantastic jaunts inspired us to stop passively surrendering to FOMO with the helplessness of two withdrawn voyeurs and instead begin crafting a virtual presence that would allow us to participate in everything we truly cared about.

Of course, the trade-off was that we had to surrender hours and data to the algorithm and the shadowy giants of Big Tech, a concession we are all inevitably forced to make—just as María could not fully escape the terms dictated by the expansionist machinery of evangelization.

Little by little, we realized the futility of wrecking our eyes by scrolling enviously through the Instagram profiles of all those who had chosen to live their lives differently, free from the rigors of a Rhode Island PhD program. Deep down we knew, just as María would not have traded her sky-blue Conceptionist habit for anything, we didn't really want to part so quickly with the prestigious university at which we had fought so hard to earn a seat. It was, ultimately, about finding a way to participate in all those fascinating lives beyond our cramped academic cubicles. It was about learning, without relying on mystical grace, how to surround ourselves with people living thousands of miles away, how to share our days with these people we had never met, and how to bilocate by returning, again and again, to the stories of the nuns who had saved our twenty-first-century lives.

Epilogue:
A Portable Convent

Our Providence era was over. It was time to pack and leave. We hadn't finished our dissertations yet, but since we didn't have any seminars or teaching assignments left, we were allowed to write somewhere else. At first, the prospect felt like a welcome respite. We hurriedly packed clothes, gave away plants, and bundled with care our small collection of relics (a brain-shaped stress ball from Brown's Counseling and Psychological Services instead of a saint's finger; not a blessed rosary, but a Neko cat mug stolen from the local karaoke bar). We were ready to break our vow of enclosure, once and for all. But neither of us could sleep on our last night in Providence, as if keeping a candlelight vigil in honor of the six years spent there. The next morning, on our way to our last meeting at the Rockefeller Library, our nocturnal thoughts still haunted us. Did we believe in life after the (academic) convent?

It's true that Providence had made us feel more miserable than María de San José in her prison at the convent of São Alberto. It had turned us into reluctant sadfishing masters. We were certain that not even a rosary bead from Saint Juana could alleviate our puffy eyes or miraculously cure our chronic back pain. And yet, Providence had also bestowed on us a friendship like no other—synching our biorhythms with more precision than those of the Carmelites Beatriz de la Concepción and Ana de Jesús—and a sense of belonging that was now, all too suddenly, about to vanish. We didn't try to hide that we were panicking, and due to our tearful, ritualistic goodbyes to our desks, it was already obvious we were sad. What now? Without the twenty-page syllabi and the teaching assistants' code of conduct governing our lives, who would tell us what to do? The only certainties left were: come the last day of next month, opening our banking app would bring no joy, emptying our 269-square-foot studios meant relinquishing a room of our own, and, worst of all, we hadn't even finished our dissertations.

It seemed, from then on, that it would be impossible not to pounce on every promise of a foolproof itinerary for our lives, and there were many: a trend guaranteeing that balancing your cortisol levels was the most reliable path to recovering your sense of purpose; a pervasive imperative to make your everyday diet orbit around the sacrosanct stress-relieving foods; the urge to design each own's "dopamine menu," a personalized list of daily activities intended to trigger calculated boosts of happiness. From Gwyneth Paltrow's *Goop Lab*'s energy healings and vampire facials to Lacy Phillips's $30 classes on "Celebrating Rejection to Harness Magnetic Projection," every corner of existence was engulfed in pledges that this was the ultimate hack that could save your life. Sitting mute and desolate on the steps of the Rockefeller Library—its brutalist architecture had never looked so hostile—it was all too tempting to believe our own wave of anguish was unique, but deep down we knew that no one managed to escape a similar existential crisis. No matter where we looked no one seemed immune to our disorientation. With burnout on the rise, a yawning gender and ideological gap, skyrocketing levels of stress, climate anxiety, and everyone falling prey to the Sisyphean cycle of app dating, who wasn't ready to embrace even the tiniest promise of serenity that the thriving wellness-industrial complex could offer? There had to be something that worked.

Staring at our IKEA bags filled with overdue books, we both knew once we returned them, all scripted steps would be over. At that point, we would have welcomed with enthusiasm the advice of anyone sharing the latest DIY strategy for survival: limiting our screen time, adding a pinch of activated charcoal to our food, or reading a self-help manual. Was entering the convent an option we considered? For a growing number of women in similar crises of the soul, it certainly was. In a 2019 *Huffington Post* piece entitled "Behold, the Millennial Nuns," Eve Fairbanks pointed out that after decades of decline, more and more young women were being called to religious life. "What on Earth is going on?" she asked. "Everything," we would have said. Everything that's going on right now would seem to urge every woman to seek the refuge of a safe space where food, shelter, and routine are secured and where there exists a community guided by a shared purpose. Were we, however, unsettled enough to ditch our twenty-first-century lives and take the vows of chastity, poverty, and obedience? Definitely not. The space within the four walls of the convent wasn't our way out, but the nuns who for centuries had inhabited it certainly were.

For years, the nuns had guided our way, so it felt only natural to seek refuge leafing through their books one last time—books that had long accompanied us, resting on our studios' dusty wooden floors. They were all there: María de San José, Saint Teresa, Catherine of Siena, Veronica Giuliani, Sor Juana Inés de la

Cruz... their biographies, hagiographies, spiritual treatises, and travel chronicles. We didn't say a word, but the tenderness with which we stacked the books, as if saying farewell, betrayed a shared anguish: Did we believe in life after them? Amid the mountain of crumbling spines and sun-bleached covers in our bags, a jacket with the face of Jerónima de la Asunción providentially emerged. With her arched eyebrows, wooden crucifix in hand, and penetrating gaze, the Poor Clare nun seemed determined to do whatever it took to pull us from our whiny nostalgia. And she succeeded. In the *History of Our Saint Mother Jerónima de la Asunción*, her companion Ana de Cristo chronicled the trials and tribulations that Jerónima and the rest of the adventurous "squadron of Poor Clares" faced from the moment they left Toledo until they finally settled in Manila more than a year later. In 1620, these nuns had left the calm of their convent behind to embark on a transoceanic voyage, facing the threats of corsairs, storms at sea, and an alarming lack of hygiene that turned mere survival into an elusive and coveted prize.

That morning, we were convinced we felt a fear as unbearable as that experienced by the gang of Poor Clares before embarking on the most daring adventure of their lives. (Never underestimate the dramatic capacity of two thirtysomethings gazing into the abyss of a life change, no matter how trivial it may seem.) As we turned the pages and left behind Jerónima's intimidating visage, the cloud of unease began to dissipate. After all, if nearly all the Poor Clares had managed to thrive in the open, far from the cozy confines of their cloister, perhaps we would too. This small group of nuns had figured out a vital truth: To survive, one must carry their convent with them. Once they boarded the ship bound for Acapulco, Jerónima and her fellow nuns transformed their space into a makeshift cloister on the high seas, a sort of portable convent.

We set sail on Holy Tuesday and if the Lord had good comfort in the first ship, it was no less in the second, which was very large and the stern chamber was larger with a very beautiful corridor and its toilet. At last, we found ourselves as if in a cloistered cell, attended by its guardians: the Mother Vicar and Sister Luisa de Jesús, who managed all affairs within; visitors who could not be excused were permitted to enter; and Sister Magdalena de Cristo, who diligently prepared the meals there.

You may leave the convent, but the convent will never leave you.
As students came and went around us, unloading their own suitcases full of books to be returned, our despair gradually subsided. There was no visible miracle, but all of a sudden, an almost miraculous conviction overwhelmed us. Our nuns would tell us what to do. The nuns we had spent days and nights with, the nuns we had ungraciously mingled with our favorite reality TV personalities, actresses, and internet crushes, were the ones who would lead us the way. Suddenly, anguish turned into enthusiasm. We wanted to seize the lapels of the librarian who mechanically scanned our books, the weary professors, the friends who inundated our cell phones with messages, and the students who wandered aimlessly in front of the Biltmore Hotel—now renamed The Graduate, where we first met. We wanted to gather everyone together and proclaim that we had discovered the recipe to create a therapeutic refuge from uncertainty, a sanctuary against unease. A portable convent for the twenty-first century.

This didn't mean there would be a specific answer to each desperate question—although we won't be the ones to judge if someone chose to follow María de San José's recipe for mastering the art of vegging out; Sor Juana Inés de la Cruz's five-step guide on crafting the perfect email, Arcangela Tarabotti's MBA on putting one's friends to work; Saint Teresa's notes on a thrifty Girl Math; or even if someone decided to honor Santa Veronica Giuliani by eating five mandarins every Friday. Rather, it meant discovering a shelter within the narratives of our nuns, weaving together celebratory genealogies that anchored us in an increasingly alienating present, knowing that (it doesn't matter in what century you're reading this in) life's trials—be they the Inquisition's harsh retaliation or the pangs of a broken heart—are only bearable when one is embraced by the warmth of a communal sanctuary. We found our way to live after the (academic) convent. In the absence of spiritual vocation and the strength or desire for the rigors of the cloister, leaving Providence became a creative endeavor: the forging of a portable convent for all of us.

—It just makes so much sense.
—It's just *convent wisdom*.

And so we left Providence with the writing of this book as our new shared mission. *It seemed impossible, given our circumstances, that we could write as much as needed to be written.* But then we did.

Acknowledgments

Many years have passed since that day when we found ourselves sitting on the steps of the Rockefeller Library, soaking up a rare ray of sunshine and dreaming of writing a book. Back then, we had already released a handful of episodes of our podcast, *Las hijas de Felipe*, and the prospect of writing together—an endeavor that had always felt so lonely—filled us with excitement. The journey to bring *Convent Wisdom* to life took longer than we anticipated, and it would have been impossible without the collective efforts of countless people. A huge thank-you to all our listeners who, from the days when we recorded in a cramped Rhode Island bathroom cushioned with yoga mats, believed that scrutinizing the lives, relics, bilocations, and anxieties of sixteenth- and seventeenth-century nuns was worth their time.

This book is the culmination of many years of readings and research, and we hope it serves as our heartfelt tribute to the countless scholars who silently support each of its pages. If Sarah E. Owens had not devoted an immense amount of time to transcribing the diary of Ana de Cristo, Jerónima de la Asunción might not have found her place in these pages—thanks for sending us your meticulous transcription! Not only this book, but our entire lives, wouldn't be the same if Tanya Tiffany had not devoted priceless hours to researching Margarita de la Cruz and her Baby Jesus collection. Without Carlos M. Eire's extensive exploration of the levitations and bilocations of some of our favorite nuns, we could have never envisioned a chapter dedicated to the physical demands of their bodies. We also extend our profound gratitude to Rebeca Sanmartín Bastida for helping us see, through her numerous books and articles, that neither María de Santo Domingo nor Juana de la Cruz—despite being born quite before our preferred centuries—should be left out of this book. A huge thank-you to Sherry Velasco for writing *Lesbians in Early Modern Spain* and uncovering primary sources so juicy we could hardly have dreamed of them. Had we not immersed ourselves in Isabella Campagnol's wonderful research, this book would have lacked its Venetian luxury and the most exciting examples of conventual entrepreneurship. We'll be forever indebted to Álvaro Enrigue for his clever, engaging, and beautiful analysis of Sor Juana's mathematical and economic sonnets. And there's no way we could have ever grasped the intricacies of Sor Juana's oeuvre and persona without Stephanie Merrim's mind-blowing scholarship. To her and her tough love, we're indebted in many ways: our notion of the sixteenth and seventeenth centuries as elastic temporalities was sparked, without our knowing, in Merrim's seminars on the Baroque as a supple, portable platform.

Our years in Providence may have been hard, but they would've been unbearable and pointless without the shelter of Brown's Department of Hispanic Studies. To the generous, loving community led by Laura Bass at the Rochambeau House, thank you. Laura's sharpness, Felipe Martínez-Pinzón's mesmerizing speeches, Michelle Clayton's galvanizing playfulness, Sarah Thomas's genius close readings—we like to think that *Convent Wisdom* has at least a bit of them all. It also owes much to our most intrepid semester with the wonderful Tara Nummedal. Betsy Wright, thank you for allowing us to be part of the incredible editorial team of the *Bulletin of the Comediantes*: Our understanding of the early modern world is deeply indebted to our extensive work in the journal.

A big thank-you to Maria Cardona, Jan Martí, and Rebeca González for helping us bring this book to life and turning it into a global publication—Saint Teresa would be proud! Without the help of Ben Brooks and Laura Ibáñez, as they know, we would've never found the right words for our nuns. Amy Guay, the editor of our dreams: thanks for being the devoted reader these nuns deserve, and for ensuring this book reaches our readers in its best possible form. Not even in our wildest academic dreams could we have anticipated such a diligent editor.

To all the nuns of today who, often in precarious conditions, dedicate themselves to preserving the writings of their predecessors, sponsoring editions, and supporting works that bring them to light—thank you. This book would not exist without your efforts. A special thanks to the Carmelite María José Pérez González for her tireless work in making the writings of sixteenth- and seventeenth-century Discalced Carmelite nuns more visible.

No PhD or book is possible without the unwavering support and love of family and friends: GRACIAS. Big shoutout to our girlfriends, for always putting up with the pitiable spectacle that we are when a deadline is missed, a footnote misplaced, or the exact date in which an Augustinian Recollect nun bit her right little finger's nail is nowhere to be found. Arden, my life's miracle, thank you for being a Marian apparition every day, every single time—a rare sexy angel packed with *filloas*, devotion, and life-saving smiles. Nerea, *mi amor*, THANK YOU for taking care of everything—from gluten-free lasagna to helping me find the perfect word—as if I were a twentieth-century man so I could focus on all my nuns. Thank you for being the best human even when life was at its worst(!). You're the best thing about being a lesbian, and that's saying a lot: *crea que estamos hechizadas la una con la otra.* ♥

To Ana,

because she challenged me. "ACT ON YOUR DESIRES," she said. Las hijas, this book, my whole post-pandemic self— nothing would be there if not for Ana's loving wisdom.

To Carmen,

for being the friend I spent years without but always needed. For sharing some of her enviable patience with me, for standing by my side through every love debacle, for possessing a prose far more captivating than María de San José's. Thank you, Carmen, for making life a truly angelic place.

Character Guide

María de San José (Discalced Carmelite, 1548–1603). Born María Salazar de Torres in Toledo, Spain, María was a posh girl turned austere Discalced Carmelite. The most loyal of friends (although she had the mood swings of a Gemini), she was also Saint Teresa's BFF. María will teach you how to unionize with the dignity of a sixteenth-century religious woman, because she knew that all work and no play makes the nun a dull girl.

Saint Teresa of Jesus (Discalced Carmelite, 1515–1582). Born Teresa de Cepeda y Ahumada in Ávila, Spain, Teresa founded her own religious order, the Discalced Carmelites, thus establishing herself as the most popular celebrity in sixteenth-century Spain. Thrifty negotiator and workaholic, stubborn and charming, Teresa is the friend who always tells you what you may not want to hear. She'll guide you through negotiating a mortgage, while also providing the candor needed to navigate the highs and lows of toxic friendships.

Ana de San Bartolomé (Discalced Carmelite, 1549–1626). Born Ana García Manzanas in a tiny village in Castile, Ana lost her parents at a young age and joined the Discalced Carmelites on November 2, 1570, when she was twenty-one. Over time, she became Saint Teresa's right-hand woman—acting as her amanuensis, nurse, and secretary. Even though she often lived in the shadow of more famous or controversial Carmelites, Ana found a special spot in Teresa's heart: "Ana, Ana, you are the saint; I have the fame," Teresa would whisper to her before her passing.

María de San José (Augustinian Recollect, 1656–1719). María was born Juana Palacios Berruecos in the Indigenous village of Tepeaca, close to Puebla de los Ángeles, Mexico. Although she didn't learn to read and write until she was thirty-two, at the request of her confessors she managed to produce more than two thousand pages recounting her life before and after entering the convent. She didn't, however, oblige in silence. This complaining nun will teach you the benefits of ceaselessly articulating, like a prayer, your "greatest repugnance for work."

Sor Juana Inés de la Cruz (Hieronymite, 1648–1695). Born Juana Inés de Asbaje in San Miguel Nepantla, Mexico, she is the intriguing face saluting you from the Mexican 200 peso bills, the heroine of a Netflix production, and possibly the most iconic figure in Latinx pop culture. This distinguished Hieronymite, exquisite writer, and intrepid philosopher will help you make your way out of your people-pleasing habits, offer you a smart alternative to the financial nightmare of your Girl Math, and teach you how to write that daunting email to your boss.

Saint Veronica Giuliani (Capuchin Poor Clare, 1660–1727). Born Ursula Giuliani in Mercatello sul Metauro, Italy, she mastered the checklist of sainthood convincingly enough to be canonized only one century after her death. Although she was of the opinion that nothing tastes as good as holiness feels—her diet included delicacies such as cat vomit and dismembered mice—she will teach you how to turn food neurosis into a refectory of your own.

Juana de la Cruz, la Santa Juana (Franciscan Tertiary, 1481–1534). Born Juana Vázquez Gutiérrez in a town near Toledo, Spain, she was a virtuoso performer whose captivating preaching shows won the admiration of Emperor Charles V. With the miraculous beads of her rosary, she established a merchandising empire that would make even Taylor Swift envious. To counterbalance the extreme fasting imposed by religious life, she indulged in vivid visions filled with candied fruit and piñatas overflowing with pastries.

Catalina de Ledesma and Inés de Santa Cruz (born ca. 1570). Born in Castille, both are far from what you would expect of two seventeenth-century religious women. Popularly known as "the Reeds" for the shape of their dildo, they were arrested for female sodomy in 1603, after neighbors correctly identified the sounds of passion heard through the walls. Inés and Catalina had to move cities, fight the prosecution of the Inquisition, and deal with the emotional ups and downs of polyamorous entanglements, but nothing could destroy their long-term relationship.

Benedetta Carlini (Theatine, 1590–1661). Born (with that name) in a bucolic village nestled in the hills of Tuscany, Benedetta dedicated herself to a life of faith at the tender age of nine. The bloody stigmata and mystical ecstasies that once earned her a reputation for sanctity were soon overshadowed by her two-year, sometimes nonconsensual affair with her assistant, Sister Bartolomea Crivelli. Her lesbianism ultimately landed her before the tribunal of the Inquisition, and centuries later, it would predestine her for Paul Verhoeven's pornographic lens.

Ana de Jesús (Discalced Carmelite, 1545–1621). Born Ana de Lobera Torres in Medina del Campo, Spain, Ana was not only a passionate advocate of Saint Teresa's legacy, but also embodied the most unwavering and devoted love of the seventeenth century. To us, she is a genuine oracle of romance, a beacon of wisdom for all long-distance relationships. Ana will provide you the essential toolkit to embrace your own anxious attachments, transforming uncertainty into strength.

Beatriz de la Concepción (Discalced Carmelite, 1569–1646). Born Beatriz Zúñiga Palomeque into a family of Spanish nobility, she said yes to the Carmelite habit at the age of twenty-one. At thirty-five, she left Spain to found the Carmelite convents in France and Flanders alongside Ana de Jesús. As the recipient of Ana de Jesús's most heartfelt and passionate letters, Beatriz de la Concepción possesses all the keys to help you navigate the challenges of long-distance relationships and, later, the sorrow of loss.

Sor Ana Dorotea de la Concepción (Poor Clare, 1612–1694). Born Ana Dorotea in Vienna, she was the illegitimate daughter of Rudolf II, emperor of the Holy Roman Empire. In 1622, she arrived in Spain to take up residence in the most prestigious convent of early modern Europe: the Convent of the Royal Discalced in Madrid. Shielded by a substantial inheritance, she ultimately squandered her fortune on extravagant devotional objects and sought-after relics.

Sor Margarita de la Cruz (Poor Clare, 1567–1633). Born in Wiener Neustadt, Margarita de la Cruz was, in fact, Archduchess Margaret of Austria, the most well-connected nepo nun of the seventeenth century—never be deceived by the austere name chosen by any nun. Secluded within her opulent convent and surrounded by an extensive collection of small polychrome sculptures of the

Baby Jesus—an uncanny seventeenth-century precursor to reborn dolls—this nun serves as a testament to the fact that, no matter what century you're reading this in, every heiress has her quirks.

Hildegard von Bingen (Benedictine, 1098–1179). Born Hildegard in Bermersheim vor der Höhe, a winegrowing district on the west of the Rhine. Polymath, natural scientist, musical composer, mystical writer, and beer brewer, Hildegard is arguably the most prolific and name-checked medieval saint—she has a minor planet, *898 Hildegard*, and a plant, *Hildegardia*, named in her honor. This fancy abbess and late-blooming entrepreneur will teach you that no entrepreneurial risk is worth taking without the support and collaboration of friends.

Arcangela Tarabotti (Benedictine, 1604–1652). Born Elena Cassandra Tarabotti in Castello, Venice, this nun had a taste for pseudonyms; you'll find her as Arcangela, but also as Galerana Baratotti or Galerana Barcitotti. She was the ultimate fashion victim (always complaining for not having at her disposal the latest trends) as well as the ultimate fashionista (resourceful enough to style her habit with a taste worthy of the most exquisite convent runway). More importantly, Arcangela, who managed to turn her sisters' knowledge of lacework into a profitable textile business, will help you source your own unexpected entrepreneurial vision.

María de Santo Domingo (Dominican Tertiary, ca. 1480–1524). Born (with that name) in Aldeanueva de la Sierra, Spain, this *beata* with an inclination for mysticism, a knack for the performing arts, and a talent for getting expelled from monasteries (she lived in at least three) is the drama queen *par excellence*. Favored with the gift of tears, María will help you ditch your guilt for belonging to the so-called snowflake generation. Thanks to her, you will finally embrace the *mater dolorosa* within you.

Saint Catherine of Siena (Dominican, 1347–1380). Born Caterina di Jacopo di Benincasa in Siena, Italy, this fourteenth-century mystic became the most iconic and revered influencer for sixteenth-century nuns, their absolute It Girl. She wrote spiritual treatises, meddled with papal politics, toured northern Italy and southern France advocating reform of the clergy, and was canonized in 1461. She succumbed, however, to rigorous fasting, and her holy-anorexia-triggered downfall will be your cue to reject the urgency to participate in the newest diet trend.

Jeanne des Anges (Ursuline, 1602–1665). Born Jeanne de Belcier in Cozes, France, she was the mother superior of a convent in Loudun that revolutionized seventeenth-century France with a scandalous outbreak of demonic possessions. She was sharp enough to turn the macabre contortions of exorcism into her ticket to a celebrity tour that would end up with a visit to the Queen of France. Jeanne, who might have been the catalyst of an early #MeToo movement, will teach you why you should never let others name your demons.

Juana Esperanza de San Alberto (Discalced Carmelite, d. 1679). Born with a name now sadly lost to us in the early seventeenth century in what is now Guinea-Bissau, old Mali Empire, West Africa, she was only six when she was enslaved and brought to Mexico. When her enslavers passed away, she was entrusted to the convent of San José in Puebla, where she worked as a servant for sixty-eight years. She professed as a Carmelite and became a nun just one year before she died. As humble as she may sound, the elderly Juana Esperanza gained a devoted fan base who would keep as relics even the pitchers she drank from. Besieged by chronophobia? Don't despair. Just find solace in Juana Esperanza's healthy acceptance of old age.

Luisa de la Ascensión (Poor Clare, 1565–1636). Born Luisa Ruiz de Colmenares in Madrid, Spain, Luisa was raised in the comfort of an upper-class family. The moment she stepped into her monastery of Santa Clara, she stood out, and she would eventually be internationally known for her mystic dexterity. But she was never a saint. This Poor Clare's life is a cautionary tale of fame, a warning against desperately seeking the blue checkmark of canonization. She was accused by the Inquisition, and even though she was ultimately declared innocent of fraud, the damage was done—she had been canceled.

Jerónima de la Asunción (Poor Clare, 1555–1630). Born Jerónima Yáñez de la Fuente in Toledo, Spain, this inquisitive nun longed since childhood to "know something about everything that existed" in the world, and her curiosity led her to travel through stormy, pirate-ridden seas to establish the first convent of religious women in Manila. She'll teach you that there's no shame in extreme fandom—she held on to Saint Juana's rosary beads with the fervor of a Swiftie who won't let go of her friendship bracelets—and that there's much pleasure in being a late bloomer who finally gets to see the world at sixty-five.

María Jesús de Ágreda (Conceptionist, 1602–1665). Born María Coronel de Arana in Ágreda, Spain, María Jesús technically never left her Spanish hometown. You may think that your FOMO is severe, but is your fear of missing out extreme enough to call upon you the gift of bilocation? María Jesús's desire to see the world and evangelize was so acute that, by miracle, she made herself present in central New Mexico and West Texas.

Notes

Introduction

5   *"I write this"*: María de San José Salazar, *Book for the Hour of Recreation*. introduction and notes by Allison Weber, trans. Amanda Powell (The Univ. of Chicago Press, 2002), 163.

5   *"I have wished"*: Ibid., 33.

5   *"I confess," wrote*: Ibid., 30.

Girlfriends

7   *"He [God] is overjoyed"*: Belchior de Santa Ana, *Chronica de carmelitas descalços, particular do reyno do Portugal e provincia de Sam Felippe* (Lisboa: Henrique Valente de Oliueira, 1675), 293.

10   *"I was then thirteen"*: María de San José Salazar, *Book for the Hour of Recreation*, introduction and notes by Allison Weber, trans. Amanda Powell (The Univ. of Chicago Press, 2002), 43.

11   *"Between equals"*: María de San José, "Instrucción de novicias," *Humor y espiritualidad en la escuela teresiana primitiva: Santa Teresa de Jesús, Jerónimo Gracián, Ana de Jesús, María de San José* (El Monte Carmelo, 1966), 566. Our translation.

15   *"Mother, please, don't make me"*: This is our translation of a popular Italian song circulating around Venice since the Renaissance: "*Madre non mi far monica, / Che non mi volgio far / Non mi tagliar la tonica / Che non la voi portar / Star tutto el zorno / A vespero e a messa / poi la madre badessa / non fa se non gridar.*"

17   *"that love and tenderness"*: María de San José, *Aviso para el gobierno de religiosas*, ed. Juan Luis Astigarraga (Instituto Histórico Teresiano, 1977), 18–19. Our translation.

17   "an outfit more suited": Quoted in Isabella Campagnol, *Forbidden Fashions*

Invisible Luxuries in Early Venetian Convents (Texas Tech Univ. Press, 2014), 82.

19 *"I recovered it"*: Jerónimo Gracián, *Escolias . . . a la Vida de Santa Teresa compuesta por el P. Ribera*, quoted in José Luis Astigarraga, "Escolias del P. Jerónimo Gracián a la Vida de Santa Teresa compuesta por el P. Ribera," *Ephemerides Carmeliticae*, no. 32 (1981–82): 350. Our translation.

21 *"It has come to our attention"*: Quoted in Barbara Mujica, *Women Religious and Epistolary Exchange in the Carmelite Reform. The Disciples of Teresa de Avila* (Amsterdam Univ. Press, 2020), 82.

21 *"It is with great sorrow"*: Teresa of Jesus's letter to Jerónimo Gracián, October 4, 1579, *Epistolario*, eds. Teófanes Egido and Luis Rodríguez Martínez (Espiritualidad, 1984), 643. Our translation.

22 *"all the shadows they saw"*: Teresa of Jesus, *The Book of the Foundations*, trans. Rev. John Dalton (T. Jones, 1853), ch. XXV, 154.

23 *"they will not have"*: Teresa of Jesus's letter to Jerónimo Gracián, October 4, 1579, *Epistolario*, 643.

23 *"I tell you"*: Teresa of Jesus's letter to Jerónimo Gracián, April 15, 1578, *The Collected Letters of Saint Teresa of Avila*, trans. Kieran Kavanaugh, vol. 2. (ICS Publications, 2007), 51.

24 *"What has displeased me"*: Teresa of Jesus's letter to María de San José, November 8, 1581, *The Collected Letters of Saint Teresa of Avila*, vol. 2, 471.

24 *"cunning fox"*: Teresa of Jesus's letter to María de San José, January 9, 1577, *Epistolario*, 390. Our translation.

24 *"firecrotch"*: "Lindsay Lohan's Infamous 2006 'Fire Crotch' Incident," YouTube, January 17, 2024. https://www.youtube.com/watch?v=Cp7tk-_4Sl0.

24 *"We're not in high school anymore"*: Emily Kirkpatrick, "Paris Hilton Says She and Lindsay Lohan Finally Ended Their Feud Because 'They're Not in High School,'" January 27, 2022, https://www.vanityfair.com/style/2022/01/paris-hilton-lindsay-lohan-feud-over-friendship-watch-what-happens-live?srsltid=AfmBOopPVBuUHM5uZuqYvF-PnCmwAxuXurcVGfAESqwk688U85DZnYcv.

27 *"my little scholar"*: Teresa of Jesus's letter to María de San José, March 28, 1578, *Epistolario*, 507.

27 *"God spare all my daughters"*: Ibid., November 19, 1576, 340.

27 *"I prefer having her"*: Teresa of Jesus's letter to Luisa de la Cerda, May 27, 1568, *The Collected Letters of Saint Teresa of Avila*, vol. 1, 48.

28 *"How can you presume"*: Teresa of Jesus's letter to María de San José, September 7, 1576, *The Collected Letters of Saint Teresa of Avila*, vol. 1, 383.

29 *"You must dream"*: Ibid., July 11, 1577, and September 7, 1576, *Epistolario*, 452, 275.

29 *"If you have so much money"*: Ibid., December 10, 1577, *The Collected Letters of Saint Teresa of Avila*, vol. 1, 712.

30 *"Your letter was a great"*: Ibid., July 14, 1582, *The Collected Letters of Saint Teresa of Avila*, vol. 2, 559.

31 *"I assure you that I am touched"*: Teresa of Jesus's letter to María de San José, July 2, 1576, *The Letters of Saint Teresa*. A complete edition translated from the Spanish and annotated by the Benedictines of Santbrook, with an introduction by Cardinal Gasquet, vol. 2 (Thomas Baker, 1921), 2.

32 *"I never kept company"*: María de San José, *A Wild Country Out in the Garden. The Spiritual Journals of a Colonial Mexican Nun*, selected, ed., and trans. Kathleen A. Myers and Amanda Powell (Indiana Univ. Press, 1999), 14.

32 *"We may have officially"*: Maria Stanchieri, "The Dark Side of Minimalism," *NSS Magazine*, October 25, 2022, https://www.nssmag.com/en/fashion/31236/nun-core-dark-minimalism.

34 *"indulge in one pastime"*: Teresa of Jesus, *The Life of Teresa of Jesus*, trans. and ed. E. Allison Peers (Random House, 1960), 53.

34 *"Youth, sensuality and the devil"*: Ibid., 55.

35 *"knew neither how"*: Ibid., 187.

35 *"I was quite alone"*: Ibid., 190.

36 *"The founding Mother"*: Teresa of Jesus's letter to Jerónimo Gracián, December 1576, *Epistolario*, 377.

37 *"For charity's sake"*: Teresa of Jesus's letter to María de San José, June 15, 1576, *The Collected Letters of Saint Teresa of Avila*, vol. 1, 346.

37 *"abomination of sins"*: Teresa of Jesus's letter to Mother María Bautista, April 29, 1576, *Epistolario*, 237.

38 *"Melancholic"*: María de la Encarnación, quoted in *Proceso de canonización y beatificación de Santa Teresa de Jesús*, ed. Silverio de Santa Teresa, vol. 1, Biblioteca Mística Carmelitana 18–20 (El Monte Carmelo, 1935), 329. Our translation.

39 *"the boat happened"*: Teresa of Jesus, *The Book of the Foundations*, ch. XXIII, 146.

40 *"They [the letters]"*: Teresa of Jesus's letter to María de San José, July 2, 1576, *The Collected Letters of Saint Teresa of Avila*, vol. 1, 355.

40 *"I was very glad to see"*: Ibid., January 3, 1577, *Epistolario*, 385.

41 *"I can truthfully say"*: Ibid., September 9, 1576 and September 7, 1576, *The Collected Letters of Saint Teresa of Avila*, vol. 1, 421, 411.

42 *"It would be a great consolation"*: Ibid., July 11, 1577, 726.

42 *"restless, wandering, disobedient"*: Francisco de Santa María, *Reforma de los Descalzos de Nuestra Señora del Carmen de la primitiva observancia hecha por Santa Teresa de Jesús*, 2 vols. (Madrid: Diego Díaz de la Carrera, 1644), book IV, ch. 30, n. 2. Our translation.

42 *"Better to indulge"*: Teresa of Jesus's letter to María de San José, July 11, 1576, *Epistolario*, 260.

42 *"Women understand"*: *The Interior Castle or the Mansions Translated from the Autograph of Saint Teresa of Jesus by the Benedictines of Stanbrook* (Thomas Baker, 1921), 37.

43 *"you say everything so well"*: Teresa of Jesus's letter to María de San José, March 17, 1582, *The Collected Letters of Saint Teresa of Avila*, vol. 2, 522.

43 *"What joy it would bring me"*: Ibid., July 4, 1580, *Epistolario*, 711.

44 *"I do not know"*: María de San José, "Carta de una pobre presa descalza," *Humor y espiritualidad en la escuela teresiana primitiva: Santa Teresa de Jesús, Jerónimo Gracián, Ana de Jesús, María de San José* (El Monte Carmelo, 1966), 351. Our translation.

45 *"And you will see"*: Ana de San Bartolomé, *Obras completas de la Beata Ana de San Bartolomé*, vol. 1, ed. Julen Urkiza (Teresianum, 1981), 598. Our translation.

Work

49 *"I went back a third time"*: María de San José, *A Wild Country Out in the Garden: The Spiritual Journals of a Colonial Mexican Nun*, selected, ed., and trans. Kathleen A. Myers and Amanda Powell (Indiana Univ. Press, 1999), 54–55.

51 *"This priest"*: Ibid., 7.

51 *"spent with rest and relief"*: Ibid.

51 *"This Father Cárdenas had"*: Ibid., 8.

52 *"Seeing how much"*: Ibid.

53 *"I am old and tired"*: Teresa of Jesus's letter to Dionisio Ruiz de la Peña, June 4, 1582, *Epistolario*, eds. Teófanes Egido and Luis Rodríguez Martínez (Espiritualidad, 1984), 880. Our translation.

53 *"exhausted at times by"*: Teresa of Jesus's letter to María de San José, December 19, 1577, *Epistolario*, 480.

53 *"as tired and sore"*: Úrsula Suarez, *Relación autobiográfica de una monja venerable*, (Biblioteca Nacional, 1984), 230. Our translation.

55 *"I felt very weary"*: María de San José, *A Wild Country Out in the Garden*, 37.

56 *"[As] the Guardian Priest"*: Ibid., 3.

61 *"It is a pity"*: Manuel Fernández de Santa Cruz's preface to *Carta atenagórica*,

quoted in Herón Pérez Martínez, *Estudios sorjuanianos* (El Colegio de Michoacán, 2015), 137. Our translation.

62 *"It has not been my will"*: Sor Juana Inés de la Cruz, *The Answer*, second critical edition and translation by Electa Arenal and Amanda Powell (The Feminist Press, 2009), 39.

62 *"Yet I protest that"*: Ibid., 83.

63 *"And thus I confess that"*: Ibid., 45.

63 *"If it [my work] is heretical"*: Ibid., 93.

64 *"If the style of this letter"*: Ibid., 103–102.

65 *"I can't do this anymore"*: Sor Juana Inés de la Cruz, *Letter from Monterrey*, Antonio Alatorre, "La Carta de sor Juana al P. Núñez (1682)," *Nueva Revista de Filología Hispánica* 35, núm. 2 (1987a): 591–673, 625. Our translation.

66 *"What is the cause"*: Ibid., 591–673, 624.

68 *"I, the worst in the world"*: Sor Juana Inés de la Cruz, "Documentos en el Libro de Profesiones del Convento de San Jerónimo," Document 413 in *Obras completas*, eds. Alfonso Méndez-Plancarte and Alberto Salceda, vol. 4 (Fondo de Cultura Económica, 1975), 523. Our translation.

70 *"It is a great evil"*: Teresa de Jesús, *The Life of Teresa of Jesus*, trans. and ed. E. Allison Peers (Random House, 1960), 60.

70 *"everything passed in laughter"*: María de San José, *Libro de las recreaciones. Humor y espiritualidad en la escuela teresiana primitiva: Santa Teresa de Jesús, Jerónimo Gracián, Ana de Jesús, María de San José* (El Monte Carmelo, 1966), 314. Our translation.

70 *"After meals"*: Teresa of Jesus, *Constitutions. Obras completas*, eds. Efrén de la Madre de Dios and Otgger Steggnik (Biblioteca de Autores Cristianos, 2012), 832, 829. Our translation.

71 *"I saw clearly"*: María de San José, *Ramillete de mirra. Resumptas de la Historia de la Fundación de los descalzos y descalzas carmelitas que fundó Santa Theresa de Jesús, nuestra madre. Año de 1562 el primer convento de monjas; y el primer de frayles año de 1577. Cuéntanse algunos trabajos que se pasaron en algunas fundaciones de frayles y monjas*, BNE, ms. 2176: ff. 45–45v. Our translation.

73 *"Do not be disheartened"*: Ibid., "Carta de una pobre presa descalza," *Humor y espiritualidad en la escuela teresiana primitiva: Santa Teresa de Jesús, Jerónimo Gracián, Ana de Jesús, María de San José* (El Monte Carmelo, 1966), 356, 359. Our translation.

74 *"May she [Teresa]"*: Ana de Jesús's letter to Francisca de las Llagas, September 28, 1611, quoted in Ildefonso Moriones, *Ana de Jesús (1545–1621). Beata* (Ediciones El Carmen, 2021), 287. Our translation.

77 *"many things [that] seem"*: María de San José Salazar, *Book for the Hour of Recreation*, introduction and notes by Allison Weber, trans. Amanda Powell (Univ. of Chicago Press, 2002), 33.

Body

81 *"One was that she should"*: Giovanni Maria Crivelli, in Rudolph M. Bell, *Holy Anorexia* (Univ. of Chicago Press, 1985), 77.
83 *"I experienced a deadly"*: Quoted in Bell, *Holy Anorexia*, 27–28.
84 *"Her stomach could digest nothing"*: Giovanni Maria Crivelli, in Bell, *Holy Anorexia*, 28.
84 *"Nothing tastes as good as skinny feels"*: Kate Moss famously used this quote in a 2009 interview with *Women's Wear Daily*.
86 *"As I sat at the dinner"*: Filippo Maria Salvatori, *The Life of Saint Veronica Giuliani, Capuchin Nun* (R. Washbourne, 1874), 65.
86 *"Is there a resemblance"*: Bell, *Holy Anorexia*, cover copy.
91 *"She had barely"*: Antonio Daza, *Historia, vida y milagros, extasis y reuelaciones de la bienauenturada virgen Sor Iuana de la Cruz de la Tercera Orden de . . . san Francisco* (Madrid: por Luis Sánchez, 1613), ff. 5v–6r. Our translation.
92 *"Now, my friends, I shall satisfy"*: Inocencio García Andrés, ed., *El Conhorte: Sermones de una mujer santa* (Universidad Pontificia de Salamanca y Fundación Universitaria Española, 1999), 343. Our translation.
92 *"ripened"*: Ibid., 372.
92 *"like little"*: Ibid., 405.
92 *"large golden"*: Ibid., 1200.
93 *"One took one hand"*: Ibid., 1299–1300.
94 *"astonished"*: *Vida manuscrita* de Juana de la Cruz, ff. 46r–46v, eds. María Luengo Balbás and Fructuoso Atencia Requena, https://catalogodesantasvivas.visionarias.es/index.php/Juana_de_la_Cruz#Vida_manuscrita_.281.29.
95 *"As an eyewitness"*: Silverio de Santa Teresa, *Procesos de canonización y beatificación de Santa Teresa de Jesús*, ed. Silverio de Santa Teresa, vol. 2, Biblioteca Mística Carmelitana 18–20 (El Monte Carmelo, 1935), 464. Our translation.
97 *"While I should"*: Bernardino Ramazzini, "De Virginum Vestalium Valetudine Tuenda Dissertatio (A Dissertation on the Care of the Health of Nuns)," *Journal of Occupational Medicine* 7, no. 10 (October 1965): 519.
98 *"The Lord seizes the soul"*: Teresa of Jesus, *Libro de la vida. Obras completas*, eds. Efrén de la Madre de Dios and Otgger Steggnik (Biblioteca de Autores Cristianos, 2012), 108–109. Our translation.

100 *"rose slightly"*: José Jiménez Samaniego, *Relación de la vida de la Venerable Madre Sor Maria de Jesus, escritora destos libros* (Valencia: por Juan de Baeza, 1695), f. 31. Our translation.

102 *"The devotion of some"*: Ibid., f. 97.

102 *"If secular justice"*: Quoted in Carlos Eire, *They Flew. A History of the Impossible* (Yale Univ. Press, 2023), 205.

Love

103 *"That you're a woman far away"*: *A Sor Juana Anthology*, trans. Alan S. Trueblood (Harvard Univ. Press, 1988), 39.

105 *"There is nothing more pleasing"*: Quoted in Hortensia Calvo y Beatriz Colombí, *Cartas de Lysi. La mecenas de Sor Juana Inés de la Cruz en correspondencia inédita* (Iberoamericana/Vervuert, 2015), 177–78. Our translation.

106 *"make pain lovable"*: Sor Juana Inés de la Cruz, *Obras completas de Sor Juana Inés de la Cruz I. Lírica personal*, ed. Antonio Alatorre (Fondo de Cultura Económica, 2009), 82. Our translation.

106 *"let no one pity me"*: Ibid., 70.

106 *"Your fingers are alabaster"*: *A Sor Juana Anthology*, trans. Trueblood, 51.

108 *"No sister may enter"*: Teresa of Jesus, *Constituciones. Obras completas*, eds. Efrén de la Madre de Dios and Otgger Steggnik (Biblioteca de Autores Cristianos, 2012), 821, 829–30. Our translation.

109 *"On the Seven Inconveniences"*: Bernardino de Villegas, *La esposa de Cristo, instruida con la vida de Santa Lutgarda virgen, monja de San Bernardo* (Murcia: Juan Fernández de Fuentes, 1635), fol. 232. Our translation.

109 *"the conversations between those who are"*: Ibid.

109 *"the affection with which"*: Ibid., fol. 233.

109 *"the restless mind"*: Ibid.

110 *"the impatience that"*: Ibid.

110 *"the anger and turmoil"*: Ibid., fol. 234.

110 *"the improper presents"*: Ibid.

110 *"the improper concealment"*: Ibid.

111 *"Love begins with unease"*: Sor Juana Inés de la Cruz, *Obras completas*, 426. Our translation.

111 *"To make fancy come true"*: *A Sor Juana Anthology*, trans. Trueblood, 79.

112 *"How long has it been"*: Federico Garza Carvajal, *Las cañitas: un proceso por lesbianismo a principios del XVII* (Simancas, 2012), 111. Our translation.

113 *"It's been about four years"*: Ibid., 111–12.

114 *"For the past three years"*: Ibid., 110.
115 *"Yes, she and the said Inés"*: Ibid.
117 *"a reed shaped"*: Ibid., 113.
118 *"For two continuous years"*: Judith C. Brown, *Immodest Acts. The Life of a Lesbian Nun in Renaissance Italy* (Oxford Univ. Press, 1996), 162.
119 *"Believe that we are"*: Concepción Torres, *Ana de Jesús. Cartas (1590–1621). Religiosidad y vida cotidiana en la clausura femenina del Siglo de Oro* (Ediciones Universidad de Salamanca, 1995), 65. Our translation.
121 *"Here, all must be friends"*: Teresa of Jesus, *The Way of Perfection. Obras completas*, eds. Efrén de la Madre de Dios and Otgger Steggnik (Biblioteca de Autores Cristianos, 2012), 254. Our translation.
121 *"Let's not speak of how much"*: Torres, *Ana de Jesús. Cartas (1590–1621)*, 68.
121 *"Asleep or awake"*: Ibid., 81.
122 *"Mother Superior [Beatriz de la Concepción]"*: Ángel Manrique, *Vida de la venerable madre Ana de Jesús* (Bruselas: en casa de Lucas de Meerbeeck, 1632). Our translation.

Money

125 *"despised money and matters"*: Teresa of Jesus's letter to Lorenzo de Cepeda, January 17, 1570, *Epistolario*, eds. Tcófanes Egido and Luis Rodríguez Martínez (Espiritualidad, 1984), 107. Our translation.
126 *"I have become such a trafficker"*: Ibid., 105.
127 *"have neither wheat nor"*: Teresa of Jesus's letter to María de San José, November 19, 1576, *The Collected Letters of Saint Teresa of Avila*, trans. by Kieran Kavanaugh, vol. 2 (ICS Publications, 2007), 533.
127 *"May the Holy Spirit be"*: Teresa of Jesus's letter to María Bautista, June 9, 1579, *Epistolario*, 615. Our translation.
128 *"You have been generous"*: Teresa of Jesus's letter to María de San José, February 8–9, 1580, *The Collected Letters of Saint Teresa of Avila*, 281.
128 *"as long as there's money"*: October 5, 1576, *Epistolario*, 297. Our translation.
131 *"There's much to be said"*: Teresa of Jesus's letter to Jerónimo Gracián, September 1, 1582, *Epistolario*, 903. Our translation.
131 *"I tell you, Your Reverence"*: Ibid.
131 *"How can these poor nuns"*: Ibid., 904.
131 *"Where will they find"*: Ibid.
131 *"It's a demonic mess"*: Ibid., September 1, 1582, *Epistolario*, 903–904. Our translation.
132 *"Don't believe the nuns"*: *The Collected Letters of Saint Teresa of Avila*, 582.

132 *"so the prioress can be"*: Ibid., 580.
133 *"I am laughing to myself"*: Teresa of Jesus's letter to Lorenzo de Cepeda, January 17, 1577, *The Collected Letters of Saint Teresa of Avila*, 631.
134 *"Affection, how often"*: Sor Juana Inés de la Cruz, *Obras completas de Sor Juana Inés de la Cruz I. Lírica personal*, ed. Antonio Alatorre (Fondo de Cultura Económica, 2009), 15. Our translation.
134 *"Love does not seek the payment"*: Ibid., 31.
136 *"fresh fish, fruits, vegetables"*: Quoted in M. Herrero García, "Tríptico madrileño. La Plaza Mayor de Madrid, los vecinos de la Plaza Mayor y la entrada de María Luisa de Orleans," in *Revista de la biblioteca, archivo y museo* 67 (1954): 140. Our translation.
137 *"collars stitched in thick"*: Almudena Pérez de Tudela, "Crear, coleccionar, mostrar e intercambiar objetos: una perspectiva general de las fuentes de archivo relacionadas con las pertenencias personales de la infanta Isabel," *Isabel Clara Eugenia: soberanía femenina en las cortes de Madrid y Bruselas*, coord. Cordula van Wyhe, 2011, 60–87. 74. Our translation.
137 *"with the sweetest words"*: Juan de Palma, *Vida de la Serenissima Infanta Sor Margarita de la Cruz, religiosa descalza de Santa Clara* (Sevilla: por Nicolás Rodríguez de Abrego, 1653), f. 224. Our translation.
137 *"Her ailments required"*: Ibid., f. 1333.
139 *"The altar you behold"*: Begoña Álvarez Seijo, "En-Clave de género. Las mujeres fuertes del Antiguo Testamento en la Capilla de la Virgen de Guadalupe de las Descalzas Reales," *Anuario del Departamento de Historia y Teoría del Arte* 29–30 (2017–2018): 143–67, 150, n. 52. Our translation.
143 *"Benedictine's 'passion'"*: Regina Sanchez and Ivonne Smith, "Entrepreneurship and Faith: What a 12th-Century Nun Has to Say to 21st-Century Entrepreneurs," *Journal of Biblical Integration in Business* 16, no. 1 (2013): 49–64.
145 *"The condemned in the tomb"*: Arcangela Tarabotti, Francesca Medioli, *L' "Inferno monacale" di Arcangela Tarabotti* (Rosemberg & Sellier, 1990), 43. Our translation.
146 *"The moment of my church"*: Quoted in Isabella Campagnol, *Forbidden Fashions: Invisible Luxuries in Early Venetian Convents* (Texas Tech Univ. Press, 2014), 41–42.
146 *"silk veils that leave"*: Ibid., 65.
146 *"it is great disorder"*: Ibid., 112.
148 *"the nuns that committed themselves to the work"*: Ibid., 116.
148 *"no less than 60"*: Ibid.

Soul

150 *"These tears are"*: Quoted in *El libro de la oración de María de Santo Domingo*, edition and introduction by Rebeca Sanmartín Bastida and María Victoria Curto Hernández (Iberoamericana/Vervuert, 2019), 46–47.

151 *"Woman, Jesus died"*: Margery Kempe, *The Book of Margery Kempe*, trans. John Skinner (PRH Christian Publishing, 2011), 211.

151 *"And in the instant that"*: Quoted in *El libro de la oración de María de Santo Domingo*, 47.

152 *"the term sadfishing"*: Rebecca Reid, "Sadfishing: Using Your Sadness to Get Comments and Shares Is Making Misery Profitable," *Metro*, January 21, 2019, https://metro.co.uk/2019/01/21/sadfishing-social-media-trend-making-misery-profitabl-8367931/.

153 *"bodily weakness"*: Teresa of Jesus, *The Interior Castle or the Mansions Translated from the Autograph of Saint Teresa of Jesus by the Benedictines of Stanbrook* (Thomas Baker, 1921), 210.

153 *"people of sensitive characters"*: Ibid.

153 *"would never stop crying"*: Teresa of Jesus, *Las moradas. Obras completas*, eds. Efrén de la Madre de Dios and Otgger Steggnik (Biblioteca de Autores Cristianos, 2012), 545. Our translation.

153 *"a real cry"*: Heather Christle, *The Crying Book* (Catapult Books, 2019), 3.

154 *"Grant me, then, some"*: Quoted in Rebeca Sanmartín Bastida, "«Dame de aquellos arroyos de lágrimas»: la performance del llano en una visionaria castellana de finales del medievo," *Poética das Lágrimas. Olhares Cruzados Sobre Textos e Contextos Femininos*, coordinated by Isabel Morujão e Geise Teixera (CITCEM, 2023), 91–106, 98. Our translation.

156 *"You beg knowledge"*: Catherine of Siena, *The Dialogue of the Seraphic Virgin Catherine of Siena*, trans. from the original Italian by Algar Thorold (Kegan Paul, Trench, Trübner & Co., 1896), 179.

156 *"You are the one who puts"*: Catherine of Siena, *Obras de Catalina de Siena*, ed. preparada por José Salvador y Conde (Biblioteca de Autores Cristianos, 1996), 25. Our translation.

156 "try to control yourself": Raimondo da Capua, *Vita miracolosa della serafica Santa Caterina da Siena* (Bernardo Giunti, 1608), 102. Our translation.

157 *"The tears of the wicked"*: Catherine of Siena, *The Dialogue of the Seraphic Virgin Catherine of Siena*, 179.

157 *"The second are those of fear"*: Ibid., 179–80.

157 *"The third are the tears"*: Ibid., 180.

158 *"The fourth are the tears"*: Ibid.

158	*"The fifth are joined to"*: Ibid.
161	*"thus, even if it isn't"*: Teresa of Jesus, *Camino de perfección*. *Obras completas*, eds. Efrén de la Madre de Dios and Otgger Steggnik (Biblioteca de Autores Cristianos, 2012), 295. Our translation.
162	*"I wish thee to know"*: Catherine of Siena, *The Dialogue*, 180.
163	*"I have already told"*: Ibid., 190.
165	*"there are 50 witches"*: Jean Bodin, *De la démonomanie des sorciers* (Paris: Iaques du Puys, 1580), 224. Our translation.
165	*"When I think of the life"*: Jeanne des Anges, *Autobiographie d'une hystérique possedée, d'après le manuscrit inédit de la bibliothèque de Tours*, Annoté et publié par les docteurs Gabriel Legue et Gilles de la Tourette (Paris: Aux Bureaux du Progrès Médical, 1886), 54. Our translation.
165	*"the shameful parts"*: Bodin, *De la démonomanie des sorciers*, 76.
166	*"As soon as he saw me"*: Jeanne des Anges, *Autobiographie d'une hystérique possedée*, 86–87.
167	*"that which she had vowed"*: Jeanne des Anges, *Soeur Jeanne des Anges, supérieure du couvent des Ursulines de Loudun: Autobiographie*, 1644. Préface, JM. Charcot, texte annoté et publié par Gabriel Legué et Georges Gilles de la Tourette (Editions Jérome Millon, 1990), 30. Our translation.
168	*"a great worry, sadness"*: Jeanne des Anges, *Autobiographie d'une hystérique possedée*, 59.
168	*"Leviathan, the chief"*: Ibid., 130.
168	*"me to pronounce"*: Ibid., 146.
168	*"were all the more dangerous"*: Ibid., 73.
170	*"the flowers that adorned"*: José Gómez de la Parra, *Fundación y primero siglo. Crónica del primer convento de carmelitas de Puebla* (Puebla: por la viuda de Miguel Ortega, 1732), f. 399. Our translation.
170	*"the bowls she ate from"*: Ibid.
171	*"Daughters of Jerusalem"*: Ibid., f. 389.
171	*"a tiny piece of flesh"*: Ibid., f. 177.
171	*"sitting on the ledge"*: Ibid., f. 397.
172	*"beautiful Black woman"*: Ibid., f. 386.
173	*"Look, Esperanza, don't"*: Ibid., f. 396.
173	*"terrible fall"*: Ibid., f. 362.
174	*"in her later years"*: Ibid., f. 394.

Fame

177 *"two small paintings"*: Cartas de algunos padres de la Compañía de Jesús sobre los sucesos de la monarquía, entre los años 1634 y 1648, tomo I (Imp. Nacional, 1861), 326. Our translation.

178 *"a dozen chickpeas"*: Fray Pedro de Balbas, *Memorial informativo en defensa de Sor Luisa de la Ascensión, monja profesa de Santa Clara de Carrión* (Madrid: por Diego Díaz de la Carrera, 1643), f. 91. Our translation.

179 *"Do you see the noise"*: Patrocinio García Barriuso, *La monja de Carrión: Sor Luisa de la Ascensión Colmenares Cabezón (aportación documental para una biografía)* (Imp. Monte Casino, 1986), 276. Our translation.

179 *"cut her veils"*: Fray Pedro de Balbas, *Memorial informativo en defensa de Sor Luisa de la Ascensión*, f. 27.

179 *"the veils?"*: Ibid., f. 26.

179 *"There couldn't possibly be"*: Ibid., f. 27v.

179 *"some branches"*: Ibid., f. 27.

180 *"I've heard it said"*: Ibid., f. 26.

180 *"virtues and graces"*: Patrocinio García Barriuso, *La monja de Carrión*, 271.

180 *"I, the King"*: *Firmas de los miembros de los conventos y monasterios pertenecientes a la Hermandad de la Purísima Concepción*, MSS/8540 (Biblioteca Nacional de España). Our translation.

181 *"Upon opening"*: Patrocinio García Barriuso, *La monja de Carrión*, 298.

181 *"Sir, if [Luisa]"*: Patrocinio García Barriuso, *La monja de Carrión*, 298, 313, 315.

182 *"great harshness"*: Sor Ana de Cristo, *Historia de nuestra santa madre Jerónima de la Asunción 1623–29*, Archivo del Monasterio de Santa Isabel de los Reyes (AMSIRT), Toledo, transcription by Sarah E. Owens. Our translation.

184 *"a ground bead of"*: Ibid.

184 *"Having done"*: Ibid.

186 *"a great fragrance and sweetness"*: Antonio Daza, *Historia, vida, y milagros, éxtasis y revelaciones de la bienaventurada Virgen Santa Juana de la Cruz* (Madrid: Luis Sánchez, 1610), ff. 51–52. Our translation.

188 *"know something about everything"*: Fray Ginés de Quesada, *Ejemplo de todas las virtudes y vida milagrosa de la venerable madre Jerónima de la Asunción: abadesa y fundadora del convento de la Concepción de la Virgen Nuestra Señora de Monjas Descalzas de Nuestra Madre de Santa Clara, de la ciudad de Manila* (México: por la viuda de Miguel de Ribera, 1713), 58. Our translation.

189 *"While immersed in"*: Ibid., 545.

190 *"squadron of Poor Clares"*: Ibid., 315.
192 *"affront to holy matrimony"*: María Jesús de Ágreda, "Relación autobiográfica (incompleta)," *Nueva edición de la Mística Ciudad de Dios*, vol. V, ed. Eduardo Royo (Herederos de Juan Gil editores, 1914), 52. Our translation.
197 *"They probably couldn't get"*: Lindsay Lohan on Jenny McCarthy's SiriusXM show (January 2019).
197 *"having been suddenly raptured"*: Quoted in Beatriz Ferrús Antón, *La monja de Ágreda. Historia y leyenda de la dama azul en Norteamérica* (PUV, 2008), 83. Our translation.
198 *"Guardian Angels"*: Francisco Palóu, *Relación histórica de la vida y apostólicas tareas del venerable padre fray Junípero Serra* . . . (Imp. de don Felipe de Zúñiga y Ontiveros, 1787), 334, 337. Our translation.
198 *"she preached in Spanish"*: María Jesús de Ágreda, *Mística ciudad de Dios*, t. I (Imp. de Pablo Riera, 1860), 207. Our translation.
200 *"the wonders of the Lord"*: María Jesús de Ágreda, *Tratado de la redondez de la tierra*, eds. Judith Farré Vidal and Beatriz Ferrús (Univ. of North Carolina Press, 2023), 110. Our translation.

Epilogue

205 *"Behold, the Millennial"*: Eve Fairbanks, "Behold the Millennial Nuns," HuffPost, July 11, 2019, https://www.huffpost.com/highline/article/millennial-nuns/.
207 *"We set sail"*: Sor Ana de Cristo, *Historia de nuestra santa madre Jerónima de la Asunción 1623–29*, Archivo del Monasterio de Santa Isabel de los Reyes (AMSIRT), Toledo, transcription by Sarah E. Owens. Our translation.

Selected Bibliography

Ágreda, María Jesús de. *Mística Ciudad de Dios*. 7 vols. Imp. de Pablo Riera, 1860.

———. "Relación autobiográfica (incompleta)." *Nueva edición de la Mística Ciudad de Dios*, t. V. Edited by Eduardo Royo. Herederos de Juan Gil editores, 1914.

———. *Tratado de la redondez de la tierra*. Edited by Judith Farré Vidal and Beatriz Ferrús. Univ. of North Carolina Press, 2023.

Ahlgren, Gillian T. *Teresa of Avila and the Politics of Sanctity*. Cornell Univ. Press, 1996.

Alabrús, Rosa María, and Ricardo García Cárcel. *Teresa de Jesús. La construcción de la santidad femenina*. Cátedra, 2015.

Alatorre, Antonio. "La Carta de sor Juana al P. Núñez (1682)." *Nueva Revista de Filología Hispánica* 35, núm. 2 (1987a): 591–673.

Álvarez Seijo, Begoña. "En-Clave de género. Las mujeres fuertes del Antiguo Testamento en la Capilla de la Virgen de Guadalupe de las Descalzas Reales." *Anuario del Departamento de Historia y Teoría del Arte* 29–30 (2017–2018): pp. 143–67.

Álvarez Vázquez, José Antonio. *Trabajos, dineros y negocios. Teresa de Jesús y la economía del siglo XVI (1562–1582)*. Trotta, 2000.

Ana de San Bartolomé. *Obras completas de la Beata Ana de San Bartolomé*. Edited by Julen Urkiza. Instituto Historicum Teresianum, 1981.

Anges, Jeanne des. *Autobiographie d'une hystérique possedée, d'après le manuscrit inédit de la bibliothèque de Tours*. Annoté et publié par les docteurs Gabriel Legue et Gilles de la Tourette. Paris: Aux Bureaux du Progrès Médical, 1886.

———. *Soeur Jeanne des Anges, supérieure du couvent des Ursulines de Loudun: Autobiographie*, 1644. Préface, JM. Charcot, texte annoté et publié par Gabriel Legué et Georges Gilles de la Tourette. Editions Jérome Millon, 1990.

Arenal, Electa, and Stacey Schlau. *Untold Sisters. Hispanic Nuns in Their Own Works*. 2nd ed. Univ. of New Mexico Press, 2010.

Astigarraga, José Luis. "Escolias del P. Jerónimo Gracián a la *Vida* de Santa Teresa compuesta por el P. Ribera." *Ephemerides Carmeliticae*, no. 32 (1981–82): 343–430.

Balbas, Fray Pedro de. *Memorial informativo en defensa de Sor Luisa de la Ascensión, monja profesa de Santa Clara de Carrión*. Madrid: por Diego Díaz de la Carrera, 1643.

Belchior de Santa Ana. *Chronica de carmelitas descalços, particular do reyno do Portugal e provincia de Sam Felippe*. Lisboa: Henrique Valente de Oliueira, 1675.

Bell, Rudolph. *Holy Anorexia*. Univ. of Chicago Press, 1985.

Bodin, Jean. *De la démonomanie des sorciers*. Paris: Jaques du Puys, 1580.

Bristol, Joan C. "'Although I am black, I am beautiful': Juana Esperanza de San Alberto, Black Carmelite of Puebla." *Gender, Race, and Religion in the Colonization of the Americas*. Edited by Nora E. Jaffary. Routledge, 2007.

Brown, Judith C. *Immodest Acts. The Life of a Lesbian Nun in Renaissance Italy*. Oxford Univ. Press, 1996.

Bynum, Caroline Walker. *Holy Fast and Holy Feast. The Religious Significance of Food to Medieval Women*. Univ. of California Press, 1988.

———. *Fragmentation and Redemption. Essays on Gender and the Human Body in Medieval Religion*. Zone Books, 1992.

Calvo, Hortensia, and Beatriz Colombí. *Cartas de Lysi. La mecenas de Sor Juana Inés de la Cruz en correspondencia inédita*. Iberoamericana/Vervuert, 2015.

Campagnol, Isabella. *Forbidden Fashions. Invisible Luxuries in Early Modern Venetian Convents*. Texas Tech Univ. Press, 2014.

Capua, Raimondo da. *Vita miracolosa della serafica Santa Caterina da Siena*. Presso Bernardo Giunti, 1608.

Carrera, Elena. "Soledad, enfermedad y discapacidad en España y América, 1530–1680: Vigencia actual de los testimonios de una veinteañera y cuarentona inquieta (Teresa de Ávila), una viuda cincuentona (Marina Navas) y una esclava negra setentona (Esperanza)." *Studia Aurea* 18 (2024): 121–42.

Cartas de algunos padres de la Compañía de Jesús sobre los sucesos de la monarquía, entre los años 1634 y 1648. Tomo I. Imprenta Nacional, 1861.

Catherine of Siena. *The Dialogue of the Seraphic Virgin Catherine of Siena*. Translated from the original Italian by Algar Thorold. Kegan Paul, Trench, Trübner & Co., 1896.

———. *Obras de Catalina de Siena*. Edited by José Salvador y Conde. Biblioteca de Autores Cristianos, 1996.

Christle, Heather. *The Crying Book*. Catapult Books, 2019.

Corwin, Anna I. *Embracing Age: How Catholic Nuns Became Models of Aging Well*. Rutgers University Press, 2021.

Cristo, Sor Ana de. *Historia de nuestra santa madre Jerónima de la Asunción* 1623–29. Archivo del Monasterio de Santa Isabel de los Reyes (AMSIRT), Toledo. Transcription by Sarah E. Owens.

Crowther, Kathleen. "The Virgin and the Globe: The Cosmography of Sor María de Ágreda." *Early Modern Women: An Interdisciplinary Journal* 15, no. 2 (2021): 29–56.

Cruz, Juana de la. *Vida manuscrita*. Edited by María Luengo Balbás and Fructuoso Atencia Requena. https://catalogodesantasvivas.visionarias.es/index.php/Juana_de_la_Cruz#Vida_manuscrita_.281.29

Cruz, Sor Juana Inés de la. *The Answer*. Second critical edition and translation by Electa Arenal and Amanda Powell. The Feminist Press, 2009.

———. *Obras completas*. Edited by Alfonso Méndez-Plancarte and Alberto Salceda, 4 vols. Fondo de Cultura Económica, 1975.

———. *Obras completas de Sor Juana Inés de la Cruz I. Lírica personal*. Edited by Antonio Alatorre. Fondo de Cultura Económica, 2009.

Daza, Antonio. *Historia, vida y milagros, extasis y revelaciones de la bienaventurada virgen Sor Juana de la Cruz de la Tercera Orden de . . . san Francisco*. Madrid: por Luis Sánchez, 1613.

Egido, Teófanes. "The Economic Concerns of Madre Teresa." *Carmelite Studies* 4 (1987): 151–72.

Eire, Carlos N. M. *They Flew. A History of the Impossible*. Yale Univ. Press, 2023.

Enrigue, Álvaro. *Valiente clase media. Dinero, letras y cursilería*. Anagrama, 2013.

Eugenides, Jeffrey. *The Marriage Plot*. Farrar, Straus and Giroux, 2011.

Ferrús Antón, Beatriz. *La monja de Ágreda. Historia y leyenda de la dama azul en Norteamérica*. PUV, 2008.

Firmas de los miembros de los conventos y monasterios pertenecientes a la Hermandad de la Purísima Concepción. MSS/8540. Biblioteca Nacional de España.

Francisco de Santa María. *Reforma de los Descalzos de Nuestra Señora del Carmen de la primitiva observancia hecha por Santa Teresa de Jesús*. 2 vols. Madrid: Diego Díaz de la Carrera, 1644.

García Andrés, Inocencio, ed. *El Conhorte: Sermones de una mujer santa*. Universidad Pontificia de Salamanca y Fundación Universitaria Española, 1999.

García Barriuso, Patrocinio. *La monja de Carrión: Sor Luisa de la Ascensión Colmenares Cabezón (aportación documental para una biografía)*. Imp. Monte Casino, 1986.

Garza Carvajal, Federico. *Las cañitas: un proceso por lesbianismo a principios del XVII*. Simancas, 2012.

Gómez de la Parra, José. *Fundación y primero siglo. Crónica del primer convento de carmelitas de Puebla.* Puebla: por la viuda de Miguel Ortega, 1732.

Herrero García, Miguel Herrero. "Tríptico madrileño. La Plaza Mayor de Madrid, los vecinos de la Plaza Mayor y la entrada de María Luisa de Orleans." *Revista de la biblioteca, archivo y museo,* no. 67 (1954): 131–87.

Jesús, Teresa de. *Epistolario.* Edited by Teófanes Egido and Luis Rodríguez Martínez. Espiritualidad, 1984.

———. *The Book of the Foundations.* Translated by Rev. John Dalton. T. Jones, 1853.

———. *The Collected Letters of Saint Teresa of Avila.* Translated by Kieran Kavanaugh, 2 vols. ICS Publications, 2007.

———. *The Interior Castle or the Mansions Translated from the Autograph of Saint Teresa of Jesus by the Benedictines of Stanbrook.* Thomas Baker, 1921.

———. *The Letters of Saint Teresa.* A complete edition translated from the Spanish and annotated by the Benedictines of Santbrook. With an introduction by Cardinal Gasquet, 2 vols. Thomas Baker, 1921.

———. *The Life of Teresa of Jesus.* Translated and edited by E. Allison Peers. Random House, 1960.

———. *Obras completas.* Edited by Efrén de la Madre de Dios and Otgger Steggnik. Biblioteca de Autores Cristianos, 2012.

Jiménez Samaniego, José. *Relación de la vida de la Venerable Madre Sor Maria de Jesus, escritora destos libros.* Valencia: por Juan de Baeza, 1695.

Kempe, Margery. *The Book of Margery Kempe.* Edited by PRH Christian Publishing, 2011.

Lavrin, Asunción. *Brides of Christ. Conventual Life in Colonial Mexico.* Stanford Univ. Press, 2008.

Lehfeldt, Elizabeth A. *Religious Women in Golden Age Spain. The Permeable Cloister.* Routledge, 2005.

Manrique, Ángel. *Vida de la venerable madre Ana de Jesús.* Bruselas: en casa de Lucas de Meerbeeck, 1632.

Merrim, Stephanie. *Early Modern Women's Writings and Sor Juana Inés de la Cruz.* Vanderbilt Univ. Press, 1999.

Moriones, Ildefonso. *Ana de Jesús (1545–1621). Beata.* Ediciones El Carmen, 2021.

Mujica, Barbara. *Teresa de Ávila. Lettered Woman.* Vanderbilt Univ. Press, 2009.

———. *Women Religious and Epistolary Exchange in the Carmelite Reform. The Disciples of Teresa of Ávila.* Amsterdam Univ. Press, 2020.

Myers, Kathleen. *Word from New Spain. The Spiritual Autobiography of Madre María de San José (1656–1719).* Liverpool Univ. Press, 1992.

Myles, Eileen. "Nun's Tale: The Selling of Sor Juana." *Village Voice Literary Supplement* 75 (June 1989): 30–1.

Owens, Sarah. *Nuns Navigating the Spanish Empire*. Univ. of New Mexico Press, 2017.

Palma, Juan de. *Vida de la Serenissima Infanta Sor Margarita de la Cruz, religiosa descalza de Santa Clara*. Sevilla: por Nicolás Rodríguez de Abrego, 1653.

Palóu, Francisco. *Relación histórica de la vida y apostólicas tareas del venerable padre fray Junipero Serra* . . . Imprenta de don Felipe de Zúñiga y Ontiveros, 1787.

Pérez de Tudela, Almudena. "Crear, coleccionar, mostrar e intercambiar objetos: una perspectiva general de las fuentes de archivo relacionadas con las pertenencias personales de la infanta Isabel." *Isabel Clara Eugenia: soberanía femenina en las cortes de Madrid y Bruselas*. Coordinated by Cordula van Wyhe (2011): 60–87.

Pérez Martínez, Herón. *Estudios sorjuanianos*. El Colegio de Michoacán, 2015.

Quesada, Fray Ginés de. *Ejemplo de todas las virtudes y vida milagrosa de la venerable madre Jerónima de la Asunción: abadesa y fundadora del convento de la Concepción de la Virgen Nuestra Señora de Monjas Descalzas de Nuestra Madre de Santa Clara, de la ciudad de Manila*. México: por la viuda de Miguel de Ribera.

Ramazzini, Bernardino. "*De Virginum Vestalium Valetudine Tuenda Dissertatio* (A Dissertation on the Care of the Health of Nuns)." *Journal of Occupational Medicine* 7, no. 10 (October 1965): 516–20. Transcribed by A. Meiklejohn and A.P. Curran.

Ramírez Santacruz, Francisco. *Sor Juana Inés de la Cruz. La resistencia del deseo*. Cátedra, 2019.

Salvatori, Filippo Maria. *The Life of Saint Veronica Giuliani, Capuchin Nun*. R. Washbourne, 1874.

Sanchez, Regina, and Ivonne Smith. "Entrepreneurship and Faith: What a 12th-Century Nun Has to Say to 21st-Century Entrepreneurs." *Journal of Biblical Integration in Business* 16, no. 1 (2013): 49–64.

San José, María de. A *Wild Country Out in the Garden. The Spiritual Journals of a Colonial Mexican Nun*. Selected, edited, and translated by Kathleen A. Myers and Amanda Powell. Indiana UP, 1999.

San José Salazar, María de. *Book for the Hour of Recreation*. Introduction and notes by Allison Weber, translated by Amanda Powell. Univ. of Chicago Press, 2002.

———. "Carta de una pobre presa descalza." *Humor y espiritualidad en la escuela teresiana primitiva: Santa Teresa de Jesús, Jerónimo Gracián, Ana de Jesús, María de San José*. El Monte Carmelo, 1966.

———. "Instrucción de novicias." *Humor y espiritualidad en la escuela teresiana primitiva: Santa Teresa de Jesús, Jerónimo Gracián, Ana de Jesús, María de San José*. El Monte Carmelo, 1966.

———. *Aviso para el gobierno de religiosas*. Edited by Juan Luis Astigarraga. Instituto Histórico Teresiano, 1977.

———. "Libro de las recreaciones." *Humor y espiritualidad en la escuela teresiana primitiva: Santa Teresa de Jesús, Jerónimo Gracián, Ana de Jesús, María de San José*. El Monte Carmelo, 1966.

———. *Resumptas de la Historia de la Fundación de los descalzos y descalzas carmelitas que fundó Santa Theresa de Jesús, nuestra madre. Año de 1562 el primer convento de monjas; y el primer de frayles año de 1577. Cuéntanse algunos trabajos que se pasaron en algunas fundaciones de frayles y monjas*. Biblioteca Nacional de España, ms. 2176.

Sanmartín Bastida, Rebeca. *La comida visionaria. Formas de alimentación en el discurso carismático femenino del siglo XVI*. Critical, Cultural and Communications Press, 2015.

———. "Juana de la Cruz's Heavenly Banquet: A Utopian Way of Thinking about Food." *Utopian Foodways: Critical Essays*. Edited by Teresa Botelho, Miguel Ramalhete Gomes, and José Eduardo Reis. Porto: Universidade do Porto, 2019.

———. "«Dame aquellos arroyos de lágrimas»: la performance del llanto en una visionaria castellana de finales del medievo." *Poética das lágrimas: Olhares cruzados sobre textos e contextos femininos*. Edited by Isabel Morujão and Gisela Teixeira. CITCEM, 2023, 91–106.

———, and María Victoria Curto Hernández. *El libro de la oración de María de Santo Domingo*. Iberoamericana/Vervuert, 2019.

Santa Teresa, Silverio de. *Procesos de canonización y beatificación de Santa Teresa de Jesús*. 3 vols., Biblioteca Mística Carmelitana 18–20. Monte Carmelo, 1935.

Suárez, Úrsula. *Relación autobiográfica de una monja venerable*. Edited by Mario Ferreccio Podesta. Biblioteca Nacional, 1984.

Tarabotti, Arcangela. *L'Inferno monacale di Arcangela Tarabotti*. Edited by Francesca Medioli. Rosemberg & Sellier, 1990.

Tiffany, Tanya. "'Little Idols': Royal Children and the Infant Jesus in the Devotional Practice of Sor Margarita de la Cruz (1567–1633). *The Early Modern Child in Art and History*. Edited by Matthew Knox Averett. Pickering and Chatto, 2015.

Torres, Concepción. *Ana de Jesús. Cartas (1590–1621). Religiosidad y vida cotidiana en la clausura femenina del Siglo de Oro*. Ediciones Universidad de Salamanca, 1995.

Trueblood, Alan S. *A Sor Juana Anthology*. Harvard Univ. Press, 1988.

Velasco, Sherry. *Lesbians in Early Modern Spain*. Vanderbilt Univ. Press, 2011.

Villegas, Bernardino de. *La esposa de Cristo, instruida con la vida de Santa Lutgarda virgen, monja de San Bernardo*. Murcia: Juan Fernández de Fuentes, 1635.

Webb, Heather. "Lacrime Cordiali. Catherine of Siena on the Value of Tears." *A Companion to Catherine of Siena*. Edited by Carolyn Muessig, George Ferzoco, and Beverly Mayne Kienzle. Brill, 2012.

Weber, Allison. *Teresa of Avila and the Rhetoric of Femininity*. Princeton Univ. Press, 1996.

About the Authors

Ana Garriga is a scholar of early modern Spain and Latin America. She earned her PhD from Brown University in 2024. Prior to joining the Department of Hispanic Studies at Brown, she completed a PhD at the Universidad Autónoma de Madrid with a dissertation on the letters of the nun Teresa of Jesus (1515–1582), for which she received the Extraordinary PhD Award. In 2014, she earned a prestigious Fulbright scholarship that allowed her to spend a semester at UC Berkeley as a visiting scholar. She joined the graduate program of Hispanic Studies at Brown University in 2016 supported by a Presidential Fellowship. She has published extensively in academic journals (*Revista Hispánica Moderna, Bulletin of Hispanic Studies*) and presented at conferences of organizations such as the Renaissance Society of America, American Comparative Literature Association, and others. While she was deciding where to attend graduate school, she met Carmen Urbita, with whom she launched the podcast *Las hijas de Felipe* in 2020.

Carmen Urbita earned her PhD from Brown University in 2025. Prior to joining the Department of Hispanic Studies at Brown, she completed her BA in comparative literature at King's College London (University of London) and was granted a scholarship to pursue a master of studies in modern languages at the University of

Oxford, where she was awarded with Distinction after completing her dissertation on autobiography and demonology in the writings of the French Ursuline nun Jeanne des Anges (1602–1665). She has presented at conferences of organizations such as the Renaissance Society of America and has published in academic journals such as *Romanic Review*. In 2016, she met Ana Garriga, and four years later, they launched the podcast *Las hijas de Felipe*.

With over sixty episodes published, *Las hijas de Felipe* has established itself as one of the most popular podcasts in the Spanish-speaking world. They have collaborated with prestigious institutions, including the Petit Palais in Paris, the Museo Pedro de Osma in Lima, the Bode-Museum in Berlin, and the Museo del Prado in Madrid.

Avid Reader Press, an imprint of Simon & Schuster, is built on the idea that the most rewarding publishing has three common denominators: great books, published with intense focus, in true partnership. Thank you to the Avid Reader Press colleagues who collaborated on *Convent Wisdom*, as well as to the hundreds of professionals in the Simon & Schuster advertising, audio, communications, design, ebook, finance, human resources, legal, marketing, operations, production, sales, supply chain, subsidiary rights, and warehouse departments whose invaluable support and expertise benefit every one of our titles.

Editorial
Amy Guay, *Assistant Editor*

Jacket Design
Alison Forner, *Senior Art Director*
Clay Smith, *Senior Designer*
Sydney Newman, *Art Associate*

Marketing
Meredith Vilarello, *VP and Associate Publisher*
Caroline McGregor, *Senior Marketing Manager*
Kayla Dee, *Associate Marketing Manager*
Katya Wiegmann, *Marketing and Publishing Assistant*

Production
Allison Green, *Managing Editor*
Hana Handzija, *Managing Editorial Assistant*
Jessica Chin, *Senior Manager of Copyediting*
Annalea Manalili, *Senior Production Editor*
Alicia Brancato, *Production Manager*
Ruth Lee-Mui, *Interior Text Designer*
Erika R. Genova, *Desktop Compositor*
Cait Lamborne, *Ebook Developer*

Publicity
Rhina Garcia, *Publicist*
Eva Kerins, *Publicity Assistant*

Subsidiary Rights
Paul O'Halloran, *VP and Director of Subsidiary Rights*
Fiona Sharp, *Subsidiary Rights Coordinator*